THE CURSE OF
CELEBRITY

THE CURSE OF
CELEBRITY

How and why our favourite stars go off the rails

Rita Wright

JOHN BLAKE

Published by John Blake Publishing Ltd,
3, Bramber Court, 2 Bramber Road,
London W14 9PB, England

www.blake.co.uk

First published in hardback in 2006

ISBN 1 84454 222 X

British Library Cataloguing-in-Publication Data:

A catalogue record for this book is available from the British Library.

Design by www.envydesign.co.uk
Illustrations by Anna Wright
Printed and bound in Great Britain by William Clowes Ltd, Beccles, Suffolk

1 3 5 7 9 10 8 6 4 2

Papers used by John Blake Publishing are natural, recyclable products made from wood grown
in sustainable forests. The manufacturing processes conform to the environmental regulations
of the country of origin.

Every attempt has been made to contact the relevant copyright-holders, but some were
unobtainable. We would be grateful if the appropriate people could contact us.

This book is dedicated to Andy, Anna, Billy, and Jessica Ann Lucey.

CONTENTS

While living on the Costa Del Sol I have met some amazing people, many of whom have become firm friends. Sally and David Cronin, Christine and Graham Stack, Anna and Chris Courtney have been especially generous and supportive. Also to Christine and Sarah, my two best muckers, who I thank from the bottom of my heart for helping me through a difficult time. Thank God for girlfriends and side-splitting laughter.

However, it has been the journalist and author Wensley Clarkson who has turned my life around. Without his belief in me I may never have realised my life's ambition. Thank you.

INTRODUCTION

The word 'celebrity' seems to be on everyone's lips nowadays, and it seems that the whole world wants to be on television. Some people, indeed, will do just about anything for their moment of fame, and those who aspire to be rich and famous but don't quite make it are left feeling less of a person. Witness the tears and tantrums of those who fail the auditions for shows such as *The X Factor*; such near-misses feel that they're abject failures.

The celebrities featured in this book *have* made it — big time. But I can't help wondering if, just sometimes, they wish they hadn't bothered. What on earth could make a supermodel mum worth £30 million risk losing everything for the sake of an illegal drug and the love of a crack-cocaine-addict rock star? Was there already a chink in her personality? Or did living a life in the 'abnormal' fast lane from her early teens prompt such self-destructive behaviour? And why did one of the world's most successful singer/songwriters compromise both himself and his career by committing a lewd act in a public toilet?

THE CURSE OF CELEBRITY

Kate Moss and George Michael were not only the pride of Great Britain but also held in high esteem around the world. Both had cracked America and both had spent more than a decade building their reputations. Just what went wrong in their minds? Why did they push their boundaries to the limit?

So many answers need to be found to so many questions, and with this book I hope to find them.

We all have problems, difficult spells in our lives when we find it almost impossible to cope. Maybe the reasons for our struggles, addictions and neuroses are to be found in our genetic makeup. Perhaps it's to do with our upbringing or our early life experiences. When times are hard, if we're lucky, we have family and friends to turn to; if not, we suffer alone. Depending on our inner strength, we either thrive or fall into mental illness.

Psychiatric help has never been more easily available than it is today, and thankfully counselling, which used to be taboo, is now known to be of tremendous use.

But what happens when your whole life is played out in the bright lights of media madness? What can you do when every move you make is scrutinised, interpreted and reported in the tabloids and gossip magazines?

In *The Curse of Celebrity*, the personalities of nine popular celebrities are profiled and then analysed in an attempt to discover their reasons for falling foul of 'the curse'. It seems that, while it's true that the media circus has to own its fair share of fame for the haloes of such luminaries becoming tarnished, there's more to each celebrity's story than this. The endurance or fragility of their reputations depends much more on their individual personalities and how they deal with blame than the intrusive paparazzi.

INTRODUCTION

The nine celebrities featured in this book have fame, wealth and power, but paradoxically they often seem powerless, trapped in the same fantasy bubble that they once craved to penetrate. Drink, drugs and rock 'n' roll take their toll on some while neurotic perfectionism makes others terrified of losing control, forcing them to embark on desperate attempts to fight off insecurities and paranoia, eventually leading to exhaustion and burnout.

As celebrities are catapulted from their relatively normal lives into a fantasy playground, it becomes increasingly impossible for them to hold on to their core personalities, to remember who they are. A void appears, and in this gaping hole a public persona grows, fighting for supremacy. The celebrity then projects a false image that they believe the public will buy into – and, of course, the public does. But now the celebrity has to live up to this image. Their life is no longer their own; they have become public property. All problems are aired and scrutinised under the bright lights of a theatre to which everyone is invited.

Sometimes, however, such public scrutiny can have a positive effect. When personal grief or vulnerabilities are exposed, some celebrities are suddenly perceived as being more human, more like the person on the street, and their public esteem is enhanced. Take, for instance, the time when Victoria Beckham was pictured looking so sad after the revelations concerning David's infidelity, and then later on when Romeo became so ill. All mothers could relate to her anxiety.

Similarly, when Kerry Katona's marriage to Brian McFadden fell apart, she suddenly found herself on a higher celebrity ranking. When the gossip magazines told misery stories about her abandonment during childhood, she became everyone's darling.

Likewise, when a celebrity puts their hand up and confesses that they're in the throes of a nervous breakdown, or fighting addiction and need rehabilitation, they are instantly forgiven by the public, with whom a positive relationship is established.

Celebrities have to endure press intrusion and a myriad of other external situations over which they feel they have no control. History tells them that death threats from stalkers and plots to kidnap them must be taken seriously. TV presenter Jill Dando was stalked and later shot dead on her doorstep. Madonna was stalked by Robert Dewy Hoskins for five years, during which time he threatened to 'slice her from ear to ear'. The lives of celebrities feed the distorted and irrational mind of the stalker.

Victoria Beckham knows only too well the terror that threats of murder and kidnap can bring. The days leading up to the 2000 Brit Awards were incredibly tense for her. On the night when The Spice Girls were due to receive a Lifetime Achievement Award, Victoria was handed a chilling message threatening her death. Terrified, she held on to the notion that the show had to go on and took to the stage. As will become clear later in this book, however, for Victoria it was one hell of an ordeal.

Then, later, an elaborate plan to kidnap Victoria and her son Brooklyn was foiled by the tabloid newspaper the *News of the World*. The security that now surrounds the Beckhams, although much needed, must at times be suffocating.

THE CELEBRITY–THERAPY LINK

Way back in 1859 a man called Samuel Smiles wrote an enormously influential book about celebrities that acknowledged how hard these individuals worked to achieve their fame. The book was entitled *Self-Help* and was an early example of mid-Victorian popular therapy and counselling. Indeed, it was this link between therapy and celebrity that inspired me to write this book.

Smiles studied the lives of celebrities who had been big

achievers in science, industry and the arts, portraying them as those aspiring to 'upward mobility'. His take on what a celebrity *was* and what a celebrity *should be* was fascinating. In many ways, the book was an attack on idleness and selfishness. Like Scott Peck (author of the bestseller *The Road Less Travelled*) in the 1980s, Smiles believed that morality and self-discipline were the attributes to which one needed to aspire.

For Smiles, celebrity carried with it public responsibilities and duties. He was a very opinionated man who disapproved of hedonistic celebrity, which he described as 'human idolatry in its worst form – a worship of mere power, as degrading in its effects as the worship of mere wealth'.

As you read through this book, you'll no doubt realise how much I agree with Smiles. Our celebrities, whatever they may say, *are* role models. They can't have the perks without the responsibilities; life doesn't work that way. Smiles wanted the man on the street to 'aspire to be like them'. With the achievement of the individual, he hoped, society would in turn grow in a positive way.

So what would the great pioneer have thought about the exposure of Kate Moss's cocaine habit? Of an iconic beauty projected on to the front page of a popular newspaper as a girl who smokes, drinks to excess and allegedly takes part in marathon orgies? What would he make of hedonistic Robbie Williams? Or George Michael's lewd conduct in a toilet? Not much, I'd say. Perhaps he would have had more respect for the likes of honest, hardworking Jade Goody, a young girl who managed to get herself out of a poverty trap and make a decent living for herself and her family and now gives generously to charities, yet was bullied by the mass media and referred to as a pig.

PUBLIC PROPERTY

The pressure and confusion that can make the lives of celebrities intolerable is twofold. Internally, they need a special set of coping skills if they are to survive the intrusion of the media. They need to keep a strong hold on who they really are, and for many this is impossible. This split between who they really are and the person they have become can be very distressing for them, because the part of them that they exhibit to the public will be constantly judged and criticised, as demonstrated by Kate Moss's fall from public grace. In a sense, Kate has been a blank canvas upon which the media outlets of the world have painted their own picture, and she has confessed that she 'lost the plot'. Can she ever, now, find a place where she is happy and contented?

Externally, the expansion of the mass media has ensured the public intimate knowledge of its heroes, leaving them no privacy. They are vaulted into the public's consciousness and the line between fact and fiction is erased.

Having to deal with this double pressure proves impossible for some. The acting genius Peter Sellers, for instance, famously declared that, after shooting a movie, 'He' simply disappeared. This would indicate a non-existent 'real self'.

Celebrities, whether they like it or not, are public property. It has always been this way, and it always will be, and it's ironic that, despite their ambivalence, celebrities both need and resent the public. What makes life more difficult for them today is the communication explosion that has made details of their lives easily accessible to the public. Television, Sky news, the internet, tabloids and gossip magazines – the list is endless. As their vanities and foibles are exposed, they become vulnerable and begin to resent the insufferable intrusion, eventually falling foul of the insidious way in which the media first elevates and then spurns them. They begin to struggle to be themselves, becoming first agitated and then, operating from a fragile sense of self, searching for ways to alleviate their pain. How they behave and which defences they implement will be unique and personal. Some, like the singer Kate Bush, will become totally reclusive, while others will live every moment in the limelight, craving attention. Those with addictive personalities, meanwhile, will turn to drink and drugs in order to find the physical state Pink Floyd referred to as being 'comfortably numb'.

This book explores the lives of ten very different characters who have celebrity status and yet often hit the headlines as much for their troubled personal lives as their talent. It's impossible to imagine a week going by without us knowing what Posh and Becks are allegedly up to, and it's difficult for us to really imagine what it must be like to walk in their very expensive shoes, so to allow some insight into their motivations in this book I pull on my experience of counselling clients from all walks of life – including celebrities, professional footballers and, more recently, gangsters who wish to go straight, along with their wives and girlfriends – and pose controversial questions such as 'Is Robbie Williams a national treasure?' and 'Just how wonderful could George Best's life and career been, had he possessed the ability to conquer his alcoholism?'

Most of us perceive Paris Hilton as having everything, but I see the bigger picture and predict potential trouble ahead – and I'll tell you why – whereas I worry about Kerry Katona's neediness and am fascinated by the sex- and food-loving Abi Titmuss. A vast amount of my time has been spent working with adolescents, many of whom have been unkindly labelled as 'attention-seekers', and this experience has informed my take on both Kerry and Abi.

Jude Law, the handsome Londoner who managed to conquer Hollywood, has already, at the age of thirty-two, enjoyed phenomenal acting success. However, just like the character Alfie, portrayed by Jude in the remake of the classic sixties movie of the same name, he appears to be a cad with the girls. After divorcing from actress and fashion designer Sadie Frost, he consequently found himself in hot water with fiancée Sienna Miller. Are we looking at a sex addict here? Or can he simply not control his anger? If anyone can cure him, it might just be sexy Sadie, the mother of his three children.

Speaking of sex, ever since the incredibly talented singer/songwriter George Michael was arrested for lewd conduct, he has had a hard time getting his career back on track. Will the troubled musical genius ever be able to make a real comeback? Indeed, does he want to? Some celebrities, like Hugh Grant, survive a sex scandal and even get a career boost out of it, while others are forced out of the limelight altogether.

In the past, the members of the royal family were the mainstay of celebrity, when they both commanded and received public respect, but times have most definitely changed on that score. Our modern-day heroes are sportsmen, artists, musicians, actors and anyone else who captures the imagination of the public. Bridging the gap, perhaps, is Paris Hilton, who was not only born into the Hilton dynasty, which gives her a certain amount of innate status, but also elevated herself to the celebrity A-list by virtue of her hard work and the controversy surrounding her home-made porn movie.

Today's celebrity, however, is more likely to be a self-made success. George Michael, Robbie Williams, Jude Law and Kate Moss have worked hard in their chosen professions, high achievers who have reached the pinnacle of their success through hard work and have therefore earned their celebrity status.

It is this preparedness to knuckle down that characterises

today's celebrities. Most are individuals with obsessive-compulsive personalities who strive for perfection, hugely motivated people who work their socks off. Every single designer for whom Kate Moss has worked has been quoted as saying that she is hardworking, dedicated and highly professional – indeed, a dream to work with. And Victoria Beckham, although perhaps not the most talented of The Spice Girls, is the one most obsessively dedicated to doing the best she could.

In this book, I've chosen to profile certain celebrities who come in for a huge amount of criticism and have been labelled as attention-seekers with no real talent, those scornfully described by journalist Piers Morgan in his TV documentary *Death of a Celebrity* as 'Z-list celebrities'. Despite their apparent shallowness, however, I believe that some of these so-called 'Z-listers' have an important place on Planet Celebrity. Take *Big Brother* contestant and now millionairess Jade Goody, for instance. Love her or hate her, this young woman, who hails from one of the poorest parts of London, has no one but herself to thank for her success. She gives hope to other kids who are desperate to break free from the poverty trap.

Meanwhile, in my analyses of both *I'm A Celebrity, Get Me Out Of Here!* contestant Kerry Katona (who began her career as a glamour model and pin-up girl) and sexy Abi Titmuss, I offer a possible explanation for how and why they are so popular.

The aforementioned trio have primarily become famous because of the attention of the mass media, and yet they receive this attention in the first place only because magazines sell when they're on the front covers. The public demand to know what they're up to because they can relate to them.

The nature of celebrity has evolved and changed massively over the decades, and nowadays its presence is inescapable. Celebrities enter our homes on a daily basis via the media, and in the absence of the solid network of the extended family our view of reality has become distorted. These glamorous characters fill a lonely void.

Freud held strong views about why certain people crave to be a celebrity, believing that they are motivated 'by the desire to achieve wealth, fame and sexual fulfilment'. This makes sense, as celebrities *are* richer, and they *do* have more opportunities for sex with other attractive celebrities. However, there is, of course, a downside, as demonstrated by the likes of Jude Law and Sienna Miller. First he cheats on her, and then she cheats on him, and then she is quoted as saying that she didn't think either of them was capable of remaining faithful. So it turns out that, while it's great to have choices, it's also tremendously difficult to resist temptation.

The simple fact that celebrities inhabit a glitzy world that's so different to everyday people sets them aside and seems to give them a licence to behave in ways that would be frowned upon if exhibited by a non-celebrity. Their excessive behaviour is ignored or tolerated and, when they seem to be suddenly hit by the 'celebrity curse', we all wonder why. George Best thought that his drinking, gambling and womanising was normal, until he learned the hard way that there are no free rides.

Have you noticed how many times people in the public eye are acquitted by a jury? Now, I'm not saying OJ Simpson or Michael Jackson was guilty of the crimes of which they were accused, but I'm sure that few were surprised when they were found innocent.

As for the consumption of proscribed drugs, it's common knowledge that artists, musicians, actors and people in the fashion industry are constantly indulging, and yet a blind eye is turned. A dilemma hit the Metropolitan Police when Kate Moss was caught bang to rights, and because of their anti-drugs campaign they simply had to be seen to be doing something.

INTRODUCTION

It's a fact that many of the millions of people who watch soap operas believe that the characters who inhabit them are real. This sense of inclusion can lift the mood of those who are lonely or isolated and make them feel that they have friends outside their homes. They really have a sense of knowing people like *EastEnders'* Peggy Mitchell or *Coronation Street*'s Ken Barlow. In this way, the rich and famous become a part of their lives and, when tragedy strikes their perceived friends, they grieve as if they have lost someone dear to them. The news bulletins and gossip magazines perpetuate this phenomenon. When Princess Diana died, Britain mourned *their* Princess, and the grief of the nation was palpable, verging on hysterical.

So is it right, then, that celebrities should be public property? If the word 'celebrity' is to be taken strictly literally, then the answer is yes. (The French word 'célèbre' means 'well known in public', and the Latin 'celebrum' is linked with 'fame' and 'being thronged'.) So here's one reason why celebrities are cursed, because the public and the media machine have great power in the making and breaking of a celebrity. They can, and do, build them up and then bring them down, and the higher the pedestal, the further the fall. Whether they are idolised or heavily criticised, the impact on their wellbeing is great.

One of the most horrendous examples in this book concerning negative criticism is the torrent of abuse *Big Brother*'s Jade Goody endured in 2002. How on earth she survived the vicious onslaught is astonishing. When she emerged from the *Big Brother* house, she witnessed banners emblazoned with the legend 'KILL THE PIG', and it would be fair to say that she was bullied by a nation of so-called adults. The chapter on Jade highlights just how inhumane the public can be.

But why is it that some celebrities fall into despair when their lives come off the rails when others survive? But then, why is it that some people are prone to depression, alcoholism and panic attacks while others seem to breeze through life? When the actor Matt Damon was asked why he was never in trouble in the tabloids and why very little was known of his private life, his answer was short and to the point: 'I behave myself and, when a photographer wants to take my picture, I smile into the camera. But there is no story to be told.' He is nothing if not disciplined.

Contrast this with a spread in *Heat* magazine under the headline 'JUDE LOSES IT IN HANDBAG JOKE', describing what happened when Jude Law lost his temper with a snapper over a joke about him carrying Sienna's handbag. This wasn't the first time he'd been criticised in the press for his petulant attitude, either.

Meanwhile, glamour girl Abi Titmuss might be on the pages of the gossip magazines showing her curvaceous assets and giving advice on how to pull a guy, but her own personal choice of men is questionable. Just what is it about Abi's personality that attracts the love rats?

It's worth noting that all the celebrities featured on these pages began their famous careers while still in their teens, a vulnerable time when their personalities were yet to be fully formed. Through analysing their past experiences, childhood messages and adolescent years, it's possible to understand why a troubled celebrity behaves in a way that's self-destructive. By extension, through understanding why they act out their anxieties and insecurities, it's possible to determine what must be done to enable them to change and grow.

Every single person in the world in unique. Long before I became a counsellor, I was a fingerprint officer at New Scotland Yard. This was back in the days before computerisation, and we had to classify and search through bundles and bundles of prints to find our criminal. Just as every fingerprint is unique, so is every person, and this fingerprint classification was a similar process to making a diagnosis. For example, a depressed woman will share similar personality traits to another, but the circumstances that led her to the point at which she sought help will be entirely her own.

Rule number one for me has always been to help my clients find a sense of autonomy, and I do this by taking a psychodynamic approach – a big word, yes, but not psychobabble; the 'psycho' bit means 'relating to the mind' while 'dynamic' (an adjective) means 'energetic, active' and 'dynamics' (an abstract noun) means 'the motive forces, physical or moral, affecting behaviour and change in any sphere'. Of course, I employ many other therapeutic models in my counselling work, depending on each client's individual needs, but my diploma was awarded for my psychodynamic counselling skills.

When I was counselling in London and the Home Counties in the nineties, I helped many artists, actresses and models who were struggling in their personal lives. The incredible pressure they were under to be the best led them to behave in neurotic ways, and because of their strenuous workloads they were suffering from burnout. Having to deal with their problems while under intense media scrutiny proved too much for them to bear. It was at this time that Robbie Williams sought help from Beechy Colclough, who saw him though a time of crisis and helped him get his life back on track. And it's with Robbie that this book opens.

Chapter 1

ROBBIE WILLIAMS

Statistics show that Robbie Williams is one of Britain's greatest pop stars. At the time of this book's publication, he has sold 40 million albums and signed the biggest recording contract in the history of British music, won ten Brit Awards and been voted the Sexiest Man Alive. It seems that everyone loves Robbie, a charming cheeky chap with a bit of an edge. But does he really love himself? I am talking here about his real self, as opposed to the public persona that he projects out to his adoring public.

Robbie's image is polarised by an addictive personality that he constantly needs to control. With his heavy drinking bouts and fondness for cocaine (he once asked Elton John to help him to give it up), he used to liken himself to the fallen hero F Scott Fitzgerald, but this romantic notion could perhaps be offset by Robbie's resemblance to the jolly latter-day entertainer George Formby, while a close look at some of his mannerisms in the video of 'Tripping' reveals that he actually looks something like Norman Wisdom!

Robbie's life has been well documented. The bookshops are filled with his autobiography, *Feel*, which is always out of the library. He's a popular boy, and people definitely want to know all about him. Yet, despite massive media coverage of his every move, it's difficult to tell how much of what he says and how he behaves is conjured up to whip the media circus into a frenzy. How much is bravado? Who the hell *is* he?

If we don't know *who* he is, we certainly *what* he is: he's a genius. Robbie Williams is a rightful celebrity who is highly talented and has achieved most of his goals through hard work.

Robbie has had many difficult experiences during his life. His parent's divorce while he was still very young and his subsequent ambivalence towards his father were especially painful. However, his spell in the boy band Take That and the troubled relationships he had during his teens with manager Nigel Martin-Smith and singer/songwriter Gary Barlow no doubt had a bigger and more devastating impact on Robbie's growing personality – so devastating, in fact, that the experiences left a deep wound on his sensitive psyche.

Much is spoken and written about how childhood trauma can cause misery later in life, but this isn't always the case. Often, dramatic events that occur later in life – say, in late teens or early adulthood – can have a similarly devastating impact on a person, especially if that person has a naturally sensitive personality like Robbie's. I'm convinced that he has never really got over the crushing disappointment of his naïve, childlike hopes and dreams being dashed.

Despite his amazing career, life for Robbie hasn't turned out quite the way he'd hoped, but he is also philosophical about his fame. He knows that his celebrity status elevated him out of the everyday struggle of the British working class. When Take That split, everyone thought that Gary Barlow, who had been likened to George Michael, would go on to have major success and that Williams, a less talented joker, would self-destruct. Of course, we now know that this forecast couldn't have been further from the truth.

Robbie has often spoken about his demons and has openly confessed to having to protect himself from himself. Indeed, the tabloids once screamed, 'robbie in drink and drugs crisis' and 'ruin of a teen idol', and Robbie himself has admitted on numerous occasions that at that time he was 'scared and confused'.

Robbie's career has had extreme lows and magnificent highs, but when is he going to find some middle ground? Where can he find some stability? He thought he'd found love with All Saints' Nicole Appleton, but this union was shattered when their baby was aborted – only to go on and have a child with Robbie's arch-rival, Oasis's Liam Gallagher, to Robbie's reported emotional devastation. Has Robbie Williams *ever* been in love? He says he hasn't.

So, after his success with Take That, and a subsequent visit to the doldrums, just what was it that enabled Robbie to claw his way back up the fame ladder? Was it his talent, his magnetic allure and his ability to entertain? Or was it the way he comes across to society? He has been described as a cool bloke with the ability to be naff, and his semi-sad eyes bear a glint that seems to say, 'Hey! Take a look at me. Don't you know I'm taking the piss?'

Robbie is an expressive guy. With just a shrug of his shoulders, he can look resigned, bored and a little exasperated, all at once. And he has been heard to mutter, with a sly smile dancing

3

around the corners of his mouth, 'This is what my world is like.'

But just what *is* his world like? What is it like to inhabit the mind of a troubled genius? And where does the entertainer who keeps on reinventing himself go from here? Will he keep going from strength to strength, or will he crash? Can he find true love, or is he destined to live out his life untrusting and isolated? To find some answers to the above questions, we first need to acquaint ourselves with the life and times of Robert Peter Maximillian Williams.

MR ENTERTAINMENT

Robert Williams began his career on the stage at a very early age when he played the Artful Dodger in a school production of Lionel Bart's musical *Oliver!* – and, in a way, it's a part he continues to play to this day. We think we know about him, but in reality we actually know very little of the singer. Could this be because he is still struggling to know himself?

His lyrics give us clues. In his song 'Feel', he repeatedly tells us (and probably himself), 'Not sure I understand.'

(You'll notice that sometimes I refer to Robbie as Rob. In fact, he can't stand the name 'Robbie', which was inflicted upon him during his Take That days by Nigel Martin-Smith, who reckoned it fitted his image of someone in a boy band better than 'Rob' or 'Robert'. For this reason, I refer to him as Rob in his personal life and Robbie in his persona as a performer. In therapeutic terms, this demonstrates just one of the splits in his identity and one of the reasons why he struggles with his sense of self.)

Long before a wide-eyed Robbie Williams strutted his stuff on to the stage singing about angels, he sat like an angel in his pram, seducing the grown-ups around him with an adorable wide-eyed expression and a beaming smile. He already knew what he had to do to get attention, to be loved, to get an ice cream: he had to perform.

Robert Williams was the first child of Peter Williams (whose stage name was Conway) and the second of his new wife Jan, who already had a daughter, Sally, from a previous marriage. In a rare article Robbie gave to the *Observer*, Robbie related a tale about his granddad being so embarrassed about his daughter (Robbie's mum) shaming the family by divorcing that he made her walk ten paces before him on the streets of Stoke. In fact, both Pete and Jan had failed marriages behind them, but it was a joyous occasion when they wed in Stoke Registry Office in 1970, and five-year-old Sally must have been delighted to be their bridesmaid.

The new family settled into their new home, a small house in Victoria Park Road, Tunstall, and soon Pete and Jan started to try for a baby of their own. After four years of trying, however, mild anxiety had been elevated to desperation, and by 1974, when Robert finally put in an appearance, they were ecstatic.

Robert was born at the North Staffordshire Maternity Hospital in Newcastle-under-Lyme, and one can only imagine the parental joy. It's not an easy thing to want a child for years before managing to conceive. As each month goes by, the need and longing grows.

Entertainer Pete was apparently so overwhelmed by the sight of his lovely wife and their newborn son in hospital that he shook like a leaf when forced to leave their sides to go to work, so much so that he couldn't drive himself to the Talk of the Midlands club in Derby, a venue where he was booked to appear alongside Frank Ifield (he of yodelling fame). Later that night, in the early hours of the morning, he crept into the hospital with flowers for Jan and sat on her bed, cradling his new baby son, overjoyed at having a little boy.

Just like many families who seem to have it all – a nice home, two cars, two happy, healthy kids and an affordable lifestyle – it would be fair to say that all was not hunky dory. While mum was at home taking care of the family, Pete was away taking care of himself and his career. Pete clearly put Pete first, and Jan was none too happy. She wanted more out of life and, no shrinking violet, was prepared to voice her needs.

Many children who grow up to be successful celebrities have ambitious parents, and both Pete and Jan expected more out of life than their neighbours, who seemed to be satisfied with much less. Pete the showbiz trouper was desperate for fame and travelled the length and breadth of the country in pursuit of his dream, whereas Jan wanted her husband at home with her and for her family to all be together. A compromise was handed to them when Pete landed a summer-season booking on the Channel Islands, where he, Jan and the children spent four idyllic months together.

During this happy time, Jan came up with the idea of her and Pete running a pub in Stoke. He was a local celebrity there, and the plan was that they would capitalise on his fame to make the pub a success while at the same time they could all be together. But this was Jan's dream, and Jan's dream alone. Career-wise, the timing couldn't have been worse for Pete. He was doing extremely well as an entertainer, and it's fair to say that, had he continued to put himself first at this time, he would have had a chance to fulfil his ambitions. Nonetheless, he gave up his career as a performer to be with his family in Stoke.

It was a disastrous decision. Pete had worked long and hard, slowly building his career in the nightclubs, but, when he stepped outside the showbiz arena and the bright lights of clubs, his place was ready to be filled by some other hungry performer.

Pete's first job had been with the police, but he was destined to trade this in to follow his heart into showbiz, and it seemed that, when he won ITV's talent-spotting show *New Faces*, he was well on his way to making his dream come true. Several years later, however, while by this time a local star, the universal fame he craved was still nowhere on the horizon and his potential was destined never to be fully realised.

Jan, on the other hand, was living a life that fed her personality. Clearly a driven woman, as well as being a wife and mother, she was broadcasting on local radio and running the Red Lion pub. Add to this the fact that she was appointed chairwoman of the National Housewives' Association and the picture of a modern-day superwoman is complete.

Meanwhile, Pete, not a happy bunny, did what he allegedly did best: he walked away. He says today he didn't mean to, but this is of little consolation to his family. His philosophy was simple: 'Life's too short to be unhappy.' Link this belief to his aversion to anything involving 'taking responsibility', including being the head of a family, and it was clear that the Williams household had a serious problem – one that usually ends in divorce.

Although Pete walked out on family life, he wasn't about to admit to abandoning his son. He recently justified his actions by admitting that leaving Rob was a terrible thing, but that he also believed his son would be better off in a happy atmosphere and, in the world according to Pete Conway, life in the Red Lion was far from happy. So, according to Pete, Rob was better off without a dad around. The reality was that, when Pete disappeared with no explanation, those he left behind suffered greatly.

Three and a half years after his departure, Pete returned – for his clothes. Jan, unsurprisingly, didn't let him in at first. When he finally managed to get a foot in the door, he thought his son would be as 'nervous and excited as me', but apparently, after shrugging a casual 'Hiya, Dad', Rob went back to watching *Batman*. It took him a while to compose himself and ask his dad where he'd been and what he'd been doing.

Pete and Rob were destined not to have a healthy father-and-son relationship. Instead, a mediocre, less-than-adequate façade slipped into the void. Just like hundreds of other kids from broken homes, Pete and Rob spent strained Saturday afternoons together. However, whereas some kids munch on burgers at McDonald's or visit local cinemas with their absent fathers on visiting days, Robert would accompany his father to the bookies' before visiting the park for a kickabout. By all accounts, the interaction between the two was forced.

So was life all darkness for the abandoned son of a theatrical wannabe? It seems not. But it also seems that the joker and the skilful impersonator that is such a huge part of the Robbie Williams persona grew out of his sense of loss. Young boys need to look up to a positive male mentor; it's not enough to have an all-nurturing mother who adores her boy. In fact, this combination of absent father and doting mother can, and often does, have a catastrophic impact on a child.

It strikes me that Robbie's 'look at me' attitude began very early in his childhood, when he quickly learned what would get him the attention he craved. Instinctively, he began to use his innate and vivid imagination to fill the void left by his absent father.

Pete has told an enlightening and endearing story about toddler Robbie standing at the top of the stairs in the Red Lion when he was supposed to be tucked up in bed. Apparently, there was a bright light above his head, and it was under this spotlight at the top of the stairs that he found his very first stage.

'I could dance before I could walk,' Robbie has said, 'and, literally before I could talk, I could sing. If I did that, people smiled and paid me attention.'

So, the child performer who was then known as Rob Williams was a seductive character long before he became Take That's Robbie Williams. In fact, Rob won his first ever talent contest at the tender age of three, and thoroughly enjoyed strutting his stuff on stage while singing 'Summer Nights' in the style of John Travolta.

The stories highlighting Robert Williams's potential are endless, but my favourite is the one his mother tells of him approaching Zimbabwean vice-president Joshua Nkomo at the age of eight and introducing himself.

'Hello,' said Robert. 'I'm Robert Williams from England and I can do impressions of black men.' He then proceeded to do an impersonation of Lenny Henry.

Nkomo burst out laughing at the gutsy kid before him, a plucky boy who wasn't intimidated by either the guns or the burly minders, and invited Rob to sit down for a chat. He signed an autograph for the youngster, who would later tell Jan with delight, 'That's the president of Africa.'

For me, this story exemplifies beautifully the Williams X-factor that we now know so well. It's certain that Robert was perceived by many as being a precocious little show-off, but he was nevertheless unmistakeably talented. One of his teachers at Mill Hill School, John Collis, remembers his instinctive talent for drama and describes how, after Robert told his deputy headmaster that he was going to be famous, the teacher told him not to waste his time on silly dreams. Knowing the Robbie

Williams of today, at this point he probably said to himself something like, 'Fuck you. Just wait and see if I don't.' What he *did*, however, was hold his head high and tell the figure of authority, 'I bet I'll end up driving a fast car before you!' I wonder how that deputy felt on watching a music video years later featuring Robbie driving a flashy sports car with a personalised number plate?

Both Pete and Jan put themselves out to make sure their son got every opportunity possible to ensure that he fulfilled his dream of stardom. Pete took him to endless auditions, and then Jan spotted the recruitment ad in the *Sun* for members of a new boy band – which, of course, turned out to be Take That. Both his parents definitely had a hand in ensuring that their only son would be propelled onwards and upwards to become the celebrity he craved to be. Rob wanted fame, and his mum and dad did everything in their power to help him find it.

The child performer who had loved to sing, dance, act, entertain and generally show off was now entering his teens, that tricky time when puberty sets in and boys begin their precarious transition through adolescence and into manhood. Rob was fourteen years old, and it had been more than a decade since he'd stood in his very own spotlight at the top of the stairs in the Red Lion.

One of Rob's defining moments on his journey through to adulthood was his portrayal of the Artful Dodger in a presentation of *Oliver!* As he marched out on to the stage, he was blinded momentarily by the bright lights. Then there was an audible gasp from the audience, and Rob Williams got his first inkling of the incredible power of the showman. *This* would fill the void. It was an addictive feeling – but it was to be his first of many such addictions, some of which would later cause him much pain and suffering. Enter fame and fortune – and vodka and cocaine...

COMING UNDONE

'I want to put 3,000 quid on Robbie Williams topping himself in the next six months.'

An EMI executive just over a year after Robbie had left Take That.

Take That's first hit was 'It Only Takes A Minute', and indeed it only took a minute for Rob – now Robbie – Williams to regret joining the band.

If Rob's account of his time in the boy band is to be believed, the experience was a horrible one. He was fifteen years old when he won the audition, and it wasn't long after that that he was wishing he'd taken his original route of becoming a Pontin's bluecoat. The chances are that he would have eventually become famous whatever road he'd taken; such was his drive and ambition, he was destined to become headline news. And just maybe, by steering clear of the likes of the allegedly controlling Nigel Martin-Smith and following a route that was less intense, he would have been spared much time in a painful psychological wilderness.

Boys typically have a tough time during the ages of fifteen to twenty, but place such a boy in an environment that's controlling, claustrophobic and somewhat intimidating and you're asking for trouble – and trouble was exactly what was waiting for the sensitive and vulnerable Rob, who was already struggling with identity and confidence issues. Yes, he could boldly march up to the African vice-president and have a chummy conversation, but deep-seated personal issues were lurking beneath the surface of his bravado, issues that would later break out into the light.

It was Jan who typed out Rob's CV, which told manager Nigel Martin-Smith that all her son wanted to do was to become famous, and in the summer of 1990 the teenaged Rob Williams became Robbie Williams, a pop star in a band of highly polished, well-marketed, good-looking boys who were destined for fame and fortune.

The moment Nigel Martin-Smith met Rob Williams, he wanted him in his band. Whatever Rob has to say about the man who he feels caused him much pain, Martin-Smith has to be given credit for the fact that he recognised the quality that has ensured Robbie Williams's continuing fame and A-list celebrity status. The manager noticed that his young protégé had that special something that set him apart from the rest of the herd.

Martin-Smith told the boys that if they gave him five years he would make them all rich. The gay impresario, who had previously managed a singing drag queen, told them that there were to be no girlfriends, no drinking, no smoking and certainly no drug-taking. They had to keep their private lives private and stay away from nightclubs, where the paparazzi and representatives of the tabloid press lurked. Martin-Smith intended to build a protective wall around his boys. His intentions might have been good, but for Rob they laid down yet another layer of defence he didn't need, serving only to stifle his outgoing personality and in turn temporarily damage his natural creativity. Add to this the fact that Gary Barlow had already snatched up the coveted label of 'talented one most likely to succeed' and it's clear that the situation was something of a poisonous cocktail ready for Rob to swallow. Yet swallow he did.

And so Robbie Williams was born – a name chosen by Martin-Smith because he thought it sounded mischievous. Rob hated it. And the unwanted name wasn't to be his only struggle with a fragile identity. He'd always had to watch his weight, and now he was told to lose it. The sexy boy-band image, it seemed, did not embrace fat boys.

The third aspect of his new identity with which he was forced to grapple was the gay thing. Initially, Take That were pitched at the gay audience, so overnight the personas of Rob, Robert, Bob and now Robbie had to try to gel into one person. He had to go on a diet and try to be comfortable in his own skin, and then he had to pretend to be gay before he was at a sexually mature age.

So what do we have here? An incarcerated fifteen-year-old supposedly not as talented as Gary Barlow (fast turning into his biggest rival) given a new name, told to change his body image, before being paraded in front of a gay audience by an equally gay boss. I defy any boy not to have a difficult time, given those circumstances!

Apparently, Nigel Martin-Smith wanted to create ambiguity, to keep the audience guessing, but this was a tall order. Did he really think he could play with young boys' sexuality without consequences? And, if he really believed that he was projecting this keep-them-guessing image, somewhere along the line the messages got very muddled because Take That's early TV performances look screamingly homosexual, with a touch of fetishism thrown in for good measure.

So what experiences did Rob have during his time as part of the Take That machine that helped to raise his confidence levels? Well, as far as image and identity went, absolutely none. But what about his vocal skills? Was he encouraged to improve his singing? Any dodgy notes he hit in the recording studio were simply smoothed over by the technicians. All this must have had a negative impact on such a confused teenager.

What Martin-Smith did do was mortgage his home to raise enough capital to nail a record deal. He then whisked the boys off to London to sign on the dotted line. What a heady moment that must have been for Rob and the other band members! But, then again, maybe not.

Apparently, Rob told his mum that he was sick of being treated like an idiot by the older band members. His already difficult relationship with Nigel Martin-Smith was going from bad to worse, and he began to talk again about becoming a bluecoat. However, an older, wiser Pete was quick to point out that, if Rob was unhappy now, he would be devastated if he left the band and they went on to have a big hit without him.

So, as miserable as he was, Robbie Williams stayed put, and of course his persistence paid off. Well, it had to really, because you just can't keep a good act down, and Take That *were* a good act.

Rob had become Robbie Williams, and not only was a star born but he also began to forge an identity with which he felt able to perform well. If Nigel Martin-Smith had wanted him to be perceived as the mischievous one, he got his wish – and a whole lot more.

While the other, more disciplined members of the group stuck rigidly to their enforced dance routines, Robbie began to break away and do his own stuff, effectively sticking his fingers up at the enforced discipline his manager had imposed and rebelling as only a teenager can. In all likelihood, it was a mixture of his naughtiness, combined with an element of satisfaction at having broken the mould, that was Robbie's winning formula.

So Robbie slowly but surely sabotaged Take That's carefully practised dance routines, all the while acting the fool. He must have had great fun experimenting with his newly formed stage identity, mixing a bit of Norman Wisdom with a bit of George Formby, as well as drafting a portion of himself into the persona. Finally, he'd managed to make part of the Take That act his very own. One can only imagine how miffed the other band members must have been to have their perfectly co-ordinated routines turned into Robbie Williams showpieces, not to mention how this might have caused the somewhat uptight Nigel Martin-Smith to react.

So what about Robbie's relationship with the undoubtedly talented Gary Barlow? At certain milestones during Robbie's life, he has come up against other males who he perceives to have wronged him. Whether they have or they haven't isn't the point here, because, when I work with someone who feels wronged, it's the feeling that we have to deal with first. This is because the feeling precedes the thought, and it's then this thinking that ultimately drives us to behave in certain ways.

Let's take a look at the dynamics of Robbie and Gary's relationship. Gary Barlow wrote most of Take That's songs and was also the lead singer on many of them, and so, like Rob, he had the requisite ego that needed constant feeding. He'd worked hard for many years, doing gigs in less than salubrious bars and clubs. Yes, his persistence paid off, but it didn't happen overnight; he'd endured rejection after rejection, having to face failure head on time and again before he too got his lucky break with Take That.

So here we have a Titanic clash of two monster egos with fragile cores. Fame, success, wealth and celebrity status were everything to these two very different boys (note the term 'boys' here, as opposed to 'men') because at the time in question, even though Gary was older than Robbie, they behaved like boys with each other. In therapeutic terms, the psychology behind this kind of behaviour is known as the 'child ego state', which means that adult feelings, thoughts and behaviour are unavailable to the subject.

In short, these two hugely talented individuals behaved like sibling rivals, and their rivalry was fuelled by their ambitious natures and their need to outdo each other. This acute competitiveness caused great tension between them, with Rob jealously eyeing Gary's position as the leader of the pack. Gary, who had dreamed of being the next George Michael, found himself having to stand by and watch Robbie charismatically steal the show with his cheeky but charming manner, undoubtedly envying his bandmate, who he might have seen as his younger brother. It was noted right at the beginning of Take That that Gary and Robbie's two very different personalities were destined to clash.

In many ways, Gary and Robbie were alike, but in others they were poles apart. Nevertheless, it's often the clash of similar personality types that causes sparks to fly, and Robbie and Gary were similar enough for this to be the case. However, if anyone were ever to suggest to Rob that he had anything in common with Gary, who used to charge him £1 every time he lent him his mobile phone, he'd most likely have a blue fit. For these two boys, it was war.

Between July and September 1993, Take That recorded their first singles, 'Pray' and then 'Relight My Fire', both of which made number one. Despite this huge success, however, Rob was not only uneasy with the whole Take That image but also, by 1994, with sixteen singles to the band's credit, he was unhappy with the fact that they were still on a measly sum of £150 per week. Surely, with the group being hailed as 'The Beatles of the 1990s', they should expect to be on a better wage?

Rob was despondent. Absolutely everything about Take That, and everyone involved in what he saw as a plastic pop scene, was literally driving him to drink. He'd been a drinker since the days when he used to be slipped beers by barmen while he watched his dad perform, but now, totally fed up, he felt more and more inclined to do as he pleased, and that included getting trashed. Whereas Gary was happy with the pop image and was sensible with money, Rob was beginning to idolise edgy bands such as Oasis.

It has been said that Rob christened the rigid management behind the band as 'Take That Towers', and he was about to rebel big time. What began as a tentative pushing of his boundaries was to end up as a flagrant flouting of rules to which he found it impossible to adhere.

It became clear that it was only a matter of time before Rob walked out of the band. If Take That was a family, it was a dysfunctional one. It's a great shame that the band never lived up to its philosophy of 'us against the world'.

HE'S THE ONE

While Rob was in the Take That machine, Jan, his mother, was sensible. She knew only too well how to run a business and had been worried for some time about her son's finances. She was well aware of how much other bands had been ripped off, and she wasn't about to see Rob's hard-earned money go adrift. As Robbie had been a minor when he'd joined the group, she'd been a co-signatory on all of his contracts, which gave her a certain amount of control over his finances. At one time, while the band were in Australia, Jan took it upon herself to question someone about Rob's earnings. When he found out about Robbie's mother's enquiry, Nigel Martin-Smith hit the roof and the relationship between him and Robbie hit rock bottom.

Robbie was about to find himself out of the band. It really didn't matter whether he jumped or was pushed; what mattered was that he was out on a limb. Instead of being one of five members of a boy band, he was soon simply 'Robbie Williams, ex-Take That'.

Out in the big bad world of rock, Robbie set about a change of image, and it wasn't long before he had changed from being a squeaky-clean teenybopper to a drink- and drug-fuelled hard nut, with a new steeliness about him. Always one to have attitude, he soon had an even stronger edge about him. In Take That, he'd been in danger of losing Rob altogether, but later, thanks to intense therapy, he would find him again.

During this painful period, Rob Williams was buried beneath layers of defence systems, most of which were destructive: booze to numb the pain and give him confidence; drugs to heighten his senses; more drugs in which to lose himself, to stop himself from feeling. The Take That experience had left him totally undone, and now he was praying he would be able to put himself back together, but he would have a long wait and would find salvation only after first floundering in some very murky waters. He might be the new kid on the block – best mates with hip rebels Oasis – but it would be some time before he found his own personal oasis in the dry and barren desert that was his life.

Where once Robbie had been disillusioned with the industry, now he was throwing himself into showbiz and his newfound freedom with all the energy he could muster, and for a while his feet didn't touch the ground. He was invited on stage at the Glastonbury Festival by mean-mouthed Liam and Noel

Gallagher. Totally intoxicated on both Champagne and a natural euphoric high, he was greeted by Liam with a mix of enthusiasm and sarcasm. 'Take fucking what?' yelled Gallagher.

Robbie Williams was having a ball, and he wanted some of what Oasis – at that time the undisputed coolest band in Britain – were enjoying. He was rebelling, although against what or whom I'm not sure he knew. Perhaps everything and everyone. It was the beginning of some real 'Fuck you, and then fuck you some more' times.

That year at Glastonbury, in the heat of the midday sun, Robbie signed one autograph 'Robbie Williams, nutter' and gave outrageously drunken interviews to the paparazzi. He projected the image of a bloke completely at odds with the boy in Take That and professed his belief that the Robbie Williams in Take That was a prat and his intention to bump him from a great height.

So what did he do? In fact, he behaved like a complete prat. He blacked out his front tooth and threw himself head first into the bright lights of his new life. Allegedly, this was the last straw for Nigel Martin-Smith. Now, as far as both he and Robbie were concerned (although for totally different reasons), Take That was history. 'I made sure I did every interview and I made sure I did every photo shoot, that every cameraman got a picture of me,' Robbie is quoted as saying of the time. 'And I made sure I did every interview pissed as well.'

Was Robbie totally aware of what he was doing? More importantly, of *why* he was doing it? Was he pressing a self-destruct button? Or was he doing what he needed to do in order to preserve his soul? In fact, I believe he was doing both.

Of course, as we now know, the PR worked. Robbie Williams had well and truly joined the media circus, and a new Robbie was born, sexy and yet vulnerable – a palatable combination with which both media and public alike fell in love.

Yet what followed was *not* palatable. The metamorphosis of 'Take That Robbie' to 'Robbie Williams Rock Star' was an ugly affair, and it was possibly more through luck than judgement that Robbie managed to survive his first two years as a solo artist. 'It isn't the sixties any more,' he observed at the time. 'People don't have to die because of their addictions; they get clean.'

Robbie has sung about having no regrets, but I believe he had many regrets swimming about in his alcohol-filled head before he got clean. Most likely stronger than the regrets, though, were the grudges, and issues such as blame and forgiveness (discussed later) clouded his judgement.

Nonetheless, Robbie didn't let such matters get in the way of his newfound rock 'n' roll lifestyle, and thus began some heady days of mixing with the likes of George Michael, Paula Yates and Michael Hutchinson in St Tropez, partying non-stop beside the sparkling blue Mediterranean as Robbie sought to escape the loneliness that had pursued him during his time in the band.

Robbie's phone was off the hook, and so was his life. He'd joined Take That at sixteen and came out at twenty, and those important and formative four or five years had taken their toll on his personality and mapped out much of who he had become. Ego and alter ego, false and true self – call it what you like; Robbie's identity was in crisis. He was in freefall, at that scary in-between stage where he couldn't go back to where he'd come from but was yet to arrive at where he was going. What made it particularly tricky was the fact that he hated the place he'd come from but didn't have a clue where he was going.

Robbie must have been having the most terrible time in his head. The inner dialogue would most probably have gone something like this: 'Oh, fuck. All I ever wanted was fame. All I wanted was to be a success, to be a somebody, to be a celebrity recognised wherever I go. Now I've left Take That, what or who will I be? Just who the fuck am I?' He must have been terrified, and news reports from that time indicate that he spent a great deal of time drunk and drugged up and was forever in tears. His new manager, Kevin Kinsella, is alleged to have said, 'He had been kicked out of Take That and he had no idea what to do with himself. Being famous had been his life since he was a teenager. It is what he did. I really don't believe he knew how to be a real person. He was terrified by the idea of it.'

By this time, Robbie's weight was piling back on and his confidence was in tatters. In fact, in all likelihood his persona was fragmenting. The only time he managed to function was when his alter ego, 'Robbie', snapped into place. Then Robbie – not Rob – would come out and face the music. Cocaine both hindered and helped him to cope with the trials of life – that is, until the biggest hindrance of cocaine usage reared its ugly head and paranoia set in.

Thankfully, Kinsella was able to feel empathy for Robbie, who needed someone to understand what he was going through. His new manager recognised the boy's confusion and saw the wounds that needed healing. Robbie was a chaotic mess and well under the curse of celebrity, suffocating and threatening to destroy his very existence. Where could Rob/Bob/Robbie/Robert go from here?

LET ME ENTERTAIN YOU

'I'm rich beyond my wildest dreams!' yelled Robbie Williams at the assembled TV crews and reporters after having signed an £80 million record deal with EMI. The question on many people's lips at the time was, how did he pull that one off? How on earth did he manage to drag his backside off the sofa of depression and leap into the record books? What motivated him to escape from his bloated alcoholic and drug-addicted state? Who, or what, helped him? He'd even managed to survive a broken love affair with All Saints' Nicole Appleton and get over the fact that their child was aborted.

I'm not suggesting that he's forgiven or forgotten, because I don't think he has. If one were to believe all one reads concerning Robbie and Nicole's romance, it would seem that at one time they were incredibly close, but the bottom line was that she didn't want to compromise her career. And, if Robbie was telling the truth when he said he's never been in love or loved, it's likely he got over the disappointment quickly. Either that or the grief remains buried. Nonetheless, life must certainly have been hard for Robbie when Nicole went on to give birth Gene, whose father is once idolised but now arch-rival Liam Gallagher, which must have really hurt.

But Robbie *did* come back from the abyss, although his rise was less than meteoric. His first solo album, *Life Through A Lens*, achieved only modest sales, but sales exploded after the single 'Angels' was released in time for the 1997 Christmas market. Amazingly, this beautiful ballad took only twenty minutes to write, yet British voters later pegged it as the second best song of all time.

So, although it didn't all happen overnight and was achieved via a road that was by no means smooth, Robbie Williams finally found success as a solo artist – a success that has turned out to be astounding. After *Life Through A Lens*, four more original albums followed: *I've Been Expecting You*, containing the singles 'Millennium', 'Strong', 'No Regrets' and 'She's The One'; *Sing*

When You're Winning, featuring the duet 'Kids' with Kylie Minogue; the million-seller *Escapology*; and a live album, *What We Did Last Summer*, which was recorded in front of 375,000 people at one of his legendary Knebworth performances.

Shortly after *Sing When You're Winning* came Robbie's extremely successful cover album of classic swing songs *Swing When You're Winning*, on which he sang an old Frank and Nancy Sinatra song, 'Something Stupid', with Nicole Kidman. The song made the Christmas number-one slot, and the Sinatra family were so impressed with Robbie's version of the song that they gave their permission for him to perform 'It Was A Very Good Year'. Millions of Robbie's fans were delighted to watch his great 2001 one-off performance at the Royal Albert Hall, where at one point it seemed that Robbie was actually singing with the great Frank Sinatra himself.

Not everyone was there that night, though. Robbie's mother, Jan, was present, but his father, Pete, was absent. Sadly, the man who had inspired Robbie's love of the Rat Pack's music wasn't present to witness his boy's success. While Robbie was enjoying one of the happiest times of his life, he had no opportunity to share it with his father. But, for all that, was Pete that bad a dad? Ultimately, only father and son can say, knowing what could and couldn't have been achieved.

So, Robbie Williams had survived – and, indeed, more than that; his career could now be described as phenomenal. The awards just kept on coming. He'd won three Brit awards as a member of Take That, and as a solo artist he went on to win another ten by the time of publication, including Best British Male Artist at the Brits in 1999, 2001, 2002 and 2003.

When asked about this incredible success, Robbie was quick to answer, with typical cockiness, 'I wouldn't have started out in music if I didn't think I could be the biggest in the world. It's all there for me if I remain tip-top.'

What does he mean by this? And how might the next chapter of this complex boy's life read? Because, in fact, although Robbie Williams is the undisputed champion of Europe, he has failed so far in his attempts to conquer America, so he really isn't the biggest in the world... yet.

The young Rob Williams had wanted to be an actor, but Take That had steered him in another direction, and his career continued to diversify. In 1999, he was the narrator of the children's film *Robbie the Reindeer: Hooves on Fire*, and in 2005 he was the voice of Dougal in the English big-screen production of *The Magic Roundabout*. Despite this burgeoning thespianism, however, in 2005 he told the *Observer*'s Paul Flynn that he had no desire to move into acting.

But then, why would he even want to cross over into the movies? He remains huge in the music industry. His latest album at the time of publication, 2005's *Intensive Care*, was released to critical approval, and the lead single from the album, 'Tripping', is certainly different, allegedly inspired in part by the legendary reggae star Bob Marley, and the accompanying video is certainly different – very pink, very camp. The track has been held by some as 'defiantly weird', and it's certainly a departure from the work he did with Guy Chambers.

Robbie now collaborates with Steven Duffy, a songwriter of whom he speaks highly. 'The guy's a genius, very trusting,' he told Vernon Kay and June Sarpong on Channel 4's *T4* programme. 'It took two years to write and record *Intensive Care*, and most of it was done in my bedroom. Steven said, "You get on the synthesisers and I'll get on bass" – although "Tripping" came from me on the bass.'

On the same programme, when asked if he thought this was his best album, he said he wouldn't be making albums if he didn't strive for the next to be the best. 'The best buzz is when I've just finished making the album.'

Intensive Care is without doubt Robbie's most autobiographical album to date. 'The lyrics are self-evident,' he admits, 'especially the line "Lord make me pure, but not yet".' He agrees that he wears his heart on a sleeve, and the lyrics reveal a great deal about his character.

Shortly, I'll be looking at how Robbie's difficulties to date have stemmed from his turbulent adolescent years, but first it's pertinent to talk a little about his apparent fear of dying, especially of dying before he has found the love that has until now eluded him.

Aside from all the physical and emotional changes that occur during our teens, we are faced with an increasing degree of independence, which can lead to confusing and conflicting emotions, especially concerning death and suicide. When facing such conflicts, some children, like Rob, express their feelings through exhibiting challenging behaviour, possibly panicking when confronting an uncertain future. Feelings of remorse and self-blame are common in such cases, as the child fears outwardly expressing his or her fears and anxieties and fights to stay in control. All of these traits remind me of Robbie Williams. It's a shame that teenagers are unaware that how they are feeling is a totally natural phenomenon; a process – no more, no less.

Robbie is no stranger to rehab, and he is now out of denial and a self-confessed 'recovering alcoholic'. He hasn't shied away from therapy; on the contrary, he has embraced the concept and braved the experience. He is a great self-analyst and wants to know who 'me' is – but I sense that he still struggles with his autonomy.

So that's my profile of Robbie, examining his primary relationships – including those with parents, teachers and mentors – from early childhood up to the present day. But these aren't the only people who have helped to mould Rob into the man he is today; his great friend Jonathan Wilkes remains close by his side. Together they sang a duet at the Royal Albert Hall gig.

But then, what about the girls? Genuine girlfriends such as Nicole Appleton and other supposed romances with stars such as Geri Halliwell, now pregnant by his screenwriter friend Sacha Gervasi.

For that matter, just who *are* you, Rob?

ROBBIE ON THE COUCH

Feel

I've always loved Robbie Williams's music but, until I researched this book, I didn't know much about him as a person and had no idea what a complex guy he is. I'd heard people label him egotistical and I'd watched his naughty behaviour as he flirted with pretty women such as Geri Halliwell and TV presenter Fearne Cotton, but I'd put his cockiness down as being all part of the act. Now that I've studied him, however, I think that, behind the hedonistic behaviour, there's someone I'd really like to meet.

Take his lyrics, for example. In one song he sings repeatedly, 'Not sure I understand,' while he also declares, 'I don't want to die, but I ain't keen on living either.' Compare these lines with the title of one of the first songs he ever wrote, 'Old Before I Die', and I think we might be getting close to the heart of the message.

It strikes me this is Rob talking through the medium of his music. It's not the Artful Dodger, and nor is it Norman Wisdom or George Formby. Whoever it is, it certainly isn't the persona of Robbie Williams who was born during Rob's days with Take That.

It is the teenage Rob who remains fearful of death. Like George Michael (see Chapter 3), he uses his music as a vehicle to give vent to a deep-seated turmoil, communicating to the masses via his talent.

Kids

'It's probably me trying my best to let go, subconsciously, of a time before Take That, when I was still a school kid. It's actually letting go of my romantic expectations of what growing older would be. When you're thirteen, fourteen, fifteen and you've got your Walkman on, and you're walking through Piccadilly Gardens in Manchester or you're at the bus station in Stoke and it's raining, then the possibility of being exactly who you want to be is at its strongest. Your expectation of sex and drinking and of taking your first E or maybe of being on the TV or in a loving relationship... the expectation of all that stuff is just so beautiful and perfect.' – *Robbie in the* Observer, *October 2005, about the mood on the album* Intensive Care.

I feel compelled to talk about adolescence, because I believe that much of what happened to Rob during his teens moulded him to become the man he is today.

As a counsellor, I often explore my clients' childhoods in

order to find the roots of their problems. Sometimes, however, there is very little to go on. Instead, I find that events during puberty, adolescence or early adult years have had a traumatic impact and that my clients have been compelled to resort to behaviour that helps them through such difficult times. Now, I'm aware that this might sound strange, a little like saying, 'Oh, he's drinking too much because he's shy' or 'She's eating too much because she's scared of having sex, so to protect herself she's added an unattractive layer of fat to keep the boys away.' But what many people fail to understand is that this kind of defensive behaviour often serves a purpose. Otherwise, why would we *have* defences?

Adolescence is a time to explore, to take risks, to make mistakes and, hopefully, to learn from them. Each time you fall down and hurt yourself, you pick yourself up, dust yourself down and get on with life. There are endless disappointments that need to be grieved for and then got over. This is what makes all the difference between success and failure. What doesn't kill you makes you stronger.

Also during adolescence, our bodies undergo puberty. Love attachments forged during this time are notoriously insecure, acting merely as a basis for sexual exploration.

Although human nature is remarkably resilient at this stage, early experiences can mar future sexuality, and the potential for both emotional and physical harm is great. Sex and love are a tricky mix: avoid them and you're emotionally only half alive; fall in love and you risk great pain.

Robbie has spoken movingly to the *Observer*'s Paul Flynn about a teenage crush and a 'giant expectation, but that giant expectation was when I was sixteen and it was with a girl who was hounded by the press last year'. Almost in the same breath, he put in that he was five years sober and six years out of a relationship, before admitting that he was getting a little panicky about perhaps being unlovable and that he would never have children. But then, in true Robbie Williams style, he counterbalances this by congratulating himself: 'Well, fucking hell, you got through your twenties without getting divorced' (eg like his mum and dad); 'there's no single mothers running around with your babies and you have no lifetime attachments to people that you hate.'

It's for sure that Robbie wasn't going to repeat his family's patterns of behaviour, but maybe on an unconscious level his parents' mistakes and his grandfather's embarrassment are unresolved issues that need to be addressed. The power of the unconscious processes, after all, cannot be underestimated; they are the hidden mass below the tip of the iceberg. However, trying to silence the voice in his head that wants to risk all for the experience of love is probably the reason why Robbie has never committed fully to a relationship. It's as if God and the Devil are fighting over his soul.

In civilised times, sex and sexuality have never been so out in the open as they are today, and the expectation of performance is high. Ever since the liberating days of the swinging sixties, we have been encouraged by society to flaunt our sexuality – but this is not an easy concept for many. As we move through the transitional stage of adolescence, growing from a child into a mature adult, a myriad of anxieties and insecurities arise: 'Can I cope in a difficult adult world? Will I be able to move away from the comfort of my family? Will I earn a decent living, and hold down a relationship?' And at the centre of this questioning self-doubt is sex.

Rob Williams left school when he was fifteen years old, after which he was transported straight into Take That. In effect, he became a member of a dysfunctional family, at the head of which was a controlling homosexual father-figure. In the early Take That videos, Robbie looks so young – and, indeed, he was; he was the baby of the group, and it shows.

Along with Robbie in this strange family was 'older brother' Gary Barlow, the supposedly most talented one, hailed as the next George Michael. During our emotional development, envy and hatred are very close on the scale, and Robbie was so envious of Gary being the frontman that he was bound to experience the 'twinned' emotion of hatred – and he certainly did. As mentioned earlier, Robbie locked horns with his 'sibling' and a mighty clash of the egos flourished.

So, if Gary had been labelled as the member of Take That most likely to succeed, what did that make Robbie? Nigel Martin-Smith wanted him to be known as 'Robbie' because the name sounded naughtier than just plain 'Rob', but the name change wasn't Robbie's choice; it didn't necessarily represent how he felt about himself. So what personality could Robbie grasp hold of and develop into something within which he felt comfortable? He was projecting the persona of a headstrong lad with a massive ego, but inside he was vulnerable, sensitive and struggling with a fragile ego.

Then there was the band's sexual image. Nigel Martin-Smith intended them to appear as having ambiguous sexuality and to keep the fans guessing about their sexual preferences, but, as I mentioned earlier, this wasn't exactly the message that was put across. Instead, even though Robbie is straight, some of their fans saw them as a gay band, during a time when Robbie was in the delicate transitional state between boyhood and manhood.

Robbie knew that he didn't belong in Take That Towers. He

wanted to leave and become a bluecoat, but he was advised against it. He was lost. And so he did what any healthy teenager does when life isn't working out: he rebelled.

Many people don't realise just how important the act of rebellion can be, especially when it's performed by a confused young boy trying to find himself. In such a case, rebellion is an absolute necessity if he is not to grow up being passive and compliant while harbouring a deep resentment.

Robbie played up terribly. He wanted to be in a band like Oasis. Then, no longer able to stand the restraints of the Take That machine, which he felt he had been bound to and silenced by for far too long, he broke free. And then he lost the plot.

However, strange as it might seem, this is exactly what Robbie needed to do. He had to break down for a while, to fall apart before he could build himself back up into a functioning adult. This is, after all, exactly what a nervous breakdown is all about, what few people realise is an essential safety switch built into our nervous systems to protect us from going totally crazy. During a breakdown phase, we get a chance to regroup, to learn new and healthy ways of coping and to rebuild our shattered lives. Sometimes we're unable to recognise when we're close to the edge and something external stimulus triggers our awareness that we've pushed ourselves to our very limits (see Chapter 2, 'Kate Moss'). Then, during our time of recovery, we can learn how to recognise our stress levels and how to manage our lives in such a way that we don't need to use chemical substances as a crutch.

Robbie got the taste for booze at a very young age, so this turned out to be his chosen addiction, while he also snorted cocaine – traditionally readily available in the music industry – thinking that it was a normal thing to do.

The combination of all this rivalry and control, with others trying to mould him into someone he didn't recognise, was a dangerous game, resulting in a fifteen-year-old boy losing his undeveloped identity. In his confusion, Rob Williams became two people: Robbie the showman and Rob the guy desperate not to get lost beneath the showmanship.

At this stage in his career, drink, drugs, food and sex were on tap for Robbie, and he went for it. After all, what young guy wouldn't? But, when he reached crisis point, he was wise enough to ask for help. He dried out, got in shape and resumed his career.

Now was the time to experiment with who he was. He could have some fun with both his image and the media. With his newfound strength, he decided he was going to give the media exactly what the media wanted. The boy had cracked it.

A choice of two paths

By the age of twenty, we have completed only five of the eight developmental phases of life. We are still incredibly naive about ourselves, others and relationships. During adolescence, we either establish our identity or we suffer role confusion, and in early adulthood we choose between a pathway of intimacy with others or isolation with ourselves.

All that we need to concern ourselves with now are Rob's feelings of isolation. I believe that, after leaving Take That, at one point he was in danger of falling into isolation, but his natural showmanship won through in the end. He genuinely seems to like people and is comfortable when surrounded by those he cares about and trusts.

I mentioned two pathways, leading to either intimacy or isolation. How we choose between these two pathways is massively influenced by events that have taken place during our childhood and adolescence, and traumatic experiences can have a massive and long-lasting effect on our choice in this respect.

Behind Robbie's early seductive behaviour of the cherub in the pram, who learned very quickly that a cheeky grin was rewarded with an ice cream, was a baby looking for love. Robbie learned very early on that being charming got him what he wanted, and today getting what he wants is still high on his agenda.

Like the other celebrities studied in this book, Robbie Williams is a highly motivated character who both works hard and plays hard. During the days before he went into rehab, the wild child who had escaped from Take That Towers played hard, but now, more than a decade later, there are fewer stories in the press about his bad behaviour. Perhaps he really does prefer to stay home with a cup of tea now instead of partying.

In October 2005, when the concert that was later released as the album *Robbie: Live in Berlin* was screened on Channel 4, Robbie asked presenter Vernon Kay what it was like to be a new dad. He was genuinely interested in the host's newborn baby, Phoebe. Co-presenter June Sarpong immediately shot back, 'Are you feeling broody Robbie?' Robbie responded by quoting a line from his song 'Make Me Pure': 'Lord, make me pure, but not yet.' This, he said, is how he feels; he wants to be pure, but there are still some demons lurking in the shadows. But maybe he needs these little devils to ensure that he remains 'Robbie Williams, the man who entertains'. He also said that he felt like a premiership football player, making it in Europe only seldom but always making it to the final. 'I think I'll go on until I'm thirty-five or thirty-six,' he predicted, 'but then my legs and bones might start going.'

For now, however, Robbie continues to reinvent himself and find new challenges with which to feed his imagination. I think that being bored drives him crazy, which is perhaps why he sometimes sings in the nude during recording session – a case of 'Hmm. What can I do now to amuse myself?'

Something that definitely turns him on is playing football, and it's been rumoured that he's had a football pitch built in the back garden of his LA home. He was quick to set the record straight about this on *T4*: 'Yes, it's true, and it's the best thing I've ever done. Well, no, the second-best thing. The first was leaving Take That. It's got built-in goals and a net over the top so the balls can't go over the wall into the neighbour's garden. There are floodlights and speakers either side of the goals, and there's a view right over the San Fernando Valley. I just send a text to everyone saying, "Footie at 6.30." And then I say, "No, sorry, you can't come. Got too many people now!"'

In the footage of this interview, Robbie is animated as he tells of how he loves the fact that Tom Jones calls out to him. 'He even knows my name,' he grins mischievously – as if he could grin any other way.

At this point, he's asked about why he's not been mentioned in the tabloids much this year, and he turns serious and appears rather bemused. 'I don't know what happened,' he confesses. 'One day last January [2004] they just weren't there any more. They'd camped out for four years, and then they'd gone. There were even rumours going around that I was dead. I even had people knocking on the door to ask if I'd died. It's different over here [in the UK], though.'

Indeed, the news in the UK today is devoted mostly to his music. OK, he's still a loudmouth and likes to hang out with comedy show *Little Britain*'s David Walliams, but the focus of media attention these days is definitely on his work.

Robbie says he wants to love and be loved in return, but he also says that his mindset is much more tuned into promoting his album and touring. So is he saying that he'll give his career his all until he reaches his mid-thirties, at which point he'll make his life pure, find a wife and have kids? Maybe – unless he's just kidding us all over again! But, if we're to believe this new, trim, cleaned-up act that is Robbie Williams in the year 2005, perhaps it's proof that the demons with which he's been grappling since his early adulthood have been exorcised, and that his days lost in the wilderness, when he was confused and lost in a pit of despair, are over.

If his Berlin concert is anything to go by, his days are definitely looking brighter. There he didn't just look fit; he was full of energy and dancing all over the stage, thoroughly enjoying himself. He actually told the audience towards the end that he was feeling more relaxed on stage than he had ever been before. Besides his newfound energy, the new music was great, the oldies made the girls cry and indeed Robbie wasn't far from tears himself. Indeed, even though he's still a young, hunky, sex-on-legs bloke, there's a new maturity about him.

I predict that, when he reaches his magic thirty-second birthday and realises that he's not going to die young after all, he'll find that young wife he's searching for and have those babies. But then, I'm something of an optimist!

Blame and Forgivness

In the emotional spectrum, blame and stagnancy are closely linked, whereas forgiveness is liberating. Bearing this in mind, it has been noticeable that, in the past, Robbie has often found it difficult to forgive others. There have been pivotal times when people he's loved have either let him down or tried to control him. For instance, it took a long time for him to forgive the father who abandoned him, his mum and Sally, his half-sister. It's such a difficult thing for a child to stand by and watch his mother suffering because of rejection; the feelings that this situation evokes can have a huge impact on a growing child. On the other hand, the fact that Rob's parents were both very strongly opinionated meant that they naturally produced an equally strong son.

I wonder whether Robbie has ever let go of the anger he felt towards the Take That set-up. If he hasn't, he must try to find a way, as anger fuels more anger when harboured for too long.

Then there was Nicole Appleton's behaviour, the aborted baby and her subsequent relationship with his arch-rival Liam Gallagher, which resulted in a child.

On the other hand, according to an October 2005 edition of the *Sun*, Robbie and Gary Barlow's long feud has now been resolved: 'They kissed and made up when they reunited for a TV documentary. Yessssss.'

Life has flung quite a lot at Robbie, but he's done an amazing job in cleaning himself up. He's survived so many curses, indicating that deep down he must have a really strong character, or his quest for fame would probably have destroyed him. He's admitted to contemplating suicide in the past, but he bravely fought his way back from the brink, largely thanks to his sense of fun and reluctance to take himself too seriously. Indeed, celebrity survival is often all about these two personality traits. He's certainly done some catching up on what was a tricky beginning to manhood that derailed his development for a while. Rock on, Robbie.

Chapter 2

KATE MOSS

In September 2005, the great Kate Moss debate began: was this great *Vogue* icon about to be frozen out of the glamorous world of fashion? Would she be sent to jail for possessing and supplying cocaine?

Then the social services became involved, and the threat of losing her daughter Lila Grace became a reality. Jetting off to a rehab clinic in Arizona was a very different prospect from jetting off to New York to be with old flame Johnny Depp, but it was imperative if she was going to get her life back on track.

By October, the same newspaper that had exposed the seedy side of Kate's life of drugs and debauchery reported that she was back – not in the UK to face any charges but on the front cover of a glossy US magazine. It had taken just three weeks for the celebrity curse to spin a circle of barbed wire around the privileged world of supermodel Kate Moss, to dump her at the bottom of the pile, rough her up and then perch her back on top.

THE CURSE OF CELEBRITY

Ever since the early nineties, when young, fresh-faced Kate first became front-page news, thousands of women have both adored her unique style and envied her slimness. The fashion and glamour industries were quick to promote her waif-like, rock-chick image, and it was inevitable that teenage girls would want to emulate her. Like it or not, for fifteen years Kate has been not only a supermodel but also a less than a super role model.

Kate was allegedly taking class-A drugs for quite some time before her habits were exposed. Publicly, she does nothing to hide her smoking and drinking habits, and she doesn't look as if she's had a square meal in her life, bringing much criticism upon her. She has been quoted as complaining, 'Now I'm not only being blamed for anorexia but also lung cancer.' But the labels hung over her pretty head in the autumn of 2005 were more sinister. At that time, she was lambasted for being a junkie, allegedly a supplier and possibly, though unfairly, an unfit mother – not exactly fitting descriptions for an icon.

So, just what led her to behave so badly? And just what mystery is lurking beneath her beautiful surface? Is there a flaw in her personality, or is she a victim of exploitation? More likely, her extraordinary lifestyle, being caught up in the celebrity circus and dissected under the bright lights of the insatiable media, has finally proved one party too much.

The lights began flashing for Kate Moss while she was still in the innocent flush of youth, when the fourteen-year-old was discovered by young and ambitious talent scout Sarah Doukas from the Storm modelling agency. From that point, Kate was elevated into a world light-years away from her Surrey hometown of Croydon. Soon, wealthy beyond her wildest dreams and jetsetting all over the world, her exquisite face became one of the most recognised of the times. Today, many people think that, if Kate failed to make a comeback, her departure would be a great loss, to both the fashion and glamour industries and her fans.

During the pop-culture context of the nineties, the young Katherine Moss found fame and fortune. but what was she destined to lose?

Kate Moss is a diva with a difference, an essentially strong girl with an iron will and attitude that would be the envy of the SAS. This attitude has worked well for her and has helped her to maintain her high-profile modelling career. Yet Kate has made the headlines as much for her wild personal life as for her busy professional one, including her well-publicised stormy relationship with Johnny Depp and her equally well-known rehab stints, first in 1998 at the Priory and then at the Meadows, Arizona. Then there was her alleged liver failure, caused by excessive drinking, and reports that she had confessed to having at times taken to the catwalk not completely sober.

Such behaviour might have seemed glamorous back when she was a free and single girl about town, but times have since changed. Now that Kate is a thirty-something mother of a small daughter, the rules are different. Where once people found her youthful and glamorous attitude appealing, they are now condemning her as a poor role model and an inappropriately behaved mother.

And then, in the wake of the UK's renewed resolve to crack down on the insidious drug culture, there was talk of the arrest of someone who could well escape a prison sentence thanks to her status as a celebrity. The person in question was, of course, Kate, whom some saw as a scapegoat while others were scathing. What was certain, however, was that the undercover operation that had exposed Kate and the shambles that her life had become had caused her to plummet into a personal and professional crisis.

The girl who had always excelled at posing with a dramatic look on her face was now floundering in her own self-made drama – a drama that was unfolding at an alarming rate. Reportedly worth around $30 million net but losing contract after lucrative contract, all seemed lost for Kate. Or was it? After all, this was Planet Celebrity, and no one can predict what can happen in the fickle world of fame.

But why did Kate's life come off the rails in such a spectacular fashion? Was the curse of celebrity to blame? To find out, let's take a look at the life of the beautiful but troubled celebrity icon Kate Moss.

Until September 2005, Kate Moss was the ultimate *Vogue* icon, and in the eyes of her disciples this remains to be the case, despite being hailed soon after by the *Daily Mirror* as 'Cocaine Kate'. Back at the turn of the twentieth century, *Vogue* magazine itself said of her, 'We all project different visions on to Kate: she can be a blank canvas for our obsessions; an icon, true, but also a cipher.'

KATE'S CAREER

As a fourteen-year-old, Kate Moss's life had been nothing more than ordinary, but all that changed when her father, Pete Moss, took her and her brother, Nick, on holiday in the Bahamas, where she had a chance meeting that would change her life.

The holiday had been a success. Kate had lost her virginity and was said to be pleased that she didn't lose it to some 'nasty bloke' from her hometown. Perhaps model talent scout Sarah Doukas caught a glimpse of this first flush of sexuality in the gangly young teenager when she spotted Kate hanging around JFK Airport while her father tried to arrange tickets back to London.

The ambitious Doukas had until recently been working for the model agency IMG, but had since started her own agency, Storm, and had been in New York on the lookout for talent, trawling the streets and bars of Manhattan, searching for the face that would launch her fledgling company. She'd had no luck, until she and her brother Simon returned despondent to the airport, where she spotted Kate. At once, she could see that Kate was different, that Kate was unusual. But, as she caught sight of her, Kate's exquisite, high-cheekboned face disappeared into the throng and was momentarily lost.

Peter Moss had managed to secure the three remaining seats on the flight that would see the end of a three-day layover. However, the seats weren't together, which left Kate sitting alone in economy class. By a twist of fate, Sarah and Simon were on the same flight, and Simon wasted no time in approaching the girl to ask her if she'd ever thought about a career in modelling. The rest, of course, is history, yet surely nothing could have prepared Kate for the future that was in store for her, a future that would include amazing highs and desperate lows.

Kate was literally plucked from obscurity, and she certainly didn't have it easy as she embarked on her new career. Yes, her rise to fame was fast, but her memory of those early years of trying to make it was awful. 'I went on eight "go-sees" a day for years, and it was hideous,' she remembers. 'No one wanted to know.' Her mother, Linda, accompanied her on the first of these 'go-sees', but the experience is said to have exhausted her and she is reported to have told her daughter that basically she was 'out of there' and that, if Kate wanted to continue searching for work, she was on her own. Kate, however, was determined to keep looking, and her patience eventually paid off.

James Brown, her friend and hairdresser back in Croydon during her teenage years, didn't think that Kate necessarily had her heart set on being a model, but then it seemed that she hadn't been keen on anything much, including school. Kate attended Riddlesdown High school in Addiscombe and it has been said that she 'wasn't an entirely enthusiastic pupil'. Homework was a rude word to Kate, who apparently viewed school as a social forum more than somewhere to gain academic qualifications and discipline, and was apparently always misbehaving and up to mischief. At this time, smoking and boozing was already on the agenda, and Brown noted that she preferred to be in the confines of his salon than in the classroom. 'She had a very nice life at home, though,' he added.

This, it appears, was true – at least, until her parents divorced. This separation had the same effect on Kate that it has on most children from split families: she was devastated. And she didn't just lose a parent; Kate stayed with her mum while Nick went to live with their dad.

Kate's life is no rags to riches story, but she does have an edginess to her that smacks of a rebellious girl who doesn't give a fuck. Although no delinquent, she pushed the boundaries from a very young age, at one time calling in sick at her boring job in order to go and have fun at a visiting carnival. She was spotted and got the sack.

Kate admits to a lack of parental supervision after the break-up of her family life. In her biography *Kate Moss: Model of Imperfection*, an 'unauthorised look at fashion's unlikeliest supermodel', Katherine Kendall writes how Kate described her childhood as rather undisciplined. From quite an early age she was allowed to act as she pleased, smoking, drinking and partying without having to hide anything from her parents. Kate felt that not having anything to rebel against meant she could think for herself and be herself.

Kate's life in the spotlight began in earnest when, at fifteen years old, John Galliano cast her as 'Lolita' at her first fashion show. 'I had to come down the catwalk by myself,' she remembers. 'It looked huge, like an aeroplane runway. I was so nervous!' It was right there that Kate's career in modelling became inextricably linked with alcohol and partying; work and play fused: 'Someone had run off with the Champagne, so me and this other person drank a bottle of scotch between us. I passed out at the table and went missing for two days. I was supposed to be back at school but no one knew where I was.'

Then, at the age of eighteen, she won a highly lucrative contract with Calvin Klein and the whirlwind began for the Surrey girl. Soon the 'attention thing' began in earnest, the same attention curse that hits most celebrities (and certainly those who feature in this book). And when asked if she missed anything about starting her career so young, she said that she just misses going to the pub in Croydon and confesses to never having been 'exactly innocent'. So it appears that her 'ladette' days began early in her teens.

Later in this book, the chapter on George Best's rapid rise to fame explains how the mood of the sixties was to have a major impact on the footballer's wild days off the pitch, and a similar thing happened to Kate in the nineties. At this time, the British indie-rock scene was just beginning to gain momentum, and the designer drug MDMA, or ecstasy, was fuelling a crazy scene. It was a resurrection of the heady, free-spirited decade thirty years earlier and a time when discipline was considered a rude word and all-night raves were embraced within the drug culture.

This exciting period saw the birth of a new breed of magazines, and first and foremost amongst these was *The Face*. Everything about the magazine was new and fresh, so it's no wonder that Kate Moss became their number-one model. For Kate's shoots for the publication, up-and-coming photographer Corinne Day joined forces with the model and Sarah Doukas, and between them they defined Kate's 'grunge' look.

When Day found Kate in a Storm portfolio, she spotted a quality about the girl that resonated with her. According to Katherine Kendall, Day said that she felt Kate was possibly a bit narcissistic, and that she identified with this, having herself been given a hard time about her shape at school. Day therefore wanted to help Kate with problems similar to those she'd had.

When *The Face*'s art director at the time, Phil Bicker, first set his eyes on Day's photographs of Kate, he knew that he was looking at the face of the magazine. Two months later, Kate was on the front cover. Her natural poses and expressive features earned her plaudits and contracts throughout the fashion world. Any photographer worth his salt will confirm how instinctive she is, how she doesn't need to be told what to do, what pose to strike; she just senses the vibe and understands what's expected of her. The girl's just got it.

Kate telegraphs her innate sense of self and her strong attitude with every move and expression. In fact, Kate Moss *is* attitude. She does exactly what she wants – no more, no less. That's how it was then, and that's how it remains today.

The writers of numerous websites argue that she isn't sexy, that the waif-like Ms Moss, with her androgynous physique, is a far cry from such sex icons as Marilyn Monroe. While it's true that she's no curvy sex-bomb, she is, as the pictures included in this book show, incredibly provocative. She seems to be at ease with her body, comfortable in her own skin, and the Moss attitude is evident in her facial expressions and body language.

Even in her most intimate photographs, Kate gives the impression that she's completely at ease with her work and is there because she wants to be, not because she's being pressured by unseen forces. There is something about her that seems to be saying, 'I'm doing exactly what I want to do, and fuck you if you don't like it.' But is that really how she feels, or was there a significant moment in her career when she *needed* to adopt this attitude, to build a wall of defence around an innate vulnerability? I think so.

Right back in the early days of being photographed by Day, she admits to being reluctant to take off her clothes. In Katherine Kendall's biography, we read how Kate talked about her early shyness, and reluctance to take her clothes off. There were arguments between her and Corinne, and having to work for weeks during her school holidays without getting paid meant that Kate found it all quite difficult.

Kendall, meanwhile, notes that Kate's pictures from around this time were 'spontaneous and natural, images of a shy, giggling girl.' But she adds that for Kate this was 'part of an act.

Therapeutically, we could deduce from these comments that the adolescent Kate's real self was joined here by her new, false, public face. It's likely that she encompassed this new alter ego into her part-formed identity, and because she was so young, and yet to mature into an emotionally secure woman, the public person became deeply integrated into the fabric of who she was. If Kate Moss hadn't found celebrity status at such a young age, she would no doubt have turned out to be a very different person.

Doukas and Day encouraged Kate at every turn, especially during times of self-doubt, and the model has spoken of how the way they styled her was all contrived and how the nude pictures that originally embarrassed her eventually became her favourites. But there came a point when they all knew that she had to move on from being the quirky schoolgirl. The problem was, she could in no way be described as a typical fashion model. For a start, she didn't reach the minimum five-foot-eight height requirement. Flat-chested and with none of the usual sexy curves, she also had crooked teeth and long, gangly legs. She also had none of the breathtaking beauty of the new wave of American supermodels, such as Linda Evangelista, who famously remarked of her kind, 'We don't get out of bed for less than $10,000 a day.'

Enter Paul Rowland, an ambitious businessman who had just opened his own modelling agency, Woman Management, in New York. His minimally furnished office could in no way be described as plush, but he was a formidable-looking character who was ambitious. However, he needed models.

In Kate, Rowland saw what Sarah Doukas and Corinne Day had seen and proceeded to launch her grunge-heroin image as if she was a supermodel. Thus the Kate Moss we know today was born.

Magazine articles in the nineties described her photographs as having an air of smugness and superiority, and certainly she became superior to most of her contemporaries. She has been described, astonishingly, as the supermodel who out-supered them all. The likes of Linda Evangelista, Helena Christiansen, Tatjana Patriz and Christy Turlington might have been immensely successful at the time, but Kate was in a class of her own, and it was the quirky, edgy attitude of her public self that made all the difference. By this time, of course, her personality was huge and she was enormously popular.

Back in 2000, during an interview for fashion magazine *Nova*, when asked if she felt exploited or if she felt that she'd lost something through being a celebrity, Kate was philosophical, pointing out that, because she's a face on a magazine, quite a lot of things have been taken from her. In particular, she spoke about her loss of privacy: 'I go away a lot. I'm not stalked by the paparazzi and I'm not in the newspapers.' (Five years on, I wonder if she's changed her mind, for it strikes me that she's rarely been out of the tabloids since the turn of the century.) In the same interview, Kate's use of vocabulary paints a clear picture of the now-famous Moss attitude as she uses phrases such as 'you're art, man' and 'heavy shit'.

Her great friend Sadie Frost, once an actress but now a fashion designer with her own Frost/French label, told Kate she could tell by her photographs that she was instinctively able to 'take direction' and would make a good actress. Kate didn't really want the compliment printed in the *Nova* piece because, she laughed, 'it sounds wanky', but she went on to say, 'If [a part] comes up that I really think would be right, I would do it.'

At one point during the interview, she asked the question, 'Does that make me a weirdo?' Maybe, on some level, she feels as if she is, and maybe that's why she tends to go out with guys who are perceived to be a bit weird themselves, feeling most at ease with slightly oddball personalities.

The *Nova* interview is revealing and totally honest, showing a Kate who had come to terms with her career, especially her position as a celebrity. On reading it, I tried to recall all the paparazzi snapshots I'd seen. Had there ever been one depicting a scowling Kate, angry at the photographers' intrusion. I couldn't think of one. So I began to take more notice of the tabloid stories of Kate and, sure enough, I noticed that she rarely puts a hand (or, indeed, a finger) up at the photographers' lenses. Her bad press isn't about her being angry at their intrusiveness; it's more about her looking rough after a heavy night out on the booze, with a fag on the go and hanging on to some drug-addict rock star. Kate simply seems not to give a damn, and much of this dismissive attitude is written all over her face. It photographs well.

Back in the mid-nineties, the most expensive possession that Kate owned was a flat in Shepherd's Bush that she rarely had time to visit. 'It was like I was on some kind of treadmill, wondering what it was all for,' she remembered in a piece for *Vogue* magazine. When her accountant told her just how much money she had earned, however, she went out and spent £800 on a Vivienne Westwood sheepskin coat – and her spending spree just went on and on.

Kate moved to the well-heeled London district of St John's Wood, gave her mum the money to buy her a lovely place in the country and then set her dad up in a travel business. Meanwhile, she indulged her passion for real diamonds and antique jewellery. For one of the magazine's photo shoots, *Vogue* journalist Lisa Armstrong reported, 'At the stylist's request, she brought a selection to the shoot: the antique diamond flower Johnny [Depp] bought her; the sapphire, diamond and ruby bracelets; the Donatella Versace bracelet which was bought for her twenty-fifth birthday; plus the huge natural pearl she'd treated herself to. Out they tumbled from a little scrunched-up pink silk pouch. "Very Kate," [stylist] Sam McKnight noted.'

When I searched through archive articles on a quest to find

answers to the question 'Who is the real Kate Moss?' I found endless positive endorsements about her attitude. Calvin Klein speaks of her as the girl who 'defines her generation', while she has also been described as 'the girl who best captured the nineties' obsession with reality and beamed it back to us via that most artificial of media: fashion photography'.

Her work ethic, too, is something of which she should be proud; there's no doubt about the fact that she's worked her socks off. Had she not, she would never have become the monumental icon she is today. And yet her voracious appetite for partying continues unchecked. She makes no secret of the fact that she is a smoker, and almost seems to brag about this now antisocial habit. That 'fuck you' attitude that she sometimes wears in fashion shoots definitely spills into her everyday personal life.

One person who knows her well is PA Rebecca White, who says she's partied with Kate around sixty times since first meeting her in 1998 and has told stories of Kate's debauched past and of how, when under the influence of drugs, Kate becomes incredibly uninhibited. Maybe this is because, almost since puberty, Kate has shared her body with the world – and it's a body whose slenderness has earned her much criticism as well as praise. It's fair to say that she was the first skinny model since the 1960s and the heyday of Twiggy, and the impact that her influence had on the eating habits of teenage girls seeking to look like her was condemned by many in the press.

As far as the newspaper reports were concerned, for a long time all we read about was Kate's jetsetting life with Johnny Depp and the likes of Liam Gallagher and Patsy Kensit, looking like a million dollars. But then, one minute she was in Hollywood or the south of France and then – wham! – she was checking into rehab, another high-profile celebrity with the ability to rush from the sublime to the ridiculous in a flash. One minute Princess Perfect, the next a victim.

THE LOVABLE KATE

Kate's old friend hairdresser James Brown is clearly a great fan of Kate's. 'There were a lot of people who were secretly satisfied that this girl who had everything could mess it up,' he remembers, 'but Kate's an old soul, and deep down she's a happy person, and nothing changes that.'

World-famous fashion photographer Mario Testino, meanwhile, observes that 'no other model inspires so much affection. She is great company and is a truly nice person.' And former *Vogue* features editor Lisa Armstrong is also complimentary, describing Kate as 'the [defiantly] non-supermodel who managed to out-super them all'. Perhaps this attitude explains why, after her fall from grace following the scandal over her drug-taking, many of the companies with whom she had contracts were didn't want to drop her. Some had to dump her due to media pressure, but that doesn't mean to say they really wanted to.

Kate knows many people, but she admits to trusting only a few close friends. She also doesn't like her own company much, telling *Nova* magazine, 'I don't like being alone at all. Human contact is very important. It's not good for your soul to be by yourself all the time.'

In this, she's absolutely right. I've long believed that, although we come into this world alone and we leave it alone, while we're here we have a great need for regular contact with others. But I think that it's exactly this fear of being alone that's one reason for her dependence on chemical substances. Her comments in *Nova*, combined with a past quote from her describing the fact that being a model is 'quite a dodgy thing', reveal Kate's vulnerable, needy side.

Five years ago, Kate was a different girl, living the celebrity dream in Hollywood and France, dating movie star Johnny Depp. She was radiant and confident, and she didn't feel exploited by the media. Despite burning the candles at both ends and extinguishing the light for a while, taking time out in the Priory to recover, she came bouncing back.

Kate is also a self-confessed people-pleaser, apparently because she thinks that everyone is waiting for her to behave like a diva. So, is this confounding of expectations characteristic Kate Moss behaviour? Does she always do the opposite of what people expect? There's definitely something exceedingly delinquent about Kate, and in fact much of her naughty but giggly child seems to be always present.

Kate is reported to have said, back in the early days of her career, 'I don't think I consciously wanted to be famous, but I probably craved the attention.' If this was indeed the case, the attention she sought soon came in abundance. When she flew back from one of her whirlwind non-stop trips, she landed at Knebworth Park, where Oasis were performing. 'Before then I knew people knew my name and that there was stuff in the newspapers, but I thought I was pretty normal looking and could just walk down the street,' she remembers. She couldn't have been more wrong, though; a bodyguard was required.

Kate had always wanted to travel and see the world, and now she was chasing modelling contracts around the globe. But there wasn't much sightseeing to be done; she was far too busy.

It wasn't all hard work, though. She was now rubbing shoulders with the rock aristocracy, and these similarly rootless people became her friends. 'I would go quite mad doing the shows,' she remembers of these days, 'running around, not eating properly. Other girls could go back to their rooms and sleep, but I couldn't. I just wanted to carry on.' She felt that she had little choice but to socialise with like-minded people: other party animals. 'People would come and stay with me and we'd be up all night,' she recalls, 'and then I would have to do nine shows the next day. It was like a circus. We were pretty naughty. To be honest, seeing what we could get away with was half the appeal.'

Kate certainly pushed herself to the limits, forever testing the boundaries that were put in place around her (although she has never denied taking heroin), and her comments quoted above illustrate just how much havoc her inner child wreaks in her adult life.

MARIO SORRENTI

At around the time that Kate met fashion photographer Mario Sorrenti, she was having a hard time, personally. Her head was filled with a million thoughts and images, nervous energy pumped around her body and the constant noise of the New York traffic outside her apartment window meant that sleep was impossible. She was prescribed Valium to help her sleep at night, but the trouble was that everything in her life was moving so fast. Overnight, what she'd at first seen as a hobby had turned into a full-blown career. She could in no way be described as an amateur, but neither was she a grown-up professional. The whole New York scene must have been quite scary for her.

The last shreds of normality to which Kate had been clinging had by now disappeared from her world. She had landed on Planet Celebrity, and it was a completely different world, where full-on drink, drugs and rock 'n' roll were considered normal.

When Mario first caught sight of this new kid on the block,

he made a beeline for her and soon they were inseparable, both professionally and personally. There was Mario, with his dark good looks, and Kate, with her streetwise beauty.

Just as it had been for Kate, *The Face* magazine had been the launchpad for Mario's ambitions. A one-time model, by the time he met Kate he had turned to his real passion of photography. He was soon in love with Kate, and he loved to photograph her.

Kate, meanwhile, found herself going from ladette to lover, and it felt strange. She hadn't considered herself to be the 'girlfriend type', yet she moved in with Mario and his family, and during this time Mario's mother, Francesca, took Kate under her wing.

Meanwhile, a wave of new creative talent was emerging on the streets of New York, including a designer named Anna Sui, who revived the hippie look. *Über-fashionista* Calvin Klein, however, was going through a quiet spell and needed to find a new angle, something or someone to relight his fire. Klein's sales had often relied on controversial advertising campaigns, such as the 'Nothing's going to come between me and my Calvins' campaign, modelled by the controversial Brooke Shields.

Klein put former art designer of Italian *Vogue* Patrick Demarchelier in charge of overseeing the new advertising campaign, and, when he stumbled upon a picture of Kate at a Barcelona exhibition, he knew instantly that she was the only one for him.

Cast alongside Kate in the new campaign was 'Marky' Mark Wahlberg, he of the urban street look and rippling muscles, and next to him Kate looked even more fragile. With Kate posing topless in Klein's men's underwear, Demarchelier captured a look that would ensure another successful campaign for the company. As with the one spearheaded by Brooke Shields, the new campaign drew whispers of disapproval, but it signified the return of Calvin Klein, and it certainly didn't do Kate's career any harm.

Then Klein employed Mario Sorrenti to shoot the ads for his new perfume, Obsession, and the results were even more controversial. Nevertheless, this proved to be yet another career jump for Kate and her lover. The striking black-and-white photos of a naked Kate on a Caribbean beach evoked fury in some circles. Devoid of makeup, her strong facial expressions were a stark contrast to the frailty of her stick-thin body. Thus the waif was born.

LOSING BOTH JOHNNY AND THE PLOT

Meeting and falling in love with acclaimed Hollywood star Johnny Depp was a pivotal moment in Kate's life. When the two met, he was a mixed-up guy, whereas she was perceived to have become a strong, streetwise girl. Indeed, she has said that her early days in the business toughened her up, but my guess is that she was pretty tough to begin with. According to Katherine Kendall in *Kate Moss: Model of Imperfection*, her brother, Nick, is reported to have said, 'When she's bitchy, she's very bitchy. That's always been in her blood.'

Kate and Johnny met in 1994 at the chic bistro Café Tabac after an awards ceremony. 'I knew from the first moment we talked that we were going to be together,' Kate later exclaimed, while Johnny is reported to have declared, 'I was never in love with anyone 'til I met Kate. I'm crazy about her. I can see myself married to Kate for fifty years.' Kate's response to this was equally devoted: 'As soon as we met, we knew we were meant to be together.' *Vanity Fair* agreed, hailing them the 'couple of the decade'.

In those days, though, Johnny was completely out of control, a hell-raiser with a self-destructive streak, whereas in contrast Kate was a fresh-faced picture of health and was definitely the most grounded character of the two. One day, for instance, Johnny trashed their hotel room while Kate stood by and watched in horror. He was later arrested and charged with criminal damage but freed after agreeing to pay the £7,500 repair bill.

And this wasn't the first time Johnny had been involved with the law. Before the hotel episode, he'd been in trouble for arguing with an LA cop, speeding and allegedly assaulting a hotel worker. He was certainly all over the place, and without a hint of respect for authority.

Kate and Johnny's stormy on/off relationship lasted for three years, until he met and fell for another stunning girl with amazing cheekbones, French beauty Vanessa Paradis. Physically, there is a striking resemblance between Kate and Vanessa, but it seems that that's where the similarities end, as Vanessa is reportedly of a calmer nature. Kate apparently fell to pieces when she heard that Vanessa was pregnant with Johnny's child.

According to those who knew him, meanwhile, Johnny seemed to grow up overnight on learning that he was to be a father, purchasing a family home in France and taking regular time away from acting locations to fly home to be with his new family. When his first child, Lily-Rose (Kate was to later name her daughter Lila Grace), was born in 1999, he was over the moon and, probably as a direct consequence of his euphoric personal life, at around this time his career took off and three of his movies – *Donnie Brasco*, *Fear and Loathing in Las Vegas* and *Sleepy Hollow* – became blockbusters. At the time of publication, he was riding high on the success of director Tim Burton's remake of Roald Dahl's *Charlie and the Chocolate Factory*. He has recently turned forty, and his party for the occasion was apparently calm and civilised – a far cry from his wild days in New York with Kate Moss. He and Vanessa remain an item and now have another child.

After their break-up, however, Kate was devastated and plunged into the depths of despair. Soon the booze, drugs, wild partying, non-stop work and emotional trauma caused by Johnny's departure became too much. She crashed and checked herself into the Priory. 'I just lost the plot,' she later confessed.

Personally, and certainly with regard to her relationships with men, Kate spent quite some time in the wilderness and for years was unable to hold down a steady relationship. That's not to say that she didn't have a beau or two to wine and dine her during that time; other males she has been linked with are Spacehog guitarist Antony Langton; Jesse Wood, son of Rolling Stone Ronnie; artist Jake Chapman; Evan Dando of The Lemonheads; Billy Zane (now with Kelly Brook); and Leonardo DiCaprio, one-time boyfriend of Paris Hilton (see Chapter 10). Then, in 2002, she announced that she was to have a baby with Jefferson Hack, editor of *Dazed and Confused* magazine. The baby wasn't planned, but Hack, who was reportedly madly in love with Kate, was over the moon. Kate also said she was delighted.

So, did the partying stop? Did Kate the supermodel calm down and take responsibility? In a word, no. Instead, she was to be seen in pubs smoking and drinking when she was well into her pregnancy.

Kate and Jefferson's daughter, Lila Grace, was born on 29 September 2002, and it has been said the celebrations, held in the maternity room, turned into a Champagne-fuelled bender.

It's at this point, I believe, that Kate's life began to really change. Having Lila and becoming a mother could have been her Nirvana, but it wasn't to be. To top it all, she and Jefferson broke up.

Now, to her horror, Kate was hitting the news more for her personal life than for her career, and the fickle world of fame was about to point a critical finger at its latest victim. Kate Moss was in thrall to the curse of celebrity.

Kate must have inherited good genes to be able to still look so great. Despite endless overindulgence of alcohol, nicotine and proscribed drugs, her natural beauty remains intact. In September 2005, when a picture of her allegedly snorting cocaine appeared on the front page of the *Daily Mirror*, a dazzling image of her was meanwhile adorning the front cover of *Vogue*. The power of makeup to give a seemingly flawless complexion is well known, but Kate is luckier than most with her wonderful chiselled features and fine bone structure and has yet to exhibit the telltale signs of smoking, such as tiny lines around the mouth. Indeed, in her recent advertisements for Rimmel, she looks absolutely stunning.

It seems that cosmetics retailers from Harrods to Superdrug wanted her to endorse their products – that was, until that fateful day when the press were tipped off about her substance abuse (allegedly by someone close to her new lover, Pete Doherty) and gave her the nickname 'Cocaine Kate'.

MOSS'S POSSE

'For years, I never thought there was anything wrong with it. We all used to get drunk at the shows. I just thought I was having a really good time, which I was. But it got too much. There was no normality. I felt like everyone was sucking me away.' – *Kate Moss in* Nova *magazine, 2000.*

In interviews that appeared in the glossy fashion and lifestyle magazines in the mid-nineties, Kate determined that she did not feel exploited, but one can't fail to note that in the next decade it all went horribly wrong. By September 2005, she was knee-deep in fertile ground, and the press were having a field day.

The exploitation was now in full swing, but who else could Kate blame but herself? Could she realistically point the finger at the fashion or glamour industries, as some of her loyal fans were doing? Maybe not. But the fact that Kate had hit the self-destruct button was not in question.

In 2004, the celebrations for Kate's thirtieth birthday were rumoured to have taken the form of a thirty-hour bash for more than 100 mates, including both her disciples and hangers-on. Her entourage, now known as the 'Moss Posse', was quite literally in full swing.

Wealthy north London's Primrose Hill will never be quite the same. The scandal that hit the news headlines in the wake of the *Daily Mirror*'s undercover operation to expose Kate as a regular user of cocaine revealed the true-life stories of some of our biggest celebrities. Panic ensued, and the likes of Sadie Frost, Jude Law and toilet-paper heiress and former Channel 4 soap *Hollyoaks* actress Davinia Taylor were pinpointed as her close friends. Davinia, who was already desperately clinging on to a marriage to husband Dave, a friend of David Beckham's, now clung to him for dear life.

Suddenly, Kate Moss was perceived by many to be both ruthless and out of control. She was portrayed as being the leader of the pack, and her followers at the heart of the inner circle were referred to as her disciples, in the sense that they were her close friends – and it seemed that she had more disciples than Jesus! Sadie, whose heart belonged to Kate, was supposedly close friend number one, while temperamental Naomi Campbell was next in the pecking order. The rest of her disciples comprised a strange mix of Stella McCartney (who was said to be furious when Kate lost her contract with H&M, as it was her collection that Kate was due to model), actress Samantha Morton and Noel Gallagher's ex, Meg Mathews. Meanwhile, musician Pearl Lowe (who reportedly suffered from terrible post-natal depression), former *Hollyoaks* star Davinia Taylor (who'd had to throw Doherty off her yacht when he nearly blew it up while lighting a magic cigarette near the engine) and ex-*Brookside* star Anna Friel (recently the love element in the movie *Goal!*) were also reported to have joined the eclectic crowd at some time or other. Jade Jagger, too, apparently used to belong, but she removed herself after Kate was caught smooching with her man, Dan, and then allegedly sent Kate a necklace on which the word 'slag' was spelled out in precious stones.

Jude Law, too, used to be part of the Posse, but he took a quick step sideways after he split with Sadie Frost and waltzed off with Sienna Miller. In fact, at one time, Jude was very much a part of the action and, when the allegations of wife-swapping and *ménàges a trois* made front-page news, he was slap bang in the middle of it all.

Is it any wonder it all went so horribly wrong for so many?

In the week before the revelation concerning Kate's cocaine habit in the *Daily Mirror*, stories of her appetite for debauchery just kept on coming. Robbie Williams told the *Observer*, 'It would never have surprised me if [she'd] committed suicide that week.'

Robbie saw the romantic side of the relationship between Kate and Pete Doherty, but others were scathing, namely the *Daily Mail*'s Natalie Clark, who wrote a particularly damning article. Robbie saw the romantic side of the relationship between Kate and Pete Doherty, but others were scathing, namely the *Daily Mail*'s Natalie Clark, who wrote a particularly damning article. She wrote, 'Many players have been lured into this dark and illicit game, but there is only ever one winner. With Kate it's not just about sex; it's more to do with power and control. A mind game as much as a sex game.'

These were harsh words indeed. In fact, the whole article was particularly aggressive towards Kate, a girl of whom, until recently, no one had had a bad word to say.

It appeared, however, that Clark held some sympathy for Sadie Frost and saw Kate as the one who had tarnished her relationship with Jude Law, as the article continued, 'Only a few years ago, [Sadie] was the beautiful wife of Jude Law, on his arm at every premiere. She made the mistake of becoming entranced by Kate, fooled into believing that you could be a "free spirit" at no personal cost.'

COCAINE KATE

At her thirty-first birthday party, Kate embarked on a torrid relationship with poet and musician Pete Doherty, formerly of rock band The Libertines. It was a union that many saw at the time as spelling her downfall, but the Moss Posse, headed by the ever-faithful Sadie Frost, could do nothing to stop her.

From the beginning, Sadie was vociferous in her disapproval of Kate and Pete's relationship. 'Pete's not the sort of guy you'd wish for your best friend,' she said. 'Kate's had a history of playing hard, and the two of them together would be a terrible idea.' It sounded like a match made in Hell, a description supported by some of Pete's antics reported in the press, including heavy drug abuse and a burglary.

At the time of publication, Kate Moss is thirty-one years old – still a young woman – but, as a mother who has been exposed as an abuser of alcohol and now class-A drugs, she can no longer elicit the same amount of public sympathy that she did back in the days when she was a fledgling model. Even so, many people in both the fashion and music industries sympathised with her plight and thought that she was being used as a scapegoat. But, when traces of cocaine were found in several toilet cubicles during London Fashion Week in February 2005 by both the *Daily Mail* and the London *Evening Standard*, this served only to confirm what most had guessed anyway.

Cocaine has widely been known as the drug of choice among certain denizens of the fashion world, being both an appetite suppressant (and thus popular with super-skinny models) and a mood enhancer (initially, at least, until the downer sets in). Indeed, the pressure on models to stay thin is enormous, and many would never be able to keep their weight down to the required limit without it.

What Kate had unwittingly done was to expose the seedy side of her industry to reveal a drug culture infesting the catwalks, a culture that has always been an accepted part of the scene.

Now the media was ablaze with stories of Cocaine Kate and celebrities' consumption of class-A drugs. Boy George was arrested. Boxer Frank Bruno, whose autobiography was due for release, spoke openly about his usage of proscribed substances, and his stories were splashed all over the *News of the World*. Grim stories and pictures of Daniella Westbrook's collapsed nose resurfaced. Celebrity cocaine users, it seemed, were suddenly big news.

And the world was asking questions. Would the police arrest Kate Moss when she returned from her month in rehab in

Arizona? Would the social services be investigating Kate's ability to mother three-year-old Lila? Or would Lila's father, Jefferson Hack, get custody?

When Pete Doherty cancelled the last three tour dates of his new band, Babyshambles, to fly out to visit Kate, I remember wondering whether Kate would ever stop carrying the torch for the crack-cocaine addict to whom she appears to be addicted.

ADDICTED TO LOVE

In many ways, the union between Kate Moss and Pete Doherty is similar to the ill-fated romance between TV celebrity Paula Yates and rock star Michael Hutchence. Paula had been in a steady marriage with Bob Geldof and was a doting mother of three daughters when she aborted her life, and together with Michael set off on a route of self-destruction. Like that of Paula and Michael, Kate and Pete's relationship was wild, passionate and potentially deadly. Particularly worrying was the fact that Kate was looking up to fifty-eight-year-old Marianne Faithfull – the original heroin rock chick – as her mentor.

Celebrity hairdresser Nicky Clarke's first magazine-cover job was with Paula Yates. He was very fond of her and described her as 'charming and irreverent', and they became lifelong friends. Paula, like Kate, began her celebrity career in her teens and was a young, enthusiastic woman who oozed sex appeal when she hosted Channel 4's *Big Breakfast* where, dressed provocatively, she interviewed celebrities on a big double bed. One of the many men she interviewed was Michael Hutchence, lead singer of Australian rock band INXS. It proved to be a fateful encounter.

Friends and colleagues who knew Paula during her teens, twenties and early thirties described her as a lovely person who, by the time she died from a drug overdose, had gone through a devastating time and wasn't the woman she used to be. Nicky Clark commented, 'Towards the end, Paula had changed. She wasn't the girl I first met. I was so sad when she died.' But how and why did this happen to Paula? Was it an excess of drink and drugs that led to her tragic overdose? Or was she already suffering from a borderline personality disorder?

Kate is not Paula, however, and there are many differences in their lives. For instance, Kate has the close-knit family that Paula craved. Undeniably, Paula had a great circle of friends, but her family situation was nightmarishly fragmented. After losing Michael Hutchence in a bizarre sex act that went horribly wrong, she found out that Jess Yates, the man who she'd always called Dad, was not in fact her father; instead, DNA tests revealed that her biological father was TV presenter Hughie Green, a man with whom her mother had had an affair. Paula was devastated. Michael had died not long before this revelation, and this seemed to be one agony too much.

Some describe Paula as being devoted to Hutchence, but in fact 'devoted' is the wrong word; she was addicted, and hers was a sick love over which she had no control. It's the same love that Kate seems to have for Pete Doherty.

Just as Kate's loyal friends tried to talk sense into her, so too did Paula's friends try to dissuade her from her self-destructive path, but their warnings fell on deaf ears and Paula descended into a life replete with class-A drugs and a sex life that has been described as 'bizarre sexual experimentation'.

Paula's initial celebrity image had been that of a ditzy and exceedingly provocative blonde. When she married Boomtown Rat Bob Geldof, she seemed to mellow for a while and threw herself into motherhood, but there is little doubt that she had many affairs during this time. She was the co-humanitarian alongside hubby Bob as he spearheaded the Band Aid and Live Aid projects aiming at eliminating hunger in Africa, but her own insatiable hunger for sex, drink, drugs and rock 'n' roll always took precedence.

When the media seized on her affair with Hutchence, Paula was once again seen as something of a wild child, and, whereas knowing that the world saw her that way was bearable, being cast as an irresponsible mother wasn't. Such allegations had a devastating effect on her, and when Geldof was awarded custody of their children she fell apart at the seams, as she adored her girls – just as Kate loves Lila Grace.

Bob Geldof knew how much Paula needed her girls, and he eventually shared custody, but soon Paula's life spiralled further downwards. Soon after she and Michael had their own child, Heavenly Hiranni Tiger Lily, Michael was found hanging from the doorway in a Sydney hotel room, having died in somewhat bizarre circumstances. Paula was adamant that he had met his death during a sexual game of auto-erotic asphyxiation that had gone tragically wrong, and the judge declared suicide.

For Paula, the implication that Michael might have chosen to leave her was too much to bear. She was convinced that he would never done so, as their love for each other was an intense, obsessive love where one simply can't let go. Of course, no one will ever really know what happened; the circumstances of Michael's death will always be open to speculation.

Following her lover's demise, Paula's real self fragmented further. Her character was vilified in the public domain, and she was perceived by many to be a lost cause. Drugs, booze, rehab, inappropriate relationships with other addicts who meant nothing to her, and an alleged attempt to hang herself all led to her ultimate death by her own hand.

In the end, the public had very little time for her, seeing her as stupid and irresponsible, instead reserving their sympathy for Bob Geldof and, of course, their girls, who no doubt miss their mother tremendously.

I'm sure that Paula didn't intend to die, but on some level there was a desperate need to escape the pain and to be reunited with the lover with whom she was obsessed. Hopefully, Kate won't fall into the same trap.

KATE ON THE COUCH

Kate Moss is fighting against growing into a responsible adult woman and mother. But, like it or not, she *is* getting older. One of the Moss Posse has revealed that, to Kate, the thought of driving a 4x4 and being a regular mum and housewife is a terrifying notion. When she was growing up, her family life was nothing spectacular, simply that of a lower–middle–class working family, not rich and not poor, and Kate doubtless found it stultifyingly boring. When she was plucked from obscurity and plunged into the world of celebrity, the concomitant lifestyle suited her personality on many counts.

Kate has been told by the world at large that she can do what she wants, say what she thinks and have whatever she wants. Her emotional state is probably akin to that of an omnipotent baby at the centre of her universe. This is a very dangerous mindset. As I mentioned in the previous chapter, our characters are only partially developed by the time we make twenty years of age, and Kate, like Robbie, was barely through puberty when she was thrust into the limelight and bombarded with attention. She was labelled one of the beautiful people and indulged in a similar way to that in which George Best was indulged (see Chapter 6). This indulgence by the media and fashion industries and the public at large has no doubt played a large part in her fall from grace.

Emotionally, Kate has a long hard climb ahead of her if she wants to return to anything approaching a 'normal' life, while physically she has some serious reparation work to do if she is to recover her health. She might still be beautiful on the outside, but her body's systems must be under a great strain. You simply cannot party all the time, taking class-A drugs, drinking copious amounts of Champagne and swigging vodka from a hip flask for years without damaging your vital organs – and Kate has confessed that her drinking began way back in Croydon at the age of thirteen, just a year before she was discovered.

Kate began to smoke at around the same time, a habit that not only ages the skin but eventually causes it to take on a muddy appearance and tiny wrinkles to appear around the mouth. And of course there are more serious risks among people – particularly women – who smoke, including those of contracting lung cancer and osteoporosis, a disease that's symptomised by the premature weakening and crumbling of bones and is exacerbated by poor diet. There's no evidence that Kate's diet is anything other than healthy, but like so many other painfully thin celebrities she possibly has reason to worry.

Kate's history of attempting to recover from the effects of her dissolute lifestyle is quite astonishing. In 1998, she spent six weeks at renowned celebrity rehab clinic the Priory because, she said, 'I've been doing a lot of work and too much partying.' Then, a few weeks later, she attended a Narcotics Anonymous meeting, and in the following year she admitted to having an alcohol problem. ('You always have Champagne before the shows,' she lamented at the time. 'Even at ten in the morning. It got to the point where we said, "We're not going out without Champagne." Terrible.') The following year, she was admitted to hospital with kidney problems, but later in the same week she was spotted in London's trendy Met Bar. The counsellors at the Priory were most concerned and urged her to return for their after-care programme. A couple of years later, Kate admitted that 'being bang on drugs' was not OK and confessed to being terribly miserable when she was indulging.

More misery was to follow, however, in the guise of love. Enter crack-cocaine addict Pete Doherty. Pete had apparently idolised Kate for years, and as a teenager had had a picture of her on his wall. How lucky did *he* get? But how long would his – and Kate's – luck last?

At the time of publication, Kate Moss is at a crossroads in her life, with three possible paths available to her. The first path would be to leave her hedonistic lifestyle behind. Jay Kay, the driving force behind funk act Jamiroquai, offered her some sound advice when, in October 2005, while Kate was in rehab in Arizona, he told her, 'Change your lifestyle and retire from the catwalk for a year. Find a true friend and, with their help, cut yourself away for a year. You have money, you're young and pretty, and no one is going to forget you.' Wise words indeed. If she could do this, there might indeed be a much better chance of survival, for both Kate and her daughter.

The second path available to Kate is to go back to her Bob Geldof equivalent, Jefferson Hack – by all accounts a grounded individual – and raise Lila Grace in a safe and contained environment. She may well be unlikely to follow this course of action, though, especially if one believes Pete Doherty's uncle Phil, who reports, 'Pete cancelled [his last three Babyshambles gigs] to fly out to Arizona to see Kate. Jefferson and Lila have already been. She is allowed one visitor a day. Pete says they are still very much in love. He is just sex, drugs and rock 'n' roll, and that's why Kate likes him. She's not bothered about Jefferson.' Other reports have it that the rehab clinic sent him packing.

The third path would be for her and Pete to get some intensive therapy and drastically modify their behaviour. However, although as a professional I'm always one to offer hope to most people and believe in the ability to change, I'm not holding my breath here. At the time of writing, Kate has recently completed her second bout of rehabilitation, and at the turn of the millennium she'd had a year of one-on-one counselling. If she was capable of making a meaningful change, she would most likely have shown some signs of doing so. Nonetheless, she *is* still young, and I've witnessed many thirty-somethings make drastic changes for the better.

The way I see it, the chances of this obsessive, addictive couple remaining together and holding down a life conducive to raising their children (Pete has a child from a former relationship) would be poor. This is a man who has had implants inserted under his skin in an attempt to cure his heroin addiction, a man of whom ex-girlfriend Kate Lewis told *OK!* magazine, 'Kate needs to realise there's very little that's actually real about Pete. I don't believe Kate can ever trust him. Pete has so much to gain from his relationship with her. Her profile means acres of press coverage he just wouldn't get in his own right.'

She really has only some good options: firstly, to take Jay Kay's advice and 'get the hell out of here for a while' and, secondly, to break the spell of the sick dependency that she calls 'love'. Even if she were to follow this advice, however, she would still have to address her egotistical and hedonistic way of life. If the stories of power and control that Kate wields over her Primrose Hill Moss Posse are to be believed, she seriously needs to address this self-centred and fickle attitude, an attitude that I'm sure is a creation more of the drugs that have poisoned her system and the people she's chosen for mentors (for example, ex-users Marianne Faithfull and Anita Pallenberg) than part of her own innate personality.

Back in 1969, Marianne Faithfull – one-time girlfriend of Rolling Stone Mick Jagger – attempted suicide, an angry episode of 'acting out' that came about as a direct result of Brian Jones's apparent death by misadventure. Marianne identified with Brian and saw his death as a kind of sacrifice. When she referred to him as her 'twin', she was displaying evidence of the loss of her real self, of her fragile identity having merged with his. When Brian's death failed to invoke a change of attitude and behaviour in the group's remaining members, the media and their fans, Marianne decided to shock the nation by taking her own life.

In her autobiography *Faithfull*, Marianne gives a fascinating insight to this loss of real self that is a worrying curse on celebrities. What with constantly being surrounded by different people, all with a different idea of who she was, Marianne states how easy it is to sleepwalk your way through it all, seduced by the idea of what you represent to others by being famous, but not really knowing where the real you is. She ended up saying no 'to life itself', feeling guilty for not being happy with what she had, but at the same time not always feeling that her life was really her own.

This false front seems to go hand in hand with living a celebrity lifestyle. It's my guess that Kate identifies with Marianne in a similar way to that in which the older woman identified with Brian Jones, which could be exceedingly dangerous for the young model.

One has to be very careful about who one mixes with, as their influence can be either a constructive or, ultimately, destructive one. It would be terrible to see the beautiful, talented Kate Moss crash permanently, as she has so much still to live for – not least her daughter, Lila Grace.

It's one thing, after all, to live your life in a state of constant around-the-clock working and partying when you're young, free and single, and that was Kate's choice (and perhaps her destiny; she likes to have control and dislikes feeling exploited), but, speaking personally, the way in which she lives her life in the public eye is a dreadful influence on other young girls who also crave fame. Good role model she is not.

I wonder, too, what little Lila is picking up from her mother, both consciously and unconsciously. Children do not have the luxury of adult language and mature mindsets, functioning instead through the medium of instincts, intuition and unspoken feelings. Lila must be aware that there's something terribly wrong in her little world. At three years of age, she will be very receptive to the moods around her, and the anxieties and concerns of her significant others will filter through into her immature psyche.

A Fundamental Celebrity Curse

When I was working at the Charter Nightingale Hospital in the mid-nineties, many celebrities came there for either in-care or outpatient treatment. Most were suffering from depression, burnout or the effects of addiction to certain drugs. Many of the rock stars I saw there, in particular, had been abusing substances for many years, and it struck me then that there really is no free ride. Your indulgence will creep insidiously up on you and, before you know it, you're trapped. To free yourself, you have to recognise that you're trapped in the first place and then take action to remedy the situation. This self-awareness and personal development is without doubt the key to recovery.

Like the late George Best, Kate has spoken of her early days of drinking, of how it all seemed normal, how all her friends did it, how it was simply accepted behaviour and how nobody really thought they were doing anything wrong. And this is one of the fundamental, dreadful curses that celebrities must endure: that their lives of indulgence are perceived to be normal. Patsy Kensit is another one-time rock chick whose life went off the rails for a while, but she now seems to have turned her life around and got her career back on track. After having a child with Liam Gallagher, from whom she was subsequently divorced, she now says that she's happy, and indeed she certainly looks a picture of health.

But now the curse of celebrity is spilling over into the lives of the everyday people who read about the lives of their idols, and they too are going on benders in pursuit of a lifestyle apparently sanctioned by those in the elevated echelons of society. Young men are looking up to drug-crazed rock stars and teenaged girls are emulating the stick-thin emaciation of the models and actresses that adorn the pages of glossy magazines.

It will be interesting to see how things work out for Kate. My prediction is that all will be forgiven – and, if the latest gossip is to be believed, she will soon be doing what her best mate Sadie said she'd be good at: acting. It would appear that Kate Moss will be making her debut acting role in the next Bond movie, and alongside quite a cast, too, including Daniel Craig in the lead role and Sienna Miller, who has been chosen for the chemistry between her and her alleged lover Daniel. This is the same Sienna who was engaged to Jude Law, who was in turn married to Sadie Frost and allegedly had sex with Kate Moss. Ahhh… celebrity!

Chapter 3

GEORGE MICHAEL

George Michael craved fame ever since he was a small boy in north London. He has since made it to the very top of his musical career and along the way has amassed an amazing fortune of £105 million, making him the thirteenth richest man in the world.

This genius singer/songwriter began his writing career at the tender age of fourteen, when he penned one of his best ever songs, 'Careless Whisper', a song that has stood the test of time, earned George a number of awards and still gets a huge amount of airplay. In fact, George's music has always enjoyed a lot of radio time, a fact that he believes is down purely to the quality of his music. It's a claim that's difficult to dispute.

After enjoying success with 1980s pop group Wham!, George embarked on a solo career. He was more than ready to make it on his own, having not only written the material for Wham! but also having been the act's dynamic lead singer. Judging by his performances, it might come as a surprise that his ambitions have always been more about writing songs than performing them, as he truly is a superlative performer. Who, after all, can forget his 'Faith'-era leather jacket and Ray-Bans?

Yet George has courted controversy every step of the way in his career, and as he developed as both a man and a musician he began to make the news headlines as much for his offstage antics as for his musical prowess.

Sexual peccadilloes have been the undoing of many a musician, from the likes of Chuck Berry and Jerry Lee Lewis to Michael Jackson. History has traditionally taken a dim view of musicians accused of sexual impropriety, and many a great artist has fallen from grace under a cloud of accusations of deviancy. And, strangely, some celebrities can withstand a sex scandal where others sink into obscurity under an odious cloud. When Hugh Grant was arrested for his solicitation of LA prostitute Divine Brown, for instance, his career actually got a boost.

Think back to when the fourteen-year-old Priscilla Beaulieu moved into Graceland to begin a five-year dalliance with Elvis Presley. It was to be another five years before her parents gave them permission to marry, but the media didn't turn a hair about the underage liaison. Incredibly, they were left alone, and King Elvis held on to his crown. How could that have happened? Was it down to good management and guidance? Or was it because Elvis was so idolised that his adoring public couldn't bear to think that his behaviour was actually akin to child abuse?

Now think back to the furore that surrounded Woody Allen when he ran off with his young adopted daughter, Soon-Yi. He was branded as strange and his wife, Mia Farrow, took him to the cleaners financially.

So what about George Michael? Just what kind of impact did

the scandal of his lewd conduct in an LA public toilet really have on his career? And how did his adoring public really feel about his subsequent admission of his homosexuality? According to *MTV News*, 'Singer George Michael has had a hard time getting his career back on track since being arrested for lewd conduct in 1998 for exposing himself to an undercover officer in a Californian park bathroom. While Michael defused the situation somewhat by mocking the arrest in the video for his 1998 single "Outside", it has to be said that his recording output since his arrest has been minimal.' So was it the gay element of George's arrest that caused his record sales to plummet, or was there already bad feeling in the industry that was simply fed by the scandal?

George Michael has changed so much since those early heady days when he and Andrew Ridgeley formed Wham!, a group that purveyed pop in its purest form. He and Andrew wanted to be huge stars, and that's what they became. George knew he had the craftsmanship with which to outdo other big groups of that time, such as Duran Duran and Boy George's Culture Club, and so he just went for it.

George is one of those immensely talented people whose creativity has been born out of trauma, and his route to stardom has been a fascinating rollercoaster ride. What follows is a history of George's life — a life that, for the best part, he has been more than happy to live in the bright lights of celebrity. Other times, however, he's backed off, turned a different corner and taken himself into the darkness. His is a fascinating story that few know about, due to his jealous protection of his personal life. 'I want to step back from all the self-publicity and promotion and marketing to protect my ability, my gift as a songwriter,' he told *Bare* magazine in 1990. 'I think that, if I've abused this gift, it's been by not using it enough. I want to change that. I've realised I need to fight to protect that gift. But, even more than that, I need to protect my life.'

A FIGHT FOR FREEDOM

'I'm too much of a control freak and really couldn't handle the idea of things coming at me and not being able to stop it. I still hear horrible stories about things happening to people on stuff like acid. It's just too extreme for me.' – *George Michael*

The young Georgios Kyriacos Panayiotou decided to create a man whom the world could love, someone who could realise his dreams of being a star, and so, at the age of nine years old, George Michael was born.

George says that he wasn't aware he could sing and had no idea he would ever be able to master an instrument. And as for dancing, forget it. Even though his Greek parents were rock 'n' roll dancers, he felt awkward and confessed to being a 'terrible dancer'.

Then, when he was nine years old, he realised that he dominated everyone he hung out with, and this made him feel uncomfortable. He didn't like being bossy. In fact, there was a lot that the young George didn't like about himself. 'I was fat and ugly and had glasses,' he told the *Daily Express* in 1990. 'I also had one big bushy eyebrow. I have now had it treated to make two eyebrows. For years I would try and grow my hair long to cover it.'

During his childhood, a tormented George was most likely often overwhelmed by the sheer struggle of life, many aspects of which were difficult. Nothing really unique there, you might say, and you'd be right; we all have difficult childhoods to some extent. However, what makes some children suffer more than others isn't so much the outside influences that affect them as what their minds do with their own anxieties and insecurities.

So sensitive is the personality of George Michael that, as I write about him, I feel as though I'm prying into his life, that I want to apologise not only for daring to peer into his world but also for having the audacity to invite an audience along. But I've been compelled to include him in this book because I want the public to get a feel of who he really is, to get a glimpse of the whole picture rather than be fed snippets of information that don't really help anyone understand the real man.

If George's childhood was racked by grave insecurity, his motivation to become a star balanced out his world. Some of his best friends in the music industry have suggested that his father, Jack, had an oppressive impact on the young boy and did everything he could to keep his only son from chasing his pop dreams. Indeed, George himself told *Bare* magazine in 1990, 'After I refused to go to a private school – which would have killed my parents, financially – my dad gave up on me, career-wise. I didn't go to a private school because my friends would have called me a sissy. Plus I would have been intimidated by it, and I really didn't want to be with those kinds of people.'

In the same interview, however, George gave an insight into just how opposed his father was to him entering the world of showbiz: '[My parents] met at a dance, and my father used to throw my mother all over the show. There are some really cool pictures of my dad that they never used to show me when I was growing up because they were afraid that I could point to them and say, "Well, look. *You* did it."'

George attended primary school in north London and then secondary school, until he was seventeen, in Hertfordshire after he and his family moved there. He described himself in primary school as 'just above average height, quite a cute kid, very popular'. So had his insecurities yet to kick in? 'Just at that age when your hormones are popping up and everything is changing,' he continued, 'my dad decided to move house, and we moved to this big place in Radlett, which is in Hertfordshire. It was a real old hole and it took a year to decorate.'

Then George met Andrew Ridgeley, and his life changed overnight. Andrew was as strong as George, and this was a refreshing change. The two of them got along famously, and they forged a close friendship. George has said that he didn't need any other friends after meeting Andrew.

Andrew was to have a huge impact on George's life. 'He looked good, got the girls and wanted to be famous,' George revealed to the *Daily Mail*, adding, 'He changed my life.'

However, George's parents, Jack and Lesley, weren't so keen on their son's best friend. In his 1990 *Bare* interview, George remembers, 'My parents used to let me bring home anyone I liked, but they didn't like Andrew Ridgeley at all. He was much more confident than they were used to my friends being; he didn't have any of the inhibitions or cautions that most people feel when they walk into someone else's home.' George was not to be told who he could or couldn't mix with, however, and his and Andrew's friendship went from strength to strength.

Although George and Andrew shared a great deal in common, they were also different in some ways. 'Andrew was a lazy bastard,' claimed George. 'He just didn't want to go to work. It was OK for him to go on the dole, because he was still living at home, but I worked on a building site, I was a DJ in a restaurant, I was a cinema usher.'

According to George, Andrew experimented with acid when

they were young but wasn't impressed with it after suffering from a dreadful trip, after which he didn't take the drug again for years. His description of what happened put George off, but George is quick to admit that there was another reason why he shied away from acid: 'I'm just too much of a control freak and really couldn't handle the idea of things coming at me and not being able to stop it. I still hear horrible stories about things happening to people on stuff like acid. It's just too extreme for me.'

George and Andrew's quest for stardom began when they used to babysit together, when they would put on records such as Quincy Jones's 'Stuff Like That' and make up little dance routines. Despite George's self-confessed lack of dancing ability, at around the age of fourteen he and Andrew began to try out their routines at school discos.

Meanwhile, George loved busking. He and another childhood friend, David Mortimer, would sing David Bowie and Elton John songs down in the underground stations, and George loved the way their voices and the guitar would reverberate down the tiled passageways.

Then *Saturday Night Fever* was released, a film that opened up new horizons for the young, impressionable George, who was a sponge for absorbing all the music that appealed to him – and both the music and the dance moves in *Saturday Night Fever* did just that.

At this time of his life, George also started to hit the nightclubs, thanks to the money he earned during his busking escapades with David Mortimer. However, despite the fact that he was enjoying his time out with his mates, doing what he loved best – singing and dancing – and generally gaining confidence, his teens were not easy years, and he struggled with many deep issues.

One gets the impression that meeting Andrew and forming Wham! saved George from both himself and his father, Jack. In his 1990 *Bare* interview, George related one anecdote about their relationship that speaks volumes: 'Me and my dad were having this big argument. We were driving in the car and I was playing this demo tape. Apart from "Rude Boy", I had done something with David, and I was plugging this thing around all the record companies as well. And I remember playing it in the car to my dad, and he was going on about how I had to realise that there was no future in this for me. He had been telling me all this for years, and I had given up arguing with him long ago; I knew he wouldn't take any notice. But now I really had a go at him. I said, "You have been rubbing this shit into my face for the last five years." I told him, "There is no way I am not going to do this, so the least you could do is give me some moral support."' One can only guess how his father felt about George finally confronting his endless put-downs and how he responded. Hopefully, he respected George for standing up to him. After all, five years was a long time for George to have to listen to such negativity.

So where was his mother while George and his father were fighting? He has said very little about Mrs Panayiotou, we do know how much he loved and admired her. In a 1993 interview with the *Sunday Times*, he confessed, 'Things were going on when I was growing up that I never understood, things that made me really admire my mum. If there's anything that I've got from her, it's that she's a rock. I've got that stability from her.' Just what George was really saying here isn't very clear, as he leaves much to the imagination. Any attempt at interpreting this statement would be doomed to failure, but it's possible to glean some insight into who his mother is and what she means to him through his song lyrics, especially those written during his solo career

As a grown man, George is now aware about how important adolescent years can be and is completely honest about the insecurities that troubled him. 'Eventually, I realised that I was used to a lifetime of putting myself down, physically,' he remembers. 'The strongest years of your life, when it comes to thinking about your looks, are between twelve and fifteen, and I felt pretty naff back then. It was almost as if I had a complex about it.' That complex was to hang over him like a dark cloud for quite some time.

George almost made his stage debut with a band called, alarmingly, The Quiffs, but bizarrely enough his looks let him down. The band members were friends of Andrew's and, when one night their drummer dropped out, George – who had some drumming skills – was asked if he would take the chair for the night. But then the guys took one look at him and decided against letting him play. 'I didn't look the part,' recalls George. 'I just looked too bad. I was crushed.'

Such rejection was all about to change, however. The manic days of Wham! were beckoning, and George and Andrew were about to find the fame they so craved. Soon the two school friends were scoring hit after hit in a variety of styles, from rap to up-tempo pop and slow ballads. George Michael was on his way.

WAKE ME UP BEFORE YOU GO-GO

The very early days of Wham! were less than glamorous. The band's first appearance was at a club named Level One in Neasden that had no stage area and where all the clientele were drunk. Trying to perform on the same level as a crowd of rowdy drunks wasn't exactly the most auspicious of beginnings, and

George later described the night as 'an absolute nightmare'.

If that gig had been a nightmare, however, their next, at Stringfellow's, was downright embarrassing. One of George's dance routines included a kick, but when he executed the manoeuvre on the night he inadvertently propelled his shoe into the crowd. In an attempt to cover up his mistake, he kicked his other shoe high into the air. And, as if that wasn't bad enough, he then found himself dancing on a glass floor in his socks. In an attempt not to fall flat on his face, he slid across the stage, pulling his mic lead behind him, but then the lead was yanked out of its socket and George was exposed to be miming along to the track.

Although less embarrassing than his exposure later on in life, the idea that people thought him a fake caused him great distress. And, although he knew that he wasn't a fake, that didn't stop him feeling like one, and this insecurity dogged him throughout his days in Wham! 'Without Andrew, I couldn't have kept up the "bright young thing" image,' he recalled in 1986 after dissolving the band. 'It just wasn't me; it was him. His personality was greater than mine.'

Nevertheless, his time in Wham! was a thrilling period in George's life, not least because it was then that he started to feel physically attractive. Suddenly, at the age of eighteen, he was 'the good-looking one' – and, for George, being considered attractive was a complete revelation.

George has openly admitted that, from the beginning of Wham!, he deliberately set out to appeal to young girls in a non-sexual way, that he didn't want to come across as a hairy, threatening bloke. That said, however, Wham! had a huge gay following, as did George himself when he went solo.

George has also mentioned that he was aware many people

thought he looked an idiot as he pranced around on stage beneath a mane of blond hair while sporting shorts and flashing dazzling white teeth, but again such an act was deeply rooted in his urge to succeed. 'They couldn't understand that it was me trying to be the ultimate performer.' So, while it might have been George Michael up on the stage, it was Georgios who was pulling his strings somewhere in the wings.

When George and the band went to Ibiza to make videos and get brown, it signalled the beginning of the end of Wham! as George realised that he would have been happier staying at home, writing songs. 'I began to feel uncomfortable with the cleanliness of it,' he told *The Times* in 1990. 'Wham! was a concept we had when we were young, at a time when we really didn't know about anything. Andrew was still completely into the lifestyle, but I was growing up a bit.'

What was actually happening was that George, being the lead singer and the songwriter, was gradually overshadowing the rest of the group, and by the time they split he was well prepared to leap into what would turn out to be a massively successful solo career. Nonetheless, he remained faithful to Andrew, declaring, 'The luckiest thing ever to happen to me was meeting Andrew Ridgeley. He totally shaped my life.'

The final appearance of Wham! in the sunshine at Wembley Stadium was spectacular, and George admits it was a huge experience for him and so overwhelming that he couldn't take the reality of it on board. On watching the video after the event, however, it finally sank in just how amazing the band's farewell performance had been, and, in a later interview with the *Daily Mail*, he noted, 'Everything in the whole series of Wham! events seemed so blessed that this was just the cherry on the cake.'

YOU GOTTA HAVE FAITH

'I can honestly say that most of 1988 was a complete nightmare for me.' – *George Michael*

The year after Wham! broke up was for George a similar nightmare to that experienced by Robbie Williams in the first year after his split from Take That, while Victoria Beckham has written of encountering similar difficulties after quitting The Spice Girls and going solo. It appears that, however much each wanted the break, they each needed some time in which to grieve over the loss of being in a group.

Like Robbie and Victoria, George's ambitious nature soon compelled him to work hard in order to further his career. His goal was to be as successful worldwide as he was in Britain, and eventually he cracked the lucrative US market, whereas Robbie struggled and Victoria failed to do the same.

Before conquering the US, however, George spent some painful times in his own particular wilderness, and he later admitted, 'Perhaps my darkest days came after the break-up of Wham!.' Like Robbie, George hit the booze big time and indulged in chemical escapism. For George, though, the vehicle to Nirvana was ecstasy, a drug that he claimed made him feel 'wonderful'. But he wasn't stupid; he knew very well that any relief the drug gave him was an illusion.

I found reading about this period in his life depressing, but then I realised that it was because much of George's music and lyrics reminds me of a time when I was feeling sad, when I would endlessly play tracks such as 'Cowboys and Angels' and 'Turn a Different Corner'. But then I'd put on 'Faith' or 'Freedom' and I would be lifted back up again. With George's songs, at least there was some balance. Of course, I wasn't the only one connecting with his stunning music; millions of others across the globe were snapping up his albums and experiencing their own 'George Michael moments'.

After Wham! split, George floundered in dark depression for about eight months, and during this time of refection he came to realise that there had been a period during his time in Wham! when he'd completely forgotten who he was. He has been honest enough to admit that this was an isolating, self-pitying period for him, and indeed a time when he suddenly realised he had a vicious temper. The anger that had been locked away began to surface and he started to lose control. It must have been extremely disturbing for a man who'd already admitted that during his teenage years he'd hated to lose control of his emotions, but that's exactly what he did. 'I got into fights with friends, threw photographers against walls, acted very macho… terrible,' he told Q magazine in 1988. 'In that period I lost my temper six or eight times. I wasn't drunk so there was no excuse for my behaviour; the people that knew me who saw it were horrified. I'd go completely out of character.'

Although George didn't say as much, in all likelihood he was totally lost and confused during this time of his life. His identity was in danger of completely fragmenting, and my professional experience leads me to think that there was some dissociation happening in his mind.

In the same interview with Q, George admitted, 'The problem was just that I had developed a character for the outside world that wasn't me, and I was having to deal with people all the time who thought it was.'

During this time, other strange things began to happen to George that must have been pretty scary. This new out-of-control aspect of George's character had a voice of its own, and he later told Q of how, when he lost the plot, his voice would drop an octave and his speech patterns would suddenly be heavy with slang.

That George managed to put himself back together is little short of a miracle, and yet it just goes to show the power and resilience of the human mind. Dissociation is a major defence mechanism of the mind that clicks in when someone is unable to deal with the trauma life is throwing at them, or indeed some trauma that they experienced in the past and that is now resurfacing.

One of the primary causative factors for this dark period of George's was the transient place in which he found himself. The person he was when he'd been in Wham! was dead – he had symbolically killed him off – but he was yet to feel the complete person he needed to be in order to feel comfortable with himself. During this period, George was suspended in mid-air.

This feeling of having no identity is felt by most people who have left one way of being behind but have yet to reach the place where they want (or need) to be. There is a time when they've leaped into the air but have yet to land on solid ground, and this sense of not being able to go back and being lost in space can be terrifying. One part of them is desperate to run back to the safety of all that's familiar while the other is terrified of going into the unknown. That said, once they've finally landed, there is usually a huge sense of relief.

In 1990, while fighting some desperate internal battles, the George who had been desperate to be the centre of attention now chose to shy away from the media and announced that he would give no further interviews. The reason he gave was that he was sick and tired of all the intrusive questions about his private life.

This dismissive attitude, known as *attention ambivalence*, crops up time and time again with celebrities. It makes one wonder, don't they *ever* take any notice of the saying 'Be careful what you wish for; you might just get it'?

George's first solo album was 1987's *Faith*, which featured a series of chart-topping singles and sold more than 7 million copies. Several of his singles enjoyed a record number of plays on Radio 1, and George likes to think that this is down to the quality of his records and his relationship with his audience. The critics were less than enthusiastic about his solo efforts, but George is philosophical about this; at Chancery High Court in 1993, he stated simply, 'My reviews have never had any effect on my sales.' This, perhaps, is just as well; if his fans had taken any notice of his critics, the chances are he would never have survived the fickle world of fame.

As I stated earlier, controversy has escorted George throughout his career, and his outspoken honesty and dogged determination have upset many in the music industry, while in his later career he would upset politicians, too. It might be fair to say, then, that his 'don't fuck with me' attitude has wound up many in authority.

As a response to not receiving what he felt to be the critical acclaim that he deserved after the release of *Faith*, which nevertheless notched up huge sales, George chose to entitle his follow-up album *Listen Without Prejudice*. However, although this album sold a million copies and included two Top Ten singles, it was considered to be a major commercial disappointment.

Then came a bitter legal battle with his record company, Columbia, when George accused them of not promoting the album as he felt they should have. He wanted to be released from his contract and said that, if he lost the lawsuit, he would refuse to record any more records.

He lost the case, and then he lost his appeal.

Undaunted, George bought his way out of his Columbia contract and signed with the music division of DreamWorks, a then fledgling entertainment corporation founded by Steven Spielberg, Jeffrey Katzenberg and David Geffen, which released his next album, *Older*, in 1996.

Was George's long period away from performing to blame for sluggish album sales? What was happening to his popularity? Was it a case of 'game over'?

What happened next threw George's world into chaos. If he'd been struggling with his music, now he was about to face a monumental personal struggle, and at the centre of the storm would be the ultimately personal matter of his sexuality. It seemed there was now to be no getting away from those intrusive questions.

I WANT YOUR SEX

'I lost my virginity at thirteen. I remember thinking, "What's all the fuss about?" I was overweight and wore glasses – and was hopeless with women. She was a right old dog. I was so inexperienced that it was embarrassingly bad.' – *George Michael in the* Sun

'When I released "I Want Your Sex" and the music video, I didn't think the image would have such a lasting effect. The image still seems to overshadow the music.' – *George Michael*

The debate about George Michael's sexuality was finally resolved in 1998 after he was arrested for lewd conduct in a public lavatory in a park near his home in Los Angeles. He no longer had a choice about whether or not to come out; the issue had been forced. By admitting he was gay and announcing that he was in a relationship with Kenny Goss, he effectively ended a long period of speculation.

George has been engaged in an ongoing struggle in all areas concerning both his image and his sexuality, struggles that it's now clear began in childhood, when he was deeply unhappy with his physical appearance. Meeting his great friend Andrew Ridgeley and forming Wham! were to be pivotal in turning around how he perceived himself. He was soon prancing around on stage, projecting an image that wasn't truly him, attracting not only a huge gay following but also an entourage of sexy young girls. He admits that there was a lot of bed-hopping in his life at this time.

There was endless debate about his sexuality at the time. Was he gay? Was he bisexual? Or was he, in fact, totally straight and fooling the media? In the end, did it really matter? Well, yes, of course it did, because sex sells music, and George had plenty of music to sell. With image being all-important, he had to pitch his sexuality just right.

As far as George was concerned, however, it was extremely important for him at the time to hang on to some part of himself that wasn't public property, and of course there's every chance that he rather enjoyed keeping everyone guessing. In 1998, he told the *News of the World*, 'At the end of the day, part of me has to believe that some of the kick was that I might get found out. Well, here I am; I got found out. I don't suppose it will be exciting any more.'

Indeed, after the incident in the public toilets, George spoke very openly about his sexual history, in terms of both his sexual preferences and how his sexuality and personal relationships had influenced his songs. In that same 1998 interview with the *News of the World*, he also admitted to never having had a gay relationship until he was twenty-seven: 'So I spent my years growing up being told what my sexuality was, which was kind of confusing. Then, by the time I'd kind of worked out what it was, I had stopped having relationships with women. I was just so indignant at the way I had been treated 'til then. I just thought, "I will hold on to this. I don't think they need to know. I don't think I have to tell them."' But then, he reckoned, it was 'as good a time as any' to spill the beans.

This must have been one hell of a situation for George to find himself in. On the one hand, he would have been relieved to have had everything out in the open, to have removed the skeletons in his closet and brought his relationship with Kenny out into the open. On the other, however, he had to give up the part of his life that he had thus far managed to keep back for himself.

In all relationships, we need to hold back something just for us. In therapeutic terms, this is known as preserving the real veridical self. Some people are so petrified about not being able to hold on to any of this real self that they obsessively control everything in their lives. Such people are known in common parlance as control freaks.

Nevertheless, issues of control are an important part of how we live our lives. Indeed, taking control of how one lives one's life is an important part of existence, as having a modicum of control means that you have some defence against being hurt. But take this tendency to the extreme and an obsession with control can prevent someone from living their life to the full. George had been swinging between the two ends of the scale, holding on and then letting go, controlling everything only to then take extreme risks. It's who he was.

In 1998, George told *Q* magazine that he had actually been openly gay with those close to him since around 1990: '[The paparazzi] don't want to hear that I am perfectly fine with my sexuality or that I have a fantastic relationship. They want to hear the hard-luck story of the poor closeted pop star. That's not what people are going to get, because it isn't like that… If it were, I would have been destroyed by my arrest. That's what they wanted.'

Although George wasn't destroyed by his arrest, he wasn't exactly happy about it, either, but he was able to make light of what could have been a catastrophe. 'It's a real embarrassment for me to go to the toilet these days,' he told *Q*. 'I have to make sure there's no one in the vicinity in case I scare them out.'

His real crime, says George, was being unfaithful to his long-time partner, Kenny Goss. He clearly loves Kenny and believes that this love is reciprocated. 'I'm not saying I have an open situation with [Kenny], but he knows how I am,' he told the *Daily Star* in 1998. He knows that I am generally over-sexed. He's been very, very good.' But have there been any other loves in George's life? And, if so, have they influenced his music at all?

The two loves about which George has spoken passionately are Kathy Jeuing and a man named Anselmo. Kathy came on to the scene in the 1980s, and George states that his relationship with her changed him a lot. With his bed-hopping days behind him, he was ready to allow someone to get close enough to share his space. 'Eventually, it comes down to whether you love someone enough to sacrifice that space,' he told the *Daily Express* in 1988, while in the following year he told the *Today* newspaper, 'I believe that if you are sleeping with a lot of girls you don't develop much as a person.'

Through his relationship with Kathy, George developed as a person and soon found that he could concentrate more on his career and other things that were important to him. It seemed that, within this relationship, he could calm down and stop the endless searching.

So just what was it about Kathy that George found both appealing and comfortable? Ironically, the young lad who had sought out female attention in his teens – and who had cleverly managed to project the right image to ensure that he pulled plenty – got fed up with being chased. 'Initially, I thought it was absolutely wonderful,' he told *Bare* magazine in 1990. 'I really thought it was fantastic. And I abused the privilege a little bit maybe – although I wasn't getting anything out of a sexual situation that wasn't being returned. In fact, it got to the point where I realised I was getting less out of it than they were, and that starts to be a turn-off.' He's also gone on record as saying that he thinks it's OK to do the eyes–across–the–room flirting thing, but that to be blatantly propositioned is a turn-off.

Kathy didn't run after him, however, and that was a turn-on. She stood apart from the other girls by not idolising him. In fact, at first she apparently didn't even like him. 'She wasn't impressed by me,' he later recalled, 'and got bugged out by being known as "George Michael's girlfriend".'

George got quite a kick out of being regarded as someone other than a pop idol by a girl, and it was refreshing for him to spend time with an 'ordinary girl' who was 'fun'. He was very aware of being a catch and found the concept distasteful; he didn't trust it, and this attitude made being with Kathy safe. He completely trusted her, though, and knew that she would never try to make money out of being his girlfriend. It was therefore probably very difficult for him when the relationship ended, as it had been a worthwhile union where both he and Kathy could grow and evolve.

The other person with whom George shared a deep connection was Anselmo, and two tracks on George's *Older* album – 'Jesus To A Child' and 'You Have Been Loved' – are about his death. 'After Anselmo died, I went through bereavement counselling, which helped a lot,' George has confessed. 'I'm not naturally depressive. I mean, I've suffered from depression in depressive circumstances, but I don't have a tendency towards it. I'm not very good at wallowing. If I'm going to feel bad, I distract myself. It was the most enlightening experience I've ever had. The minute someone you really love is irretrievably lost, you understand life in a different way. Your perspective changes. You understand how short life is, how incredibly painful it can be. But once you've seen the worst of things, then you can see the best of things.'

Anselmo's death was a terribly painful, shocking experience for George and one that had a deep impact on him. Such a loss was bound to change George, and he lapsed into depression, but then he wouldn't have been human if he hadn't. What many people don't realise is that feeling depressed can be a healthy thing and is a natural part of a healing process.

Following the loss of Anselmo, George used his depression in a positive way. Firstly, he wrote down all of his emotions and then composed the two beautiful songs listed above. Secondly, he acknowledged his grief and just went with it, *through* it, and then came out the other side. Indeed, this is really the only real way to get over the loss of a loved one. Anyone resisting this process will remain entrenched in a pain that grows and spreads like a cancer.

A puzzled George began to ask himself one question over and over: 'What's more important: to have a long and healthy life or to enjoy every day as it happens?' It's a good question, and an age-old one. George has confessed to being obsessively invested in his future, but after Anselmo's death he confessed to the *Big Issue* in 1990 that he wasn't sure he should spend so much time worrying about it, as there might not be a future. Similarly, he has also admitted to believing that he'd never live to an old age, which is a common way of thinking, especially among teenage boys.

One thing that doesn't need to be debated is his love for Anselmo. In 1998, he told the *National Enquirer* that Anselmo was the love of his life and claimed, 'He was the one who taught me that I was gay. Anselmo lived life on the edge – and he infected me with that excitement.' When he hooked up with Anselmo, it was the first time George had got together with someone who he thought loved him, and he gave that love straight back. They clearly mirrored each other and, because they had shared such a deep, all-consuming love, the grieving process seemed to go on forever.

It was a time for George when listening to music was 'dangerous' and threatened to take him into a familiar dark place. He knew he was too fragile, and in this sense he was taking care of himself. The self-awareness he had learned in his counselling sessions was now guiding him, and this made all the difference to his state of mind. At the end of 1994, eighteen months later, his demons were finally exorcised when he wrote 'Jesus To A Child', an achievement of which he simply says, 'Phew!'

So we have Anselmo to thank for 'Jesus To A Child' and 'You Have Been Loved', while George has a lot to thank Anselmo for.

OLDER

'I know fans will be disappointed that I've given up the ghost and I'm not sprinting from one end of the stage to the other any more, but I just can't do it. I've got a bad back. That's what *Older* really means. My discs are going. "He's gone from gold discs to slipped discs."' – *George Michael*

The success of his album *Ladies and Gentlemen* meant a lot to George, and he likes the fact that it shows two very different sides of his appeal. He told Q magazine in 1998 that he reckons it consists of 'fuck-off pop records people can't resist and songs that make people feel'. He was also pleased that Sony were bringing it out at a reasonable price.

It was around this time that George went through a difficult time of trying to get out of his record contract with Sony, after which he formed his own record label, Aegean. 'Having my own record company is really about having a corner of the industry where artists know they can come if they want the kind of respect and freedom to do what they want,' he told Capital Radio in 1997. 'Basically it's about fifty-fifty, you know; it's all about [the artists being able to do] their best work and being free to leave if they are not happy. The success of the label is really about my decisions, my choices, who I think has got the talent to do this, so really, if I fail miserably, it will all be down to me.'

I have the urge to stop here on this positive note, to finish George's profile at a point where he is feeling in control of his own destiny. However, life's not like that, and this isn't fiction, so I'm forced to move on to more controversy and to highlight the power of repeating patterns.

LET'S GO OUTSIDE AND SHOOT THE DOG

'Pop singer George Michael is reportedly being sued for $10 million by the police officer who arrested him for committing a lewd act in a public rest room in California. Beverley Hills cop Marcelo Rodriguez said the singer slandered him in interviews, according to Association Press. George Michael pleaded "no contest" to the 1998 charge and was ordered to perform eighty hours community service, undergo counselling and pay an $800 fine.' – MTV News, *14 September 1999*

When George was sued by the cop who had arrested him in that LA toilet, he couldn't believe it was happening. He admits that he took a risk on the day he was arrested – indeed, some might say he's the ultimate risk-taker – but he might have had a point when he confessed bemusedly to Q magazine, 'I don't understand why it's more legal for a cop to go into a toilet and wave his dick at people than it is for someone who wants to do it.' Yet he dealt with it, and he got over it. Speaking to Q again, he said, 'I've had the privilege of being seen in my worst possible incarnation and people being all right with it. If you've been the soundtrack to somebody's life, they'll be a little more forgiving. I responded with honesty. People said, "Fuck it. We don't care."'

It seems that George cares quite a bit, though, particularly where his lover Kenny is concerned. He says today that he's unlikely ever to put himself in another compromising position, yet he's not so convinced that someone won't try to humiliate him again. The curse of celebrity, it appears, has claimed another victim. Had he not been famous, George said that it's likely he would have given Rodriguez a run for his money in the courts, just as he did with Sony. As he told Q, though, 'Not on worldwide television. It's not an option for a celebrity.'

In fact, over the years, George had become a kind of superstar, which made it even easier for his adoring public to forgive him. Once more, his critics damned him but his fans stood loyal.

So the music went on, and for whatever reason – probably as a way of dealing with the humiliation and out of a need to redirect his anger – George released 'Outside' as a single. The song's video spoke for itself and left no one in any doubt about what George was saying as he stuck up two fingers to authority – again.

'Controversy erupts over George Michael's video showing Bush as an idiot and Blair as a lap-dog in "Shoot the Dog".' – MTV News, *3 July 2002*

It was at this point that George began to stray into the world of politics and, when the video of his song 'Shoot the Dog' hit the screens, many critics predicted that it would spell the end of his music career. Of course, they'd been predicting his downfall for years, although it could be argued that he'd gone just a tad too far this time. 'Shoot the Dog' was a protest song about the war in Iraq in which George criticised British foreign policy (at least that pertaining to dealings with the Middle East) as being too closely aligned with that of America. However, George was quick to defend his video, which showed him astride a nuclear missile, claiming to *MTV News*'s Kurt Loder that both the imagery in the video and the lyrics to the song had been misinterpreted. He confessed, however, that the clear message to Tony Blair was that he had been remiss in some of his homeland duties and that the British people were feeling just as threatened as the Americans by the situation in the Middle East.

In the same interview, he denied that the song's lyrics referred to the heinous terror attack in New York on 11 September 2001, arguing that the lyrics had been written beforehand. He also claimed that he'd never intended to release either the single or the video in the US 'out of respect for those who suffered any loss in the attack', and that he wanted to avoid any misunderstandings. 'The incident [in New York] was so appalling and the shock was so fresh that I think it would have been totally disrespectful,' he observed, 'because the song was really about the West and the fundamentalists' world. It wasn't about any one event.'

So the young 'geeky boy' of Greek heritage from north London had come a long way. He'd learned lots of lessons and grown in a myriad of ways − taken ecstasy, smoked plenty of dope and drank copious amounts of red wine, bed-hopped his way through the eighties and had sex with girls, women and, eventually, men. He'd learned to have faith in others and fought for both his freedom and that of others. But to what extent did his formative years mould him into the gay icon he's become?

George Michael has a God-given gift, but he's also been cursed with the kind of celebrity status that has killed off weaker men. He has been criticised and judged harshly, and he has courted controversy like no other performer in our modern-day society, yet no one can ever take away his phenomenal musical success. Reportedly worth $ 105 million, he has sold over 70 million albums worldwide and has notched up a dazzling string of chart hits, both with Wham! and as a solo artist. But for every arena he has packed out and for every album that has gone platinum, he has had to fight many of his own personal corners, visit more than enough dark places and battle with unthinkable demons, and his losses have been varied and many. Often confused and puzzled, he now seems to have come to rest in a peaceful place.

Nowadays George releases his music via the internet, and his recent brief appearance at Live 8 confirmed just how many fans he still has out there. Love him or loathe him, he's certainly worth analysing.

GEORGE ON THE COUCH

Whether Georgios Panayiotou liked it or not, he was born with Greek blood running through his veins, but as a small boy he didn't like the face that gazed back at him from the mirror, so he chose to give birth to George Michael, someone he felt was worthy of receiving love. George's quest for a physical identity with which he could feel comfortable gave rise to an acute anxiety, an anxiety that would accompany him through his teens and early twenties.

When he met and shared a requited love with Anselmo, this was a hugely defining moment for George. With Anselmo, he could look into a face he loved and see that love reflected straight back at him. In Anselmo, he had found a mirror image that completed him and satisfied his once insatiable appetite for love and sex. 'For the first time I got together with someone I thought loved me, I actually felt that I loved him,' he later told Q magazine. This is a typical statement from someone who has found himself through the eyes of a loved one.

To understand what happened to George when he and Anselmo fell in love, we need to go back to his early infancy, a time when a baby either learns or fails to learn all about giving and receiving love.

Think of a baby gazing up into the eyes of his mother as he suckles. As well as receiving the milk he needs to thrive, he is also looking into his mother's eyes, in search of recognition of himself. He and his mother are one, and he appears to be in a drunken state, full of the most amazing feelings. There is a speechless communication, a sense of intense belonging, of being contained somewhere that's safe and where all his needs are met. With such a providential start to life, the experience actually becomes part of that person, built into the fabric of his personality, against which all other experiences will be measured and judged. It's fair to say that babies are as likely to fail to thrive through a deficiency of love as through one of food. The baby has a powerful need to be at the centre of the mother's attention.

Yet these early experiences are loaded with potential problems. However much our parents might want us, they are often ambivalent about pregnancy. They may be excited but at the same time terrified of the responsibility it represents. And mothers' experiences of both pregnancy and childbirth differ enormously; even before birth, while still in the womb, the baby might sense internal emotional reactions from the mother.

What we do know is that the experience of being loved is built into the growing body of the infant, and somehow this instils a need in most humans to search constantly for this loving experience to be repeated throughout their lives.

Love is a hugely complex and complicated emotion, and how we perceive the messages we receive are as important as the actual messages. This is a fundamental truth, and with most of my clients, once they've gained a real understanding of this, much of my work is done. When they realise that the most important issue is how they have perceived their experiences, they can change how they feel, think and, ultimately, behave. If you've perceived something, you can alter your perception. Likewise, you can't change what has been done to you, but you can stop it from hurting you for the rest of your life by changing your thought processes.

Oliver James, author of the insightful (and often disturbing) book *They F***You Up*, writes about how the phenomenon of babies picking up these early experiences and messages from their mothers has a scientific basis: 'If one's mother was depressed, the thoughts and feelings that this engendered became established as measurably different electro-chemical patterns in the frontal lobes of the right side of the brain. Psychologists know that these patterns are not inherited because they are absent at birth and only show up if the mother behaves in a depressed fashion when relating to the child. Whilst not immutable, the earlier these patterns are established, the harder they are to change. Unless something radically different has happened in the interim, they are still present years later. Dysfunctions in the right brain have now been linked to numerous mental illnesses.'

Now, I'm not for one minute suggesting that George Michael is remotely anything like mentally ill; I've chosen to share this amazing knowledge simply as way of communicating the fact that the brainwaves and chemistry of the body are hugely influenced by our time in infancy and that this phenomenon re-presented itself when George fell deeply in love with Anselmo. In fact, it's a phenomenon that all human beings experience. The majority of my clients' pain comes from their need for love and their inability to cope with their disappointments, losses and ultimate frustrations, emotions that are linked to the levels of chemicals swirling around in their bodies.

To be able to cope involves understanding that life is as much about suffering as it is about being happy. It's about saying, 'What have I learned about me from this painful experience?' Analyst DW Winnicott states, 'The human being's development is a continuous process. As in the development of the body, so in the development of the personality, and the capacity for relationships, no stage can be missed or marred without ill effect.'

It is important to understand this concept if one is to understand one of the fundamental motivations of humans, just as it's imperative to know that the extent to which our parents love us, firstly without judgement and condition and then gradually for who we are, will make a major impact on how we feel about ourselves in love-based relationships and how accurately we see those we grow to love.

During the second year of our lives – the terrible twos – there is a major developmental shift when we go through the transition from being the centre of attention towards a recognition of others and building a capacity to love. A child needs a sense of self-esteem to be able to love others as separate entities.

George, like all other babies, was subject to this complex process. As a baby, he was at the centre of his mother's universe; her world would have been his world. When he gazed into her face, he would have been filled with an all-consuming love – the same feeling that he was searching for and, indeed, thought he'd found with Anselmo. It was this realisation of a lifelong search that made their love affair so all-consuming for George.

But what about his other relationships? Let's begin with the relationship with himself. For a start, why exactly did he feel the need to kill off Georgios Kyriacos Panayiotou? What didn't he like about him? His Greek parents certainly gave him a very Greek name, and it's likely that George was deeply unhappy with this Greekness. He certainly disliked his physical attributes, including the dark hairiness often associated with those of Greek descent.

It's highly likely that the thick, bushy eyebrows he manages to joke about today were a real source of embarrassment in his formative years. Boys, generally more so than girls, hate to feel embarrassed or ridiculed, emotions that drive deep into their psyche, and they'll do just about anything to defend themselves against these annihilating feelings.

But there is another association with his Greek inheritance that had a negative impact on George: his father. Now, Jack Panayiotou no doubt loved and still loves his son, but he embarked on fatherhood with the same limited set of parenting tools as every other mother and father, and everyone makes mistakes. There is, after all, no such thing as a perfect parent; we can only be what Winnicott describes as 'the good-enough parent'.

Whatever caused Jack's relationship with his son into difficulties, he no doubt had his son's best interests at heart, but he was probably also considering his own best interests, and their relationship was consequently fraught with difficulties. Despite having enjoyed rock 'n' roll dancing with his wife, Lesley, Jack was determined that his boy was not going to go into the music business, and his negative words and behaviour had a huge impact on George, who harboured a slow, simmering and growing rage. Could there be another 'angry alter ego' residing in George's troubled mind? Might this be that aspect of his personality that emerges at times of stress, the George who loses control, who lashes out and whose voice is several octaves lower?

It's likely that this 'other George' was caused by high levels of the hormone cortisone being released into George's bloodstream as a direct result of his being in a highly stressful state. One reason for this could be that, as a child, he lived in a stressful environment. For any child living like this, their hormonal levels will fluctuate so much that they will either have too much or too little cortisone released into their system, and this chemical trait is often carried through to adulthood, with specific hormonal levels reflecting certain types of childhood experiences. For example, adults who were sexually abused as children have high levels of cortisone in their bodies, while neglected children have lower levels. Elevated levels of cortisone give a person a natural high, whereas low levels cause them to shut down emotionally.

Many celebrities have high adrenalin levels, which indicates that they also have high levels of cortisone. Such people seem to be on an emotional high from which they find it difficult to come down. If it's true that the first six years of our lives play a critical role in shaping who we are, both physically and psychologically, it might also be true that those likely to become rich and famous are those with high levels of cortisone, which judging by his behaviour almost definitely includes George Michael.

In order to build up his own identity, George had to rebel against his father and had to get as far away as he could from being anything like him, which included dyeing his hair blond.

George speaks about his mother in a very different tone, however. The love and respect he professes towards his mum is heartfelt. She was a rock from whom he gained his stability.

Even so, there's probably a lot George isn't saying about the interaction between his parents. It would be intrusive to second-guess attitudes and behaviour patterns in the Panayiotou household, but it's probably that the atmosphere there was often fraught with conflict. Jack's strong personality would have clashed with that of his equally determined son – especially where George's education and choice of vocation were concerned – while his mother might have stood by, really quite upset by all the male testosterone flying around her home.

George, however, was made of strong stuff. Instead of giving in, he rebelled. He won the battle of which school he was going to attend, and then he met Andrew Ridgeley and struck up a friendship with him against his parents' wishes. That was the catalyst that caused the rest of his life to change. George found in Andrew all the things that were missing in his own persona. They fitted together perfectly. Andrew's character was, in many ways, just like George's: larger than life. They wanted the same things – most of all, fame.

George saw good-looking Andrew as having all the goodies in the bag, believing that his friend had it all. But he wasn't jealous; instead, he used any envy he might have felt towards Andrew in a positive way and tried to become more like him. George's optimism, motivation and hard work took him on a journey into fame and fortune and saw the birth of a new aspect of his personality: the sexy performer seen cavorting on stage in Wham!, the man he described as 'that bloke poncing around with the pretty blond hair, the shorts and teeth'. However, he then added, 'Don't they realise this is not me?' And, of course, it wasn't; it was a sub-personality that worked well for him for a while. Georgios had turned himself from a Greek geek into George Michael, the ultimate performer. The real George Michael was still in there somewhere, writing hit songs and craving to come out and be heard, acknowledged and understood. Inside was the real creative genius, subsumed beneath the dazzling outer shell of the glitzy performer, who was almost certainly born out of George's insecurities and fears.

In 1993, George issued a press statement, describing how, back when he'd chosen to kill off Georgios, his biggest fear was that his huge ambitions 'would stay just out of reach for the child I saw in the mirror'. In the same statement, he said that the

George Michael who had worked non-stop for him for almost a decade now had to go, so he killed him off, too. How clever. What a genius. 'Thanks very much, but bugger off now; your services are no longer required.'

At this point, some people reading this might be thinking, 'What's she on about? That's mad!', and, yes, such behaviour might seem a little crazy – indeed, even George admitted that many might find it strange – but this is the nature of the human mind's wonderful defence systems. In psychological terms, this creation of different aspects of a personality is known as *splitting*, which occurs when someone splits away part of their personality from the other parts in order to protect their sanity. It's a trick at which George has proved to excel, and much of the time it's worked well for him. Like everything in life, however, there's no such thing as a free lunch and, when someone who has undergone this splitting gets a little stronger, they will need to reunite the split-off aspects of their personality, and this process can be acutely painful, emotionally.

When George's Wham! days were over and he dumped 'the performer', he fell into a deep depression and he grieved over the loss of the man he had become. There was a great big black hole where the Wham! man had resided, and that void had to be filled with something or someone else.

Throughout my career, I've seen many people trying to fill such voids in their lives, often with booze and drugs, searching frantically for a place where they can feel, as Roger Waters put it, comfortably numb. I've worked with men who can find this womblike place only under the influence of heroin or crack cocaine and girls who seek relief from the pain in the beds of men, only to be left feeling even more empty when they're alone once again. This way of hooking into a negative way of defending oneself against pain and suffering is a dangerous road to walk, but one that most of us find ourselves on at one time or another in our lives. As I mentioned earlier, life is as much about suffering as it is about being happy and contented.

George's addictions have accompanied him in some shape or form throughout his life, and after Wham! broke up he drank to excess. When he suffered another bout of depression after losing Anselmo, however, he changed the way he coped with the loss. Instead of running headlong into destructive behaviour, he faced his grief head on and shared this pain with a trusted person. He then used the traumatic experience to create two beautiful songs. He had, in short, grown up, and added maturity and discipline to his character.

But, of course, life is all about learning, and George still had lessons to learn, yet again under the gaze of the world. But why in God's name did he risk his career, reputation and love for his boyfriend Kenny Goss? Because he could.

Ever since his teens, George had divined from the actions and words of those around him that he was somehow special, somehow different, and when he found celebrity status he began to feel omnipotent, a belief that came to be reinforced with his vast wealth. But somewhere deep within his subconscious, this must have felt uncomfortable, and so, just as a small child would, he experimented with how far he could push his luck. Having boundaries makes a person feel safe, makes them feel that they know where they are, but George had no sense of where his boundaries ended, and so, in an attempt to find it, he pushed his luck and was arrested. He'd found the boundary in a painful but, in some ways, liberating way. He certainly knew he couldn't go any further without landing himself in hot water or even jail.

It's likely that George Michael felt like a fraud. After all, the name on his birth certificate was 'Georgios Kyriacos Panayiotou', not 'George Michael'. When people dissociate from an identity they no longer wish to own, or distance themselves from painful situations, they simply become somebody else, someone who they feel more comfortable being. George became adept at pretending to be the man everyone loved and admired, and yet somewhere within the ego he constructed it's likely that he felt like an impostor, a fraud always in danger of being caught, which could be the reason why he took so many risks and pushed his boundaries to the limit, constantly challenging the authorities. He might even, on some level, have wanted to be caught and exposed as an impostor, having decided that he could no longer live the lie and lead a pretend life with little sense of reality.

In my experience, most people feel a fraud to some degree, sensing that they're going to be 'found out' even when they've done nothing wrong. I know there have been times when I've seen a police car and thought, 'Oh, God. What have I done?' But it's how much this feeling dominates someone's personality that's the important issue.

When the gulf between reality and fantasy is wide, the 'fraud' lives in a lonely bubble with no real contact with others, an experience that has been described to me as being suffocating. It makes one wonder how long George had been acting out in public places, daring himself to be caught. Was he unconsciously searching for relief from the solitary confinement of his lonely bubble? (Remember, this is a theory rather than a diagnosis. As with all the celebrities analysed in this book, I'm giving *my* expert opinion.)

It's also that George has become addicted to the elevated levels of hormones that he's been experiencing for the last twenty-plus years. With such an exciting life in a world where there is always something going on, the levels of these hormones will remain high for most of the time, but, if the level drops at all and he becomes calmer, his body might crave the high. If this calmness is experienced as boredom, he might well have a tendency to create a drama in order to escape feeling bored. So maybe he was just bored on the day he took himself off to the toilet in the park, and was simply looking for some action. There is, after all, a large element of danger involved in going to a public place for sex, and George might well have been getting an adrenalin fix. Yes, he was looking for sex. I don't dispute that for one moment. In fact, he confesses to being over-sexed.

Why should that be? Could it be that one of the reasons he loves sex so much is because it fills him up, emotionally, and makes him feel alive? Sex, like food, offers instant gratification. You can't feel bad when you've got a bar of chocolate in your mouth or a penis inside you, or yours in someone else; this is a scenario that's a far cry from an isolated inhabitant of a lonely bubble with no contact with others. Existence in the bubble is like a living death. And in my experience, most gay people love danger. They have an edge to their personalities, and many are risk-takers.

There is an ongoing question in society as to whether one is born gay or one has gayness thrust upon them, that life messages and learned behaviour compel one to homosexuality. Is our sexuality down to our DNA or our environment? Nature or nurture?

What we do know is that our sexual preferences and behaviour are hugely affected by our early childhood relationships. (Genetics, it would appear, has very little, if anything, to do with it.) The whole picture is made up of

109

myriad different things, from oral sensual needs to fascination with excrement, flirtation and sex play with siblings. The sexual behaviour of boys can be particularly affected by the pattern of care that they receive. Neglect and disharmony between parents can make them promiscuous, as can sexual abuse, and often the differences between sex and love are confused. And the family messages that we receive and labels attached to us in later childhood certainly influence how we feel about ourselves, affecting our confidence levels about our looks, the way in which we cope with adolescence and how promiscuous we are.

So there's a whole cocktail of factors that might be behind George Michael's homosexuality, or indeed that of any person. But does a person's sexuality – homo or hetero – make any difference to their psychological profile as a whole? No. The bottom line is that, as long as people find a place in which they're comfortable within their own skin, it really doesn't matter how they defend themselves from the harsh reality of life. I sincerely hope that George has found this comfortable place and has exorcised his demons.

George might upset critics and politicians, but that's just George expressing his feelings and beliefs. He has that right. And something great about being a celebrity is that you have a voice that's heard by the world. That might not be a fantastic thing when you want to have sex in a public place, but it's pretty damn wonderful when you want to change something you feel could well do with changing.

Chapter 4

JADE GOODY

Jade Cerisa Lorraine Goody was born in Bermondsey, south London, on 5 June 1981. Her mum, Jackiey, was twenty-one years old at the time and had already delivered one baby boy into the world, but Jade's older brother, Brett, had been adopted and taken off to lead a new life in Australia. However, Jackiey was determined not to give up her little girl. Instead, against all the odds, she fought tooth and nail to keep her family together. Luckily for her, little Jade proved to have the same fighting spirit.

It has been widely reported that Jade's father, who had been just eighteen at the time of her birth, was a volatile character, and indeed it wasn't long after her birth that he was in prison. Jade was to have a difficult relationship with him in the early years of her adulthood, and despite several attempts at reconciliation it seems that he simply wasn't made of the necessary fibre to play the role of a solid father-figure. When he died suddenly in September 2005, it must have been a dreadful blow to Jade.

However, it was in 1986 – back when Jade was only five years old – that the relative calm of the Goodys' Bermondsey household was shattered when her mum and favourite uncle were involved in a fatal motorcycle accident. Her uncle was killed outright and Jackiey, seriously injured, was rushed to the Intensive Care Unit at London's Guy's Hospital, where by some terrible coincidence Jade's nan was lying in another ward, dying of cancer.

It doesn't take much imagination to conjure up the sad image of young Jade sobbing in the waiting room, afraid and alone, but she was made of strong stuff. Indeed, her strength would later be stretched to its limits, not only because of this event but also because her resilience and ability to cope was going to be tested time and time again throughout her childhood. Every time Jade has been knocked down, she's got right back up again and made the best of things. In all likelihood, it was this steely determination that led her to fame and wealth – and she is, without doubt, wealthy, reportedly having amassed over £1 million, much of which she has invested wisely.

Love her or hate her, no one can take away the fact that Jade Goody, winner of the third series of *Big Brother*, has become the most successful reality-show celebrity, and the magazines and tabloids fly off the shelves whenever she's featured on their front covers.

I must admit that, when I saw her on *Big Brother*, I would often cringe at her lack of dignity. ('Where's the girl's *pride*?') Rarely had there been a woman so ridiculed on a TV show, and her ability to put herself down was extraordinary. Her naked 'kebab belly' (her own description) was not a pretty sight. And what was all this new language? It was all 'minging' and 'chipsticks'! Today, of course, these words and others are fondly referred to as 'Jadeisms'. Indeed, these days the UK seems to be genuinely fond of Jade, if not obsessed with her — a far cry from her *Big Brother* days, when the public lapped up the media's cheap shots at her. And when she left the *Big Brother* house in 2002, she was met by people carrying placards bearing such cruel messages as 'kill the pig' and 'slaughter the pig'. She seemed to have been cast in the role of Piggy in William Golding's *Lord of the Flies*.

Neil Simpson, author of *Jade's World* — a fascinating story — very cleverly highlights the uncanny similarities between Jade and John Merrick, better known as the Elephant Man. Like Merrick, he points out, Jade was cursed with a tremendously difficult childhood, and like him she was determined to escape a life of poverty and make something of herself. Both became the victims of cruel mob hysteria, and both became circus freaks — Merrick literally, joining the fairground freak show run by the infamously cruel circus manager Sam Torr, and Jade figuratively, laying herself bare for the viewing public tuning in to *Big Brother*. Fortunately, the finales of both stories have a rich and warm feelgood factor.

With so many celebrities, body image is a major issue, and Jade is no exception, having struggled with her weight. What a bore to have your body under such scrutiny and ogled at by a nation obsessed with the rich and famous. What a curse! But wasn't this exactly what she'd wanted? Didn't she crave the attention, like so many other celebrities?

When she was younger, Jade loved to read the gossip magazines and always dreamed of being rich and famous, but what's life like for her now that she's front-page news? What's life under the bright lights *really* like? Does she want to remain big news, or would she prefer to take a back seat and run her new Harlow beauty salon, tellingly named Ugly's?

These are all interesting questions, but I think that one of the most intriguing questions asked about Jade Goody is, just what is it about the girl that everyone loves? For me, though, a more burning question is, of which celebrity curse is Jade in most danger of falling foul?

To answer some of these questions, let's take a look at her life, which all began in southeast London.

THE BERMONDSEY GIRL

There's little doubt that Jade Goody was loved. Although her family was poor and beset with problems, they were good, honest people with big hearts. Jade turned out to be something of a trouper, which is just as well, considering the testing trials that life has thrown at her. A weaker child might well have buckled under the pressure – but not Jade. She had a strong personality and a big mouth, and she just got on with things. While not particularly bright, academically, she nevertheless shone – like a star. And, although she has demonstrated huge reservoirs of resilience, that doesn't mean that she didn't suffer, because she did – so much so, in fact, that when she recalls her life as a child she finds it almost impossible to speak about some of the things that happened to her at that time.

Jade's family has always been at the centre of her world, but due to her difficult circumstances she was forced to grow up far too quickly. Incredibly, though, she never lost her innocence in the way many do when put under too much pressure too young. In fact, her childlike innocence is still very much a part of her character and seems to be one of the facets of her personality that the public finds so endearing. Read the following true story and imagine the scenario:

A little blonde, blue-eyed girl is skipping happily along the road. She is five years old and, although she's just had a lovely time at her friend's flat, she's looking forward to seeing her mum. Because her daddy is in prison, her mum means everything to her. She also has a grandmother, on whom she dotes, and a favourite uncle. Not all in the garden is rosy, however, because they don't have very much money, but they get by.

When she reaches her home, there's a crowd of neighbours waiting for her. They tell her that there's been a terrible accident. Her mum was out with Uncle Martin, and now he's dead and her mum's in the hospital. She, too, might die.

When the little girl gets to the hospital, she's told that her nan, who is already being treated at the hospital for terminal throat cancer, has died. The news about her beloved son's fatal accident has, it seems, speeded up her own death.

The little girl cuts a pitiful figure as she sobs on the bench in the corridor, waiting to see if her mum is going to die as well.

The little girl is, of course, Jade Goody and, while her mother didn't die, she was desperately ill and remained in hospital for two years before she came home to be cared for by Jade. While her mother had been nursed in hospital, Jade had been cared for by their extended family, but now she would be caring for her mother. It must have been extremely unsettling for the young girl. 'For the first nine months, Mum was pretty much out of it,' she later admitted to journalist Neil Simpson. 'I'd sit by her bedside and chat away, but things were really bad as Mum had so many hospital drugs in her. She even forgot me at one point.

She forgot she had a daughter because her memory had been affected by the accident.' In my book, if you can survive that, you can survive anything. Can being the subject of a 'kill the pig' banner when you're twenty-one compare with your mother forgetting you exist when you're just seven years old? I don't think so.

Jackiey had been left an invalid, having been blinded in one eye with a left arm that was permanently paralysed. Caring for her was a round-the-clock job for Jade, but she got on with it selflessly. 'I had to wash her, shave her armpits, do her hair for her. It was hard but because it's your mum you don't mind.'

This kind of selfless behaviour was evident on at least two occasions in the *Big Brother* house. The first occurred when all of the contestants, apart from Jade, had taken part in a marathon drinking binge. Meanwhile, Jade cleaned up the house, helped housemate Jonny to bed and kindly comforted the drunken Kate, who hadn't exactly been supportive of Jade.

The other example of her thoughtful nature concerns the chickens that the housemates kept and for which they were responsible. Jade, it seemed, was the only one of the housemates prepared to venture out in the pouring rain to feed them. As *TV Times* deputy editor Roger Felton said of her, 'That proved that she's got heart and is not just in it for herself.'

This same big heart pumped away furiously while caring for her disabled mother, a woman who – it has to be said – was not always an easy patient. To look at the situation from Jackiey's perspective, life must have been pretty grim for her even before the accident, and when the crash occurred she must have felt like her life was over. Physically, she must have been in terrible pain for a long period of time. Most of us know what it's like to have a blinding headache and how irritable it can make us. If the irritability continues, we get angry. By the same token, a prolonged period of illness, during which you're totally dependent on others, almost inevitably leads to angry outbursts. 'Daughters are always going to have arguments with their mums, but it was worse for me because there was a lot of frustration there,' Jade later confided in Neil Simpson. 'Mum would shout and then break down and cry with guilt because she knew I was only trying to help. I had to learn from a very young age that you have to be understanding.'

Of course, what Jade didn't realise at the time was that undergoing this experience would stand her in very good stead when she grew up and had to face people who weren't quite so understanding.

In the *Big Brother* house, for instance, housemates Kate and Jade were poles apart in character, the latter never trusting the former and later describing her as 'sly and a manipulator'. 'One minute she would talk to me, and the next she would go off me,' Jade told the *News of the World* on quitting the *Big Brother* house. This kind of attitude was alien to Jade, who couldn't understand her housemate's problem with her. Jade, in contrast, seems to be a tolerant individual with a great sense of fairness. But where does this tolerant nature come from? Does she derive it from her own nature or from her upbringing? It's a question that will be examined later in this chapter. For now, we need to stay with her difficult childhood, because it's for sure it had to get worse before it got better.

Accidents happen in troubled homes, maybe more often than in happy ones, and the members of the Goody household had more than their fair share of dangerous incidents. On one occasion, eight-year-old Jade walked into the kitchen, where her mum was cooking dinner, only to see that her mother's hand was in the pan. Having no feeling in her paralysed arm, Jackiey literally fried her hand.

Worst than this, Jade and her mother took to using candles to light their flat in order to save electricity. One morning, Jade awoke to find flames licking the side of her wardrobe and screamed to her mum to wake up, but Jackiey's disabilities made it difficult for her to move at all, let alone quickly. Somehow, in her adrenalin-fuelled panic, Jade managed to drag her mum out of her bed and carry her through the smoke and flames. She saved the pair of them.

If anyone tried to blame Jackiey for any of this, however, or suggest she wasn't capable of mothering her little girl, Jade would vociferously defend her mother. The last thing she wanted was to be taken into care, although there were more than enough incidents that might have warranted the intervention of social services.

On one such occasion, after lashing out at her child during the smallest of arguments, Jackiey struck Jade. It was probably a minor incident, but it was the last straw and the volcano of anger that had been bubbling slowly inside Jackiey suddenly erupted, and Jade was directly in its patch. Jackiey's frustration at not being able to take care of herself finally got the better of her and she beat her daughter. The next day, when Jade went to school black and blue and couldn't sit down without wincing, the teachers knew something was wrong.

To give Jackiey her due, however, she knew instantly that she'd crossed a line and was so scared that she'd harm her daughter again that she called social services. 'She actually wanted them to put me on a risk list,' Jade later revealed. 'I now know that social services decided not to do that, and I'm so glad. Me and Mum are a team. We're a family.'

The bond between child and parent is a sacred one, and Jade recognised that her family had to stay together, even when at times this seemed unbearable. It's a belief that's common in my line of work. Having worked with many families who are struggling with various problems and difficulties that could destroy them, I've heard them affirm again and again how much they want to stay together. And, while they have no doubt saved many children from dire physical and emotion abuse, I've witnessed more than one case where social service have taken it upon themselves to intervene where it would perhaps have been best to leave well alone. I wonder how Jade would have turned out if social services, instead of having the sense to see the whole picture of their lives, had separated Jackiey and her daughter and placed Jade into a care home. It doesn't bear thinking about.

JADE LEARNS TO SIGN HER NAME

The news broke in August 2002: Jade Goody needed to have handwriting lessons so that she could sign autographs consistently. Was she preparing herself for the fame ahead, getting ready for the day when she left the *Big Brother* house to face her adoring public? Had she been tipped off to the news that tens of thousands of postcard-sized pictures of her had been printed off and were about to be distributed to her fans?

It transpired that this wasn't quite the case. An article in the *Daily Express* reported that in fact Jade had several ways of signing her name, which apparently was causing problems, especially when she had to sign her name on official documents.

Jade admitted that her spelling, too, was so poor that, when she was a youngster, she'd used to add an extra E to her surname, and confessed that joined-up writing wasn't exactly one of her strengths. Such shortcomings aren't exactly surprising; instead of

119

paying attention in the classroom, she'd been sleeping, having been up all night looking after her mum.

When she was in the *Big Brother* house, however, Jade's difficult childhood and the reasons for her lack of schooling weren't yet common knowledge, so she was the perfect figure for the other contestants to poke fun at. Indeed, the UK as a whole joined in the fun and ridiculing Jade became a national pastime.

One thing that many wanted to know was, just how did Jade Goody manage to beat incredibly stiff opposition to become a contestant on *Big Brother* in the first place? What had motivated her to apply? Well, it appears that Jade, like most of the other celebrities featured in this book, dreamed from an early age of being famous. Her mother has described her as 'happy and ebullient, always smiling and ready to sing and put on a show', and one of her fondest memories of her daughter is of the day the two of them visited a festival held by the local council at which the songs and dances of the hit musical *Fame* (Victoria Beckham's favourite) were being performed. Jade got up on the stage and joined in.

Later, at the age of five, Jade got herself a small part in the TV series *London's Burning* and soon demonstrated her urge to be on the television. The girl who used to watch *The Smash Hits Poll Winners' Party* in her Bermondsey home and wished she was there just went for it.

When she was told by a friend about an advert asking for contestants for a new series of the UK's fabled reality-TV show *Big Brother*, the now celebrity-obsessed Jade got excited. She'd seen contestants of the previous two shows dressed in designer clothes, doing the rounds of chat shows and attending the film premieres, milking every second of what they were quick to realise might well be only five minutes in the limelight.

JADE GOODY

Although she enjoyed her job as a dental nurse, Jade sometimes found the mundane routine boring, so she decided to apply to appear on the show. At the very least, she reckoned, she could have an all-expenses-paid holiday. And, apart from missing her mum and boyfriend Danny, she had nothing to lose.

The selection and elimination processes to get into *Big Brother* are far more intense than most people realise. For a start, the initial application form given to hopefuls for *Big Brother* 2002 was nine pages long and requested details about each applicant's personal life, relationships, education and employment. Here are some examples of the questions that appeared on the form:

1. What might people dislike about you?
2. What is the worst thing you have ever said to anyone, and why?
3. If someone made a film of your life, who would play the lead role?
4. If you could have a famous person (dead or alive) as your mother and father, who would it be and why?
5. Write the headline you would least like to see about yourself if you are in the house.
6. Write the headline you would most like to see about yourself.
7. Describe your parents.
8. Which five words best describe your childhood?

Predictably, the last two questions proved particularly difficult for Jade to answer, but eventually she wrote that she would have loved to have had James Bond actor Sean Connery as her dad and Italian actress Sophia Loren as her mum, then named

EastEnders actress Patsy Palmer as the person who she'd like to see play the part of her in a movie.

Next Jade had to submit a two-minute video of herself. For her submission, while other hopefuls were handing in cleverly produced videos, Jade had thrown together a basic and, indeed, slightly risqué homemade movie that was, like her, completely honest, original and upfront. The footage shows her wearing tight blue jeans, an equally tight white T-shirt (showing off her pre-kebab belly, of course) and a sparkly bling-bling belt. Fluffing up her big hair, she positions herself in front of the camera – set up on a tabletop – all the while giggling nervously. Then, after a final check of her makeup and a last-minute lipstick application, she records her party piece.

Looking at the camera and chattering away at full speed in her brash south-London accent, she shows Big Brother how she can put her body through an elastic band. Then she grabs her boobs (pre-surgery, of course) and thrusts them towards the camera while gabbling as fast as a speeding train, 'I get called Pamela Anderson because of these. An' I get called Claudia Schiffer. Me mates take the piss out of me 'cos I wanna be a so-called model. I'd be great for the show *Big Bruvver* 'cos I've got a great personality. I'm very, very bubbly and I'm very outspoken.'

She barely comes up for air before continuing, 'Everyone on *Big Bruvver* will vote for me, I'm sure of it. Not because I'm sure of meself or anyfink but just 'cos I'm an original. There's not anuvver like me. I'm unique.'

Jade then decides to sing a little song, without much of a tune but in a pretty good voice. 'Get me out of Bermondsey and put me on TV/So, Davina and all your friends, pick me.'

The selection committee had requested a video in which each contestant showed them 'how you really are' and, in the case of

Jade, that's exactly what they got. And although she still had a very long way to go in the selection process, with endless forms to fill in and interviews held at secret locations to preserve confidentiality, the chances are she'd pretty much cracked it with her unique video show. The footage has recently surfaced and has been shown on daytime chat show *Richard and Judy*, where it caused much hilarity.

All through the long and difficult *Big Brother* selection procedure, which involved some frankly terrifying tests, she kept telling herself, 'Just be yourself. Just be yourself. I'm perfect for this programme. That has to show through.' It's a chant. A mantra. Positive visualisation at its highest level. All the time she was repeating this to herself, she was raising her confidence levels and pushing her naturally optimistic attitude to its limits. By hook or by crook, she was determined to get on *Big Brother*, and she was willing to put herself through torture to get there.

Big Brother producer Deborah Sargeant said of the show, 'We are very selective with the under-twenty-ones. Although in theory we'll take anyone over eighteen, they have to be especially good to make it through if they're under twenty-one.'

After jumping through all the hoops the *Big Brother* production team had required, Jade spent days in a state of nervous anticipation, finding it impossible to concentrate on anything else. This could be her big break, and she knew it. Eventually, when *Big Brother*'s executive producer, Phil Edgar-Jones, called her to tell her that she'd made it into the house, he later reported that he thought she was going to collapse when he broke the news. She hyperventilated, and he had to ask her to sit down and take some deep breaths.

So the girl had gone for it, and she'd done it, having beaten a record-breaking number of hopefuls in the process. But, as anyone who watched *Big Brother 3* knows only too well, Jade had to endure a lot, both inside the house and outside at the hands of the media. How does the saying go? Be careful what you wish for; you might just get it.

JADE IN THE HOUSE

Jade once claimed that her specialist subject on *Mastermind* would be 'shoes and handbags', while also declaring that she adored shopping and that gossip and being healthy made her happy. She is no doubt not alone in having such simple pleasures. How, then, did it come to pass that, during the same summer, the following was said on national television about Jade: 'They had 150,000 applicants and, in the final equation, Jade. How did that happen? God, she's annoying. If it wasn't cruel to kick a pig, you would.' And this was one of the kindest things that presenter Graham Norton had to say about her. Why? How could this nightmare be happening?

By the end of the first week of *Big Brother 3*, Jade was at the bottom – and by a long way – of the official online poll charting the most popular housemates. At the same time, the media hate campaign had begun.

Big Brother 3 was a runaway success, earning a much greater audience share than *Big Brother 2*. The viewers tuned in by the hundreds of thousands, even though the competition was fierce and it was screened during the August holiday period and the football World Cup was in full swing. Of course, it was the uniqueness of Jade Goody that made all the difference.

The show featured all the usual ingredients that have made reality-TV shows so popular today: flaming rows, furious competitiveness, dreadfully childish behaviour and the tantalising prospect of some onscreen sex. But, when Jade and her Jadeisms were added to the mix, the dish became a *cordon bleu* extravaganza.

When Jade stripped naked live on television, she took the show to new heights – or, possibly, lows. But she didn't strip off solely for the sake of sensationalism, and neither did she do it to show off her body in the hope of earning herself some modelling work after the series had concluded.

Let's take a look at how the strip came about. It's a fascinating story, but it's also an example of human behaviour at its worst.

All the housemates are assembled in the living room area. Lounging around on the comfy sofas, they are having a boozy night. They decide to play word association, which, although a simple game, does require a certain degree of knowledge. Given Jade's lack of schooling, she was at a disadvantage from the beginning, and her housemates were no doubt aware of this.

Poor Jade is losing. As if this isn't bad enough, the boys then decide that, as a forfeit, each time a wrong answer is given the person who gave it has to remove an item of clothing. Jade is given some particularly difficult questions and, with every item of clothing she sheds, the more exposed and vulnerable she becomes.

When she gets down to her knickers and screams that, no, she can't take them off, she is met with laughter and is told that she has to remove them. It's the rules.

Eventually, the knickers come off and Jade is left there, sitting naked, washed in the laughter and cheers of her fellow housemates.

According to a Channel 4 spokesman, a record 5.8 million people watched this spectacle, but ultimately Jade has had the last laugh. While this episode of her life might have been mortifying at the time and might still cause her some embarrassment, this scene was later voted the best from all five series of the show.

Jade's personality evoked strong public reaction, the worst of which was demonstrated by the 'kill the pig' placards that met her on leaving the *Big Brother* house. Indeed, the dreadful mass-hatred that circulated in the tabloid press while she was in the house is still talked about today. 'It may be fun to hate her,' wrote one girl on an internet message board, 'but some comments made about her intellect and appearance will probably stay with her for the rest of her life. It's like being bullied by a whole nation of bullies.'

She has been given the honorary title 'National Celebrity Treasure', but others are less keen to dish out plaudits. Again on an internet message board, one very angry Irishman protested, 'Choosing Jade as a housemate was irresponsible of the producers. What did they expect from such a horrible childhood, with little knowledge about the world except for her to make a fool of herself on camera? It was a low swipe.'

So what on earth did life have in store for Jade when she left the confines of the *Big Brother* house? And just how would her portrayal in a cruel and vicious media affect the young Bermondsey girl? Of the stripping incident, the *Daily Mirror* reported, 'We saw fat-rolled Michelin girl Jade in all her preposterous lack of glory, naked as the day Frankenstein made her. Mothers should cover their children's eyes – and their own. A pig lookalike unveiling cascading mountains of blubber while downing industrial quantities of wine.' It's a great piece of creative writing but a terribly vicious comment. Could the vulnerable dental nurse get past such comments?

LEAVING THE HOUSE

Some people believe that, if one is to be able to survive abusive situations, one must become thick-skinned. This might or might not be true but, whatever the case, it doesn't apply to Jade. She doesn't come across as being thick-skinned at all. In fact, she gives an impression of being very receptive, emotionally, and it must therefore have been the most bizarre moment of her life when she stepped (in fourth place) out of the Big Brother house and into the craziness of the outside world. In her early days in the house, she asked, 'What does hostile mean?' Well, she was about to find out.

When Davina McCall yelled out Jade's name, the swelling crowd waiting outside erupted. (It was later reported that the screams could be heard two miles away.) Jade was terrified and clung on to Alex as she left the house.

As she re-entered the outside world, she was blinded by harsh lights and flashbulbs. 'I can't believe it,' she kept repeating. 'I can't believe it.' Then the show's host, Davina McCall, rescued her and guided her by the hand past the offensive banners, although she still heard calls of 'Jade, you're a minger'. Ever the optimist, though, she knew that, despite all the cruelty being hurled at her, she was a winner. She might not have won the contest, but that didn't matter; the humble Bermondsey girl was now a celebrity. Wearing a pale-pink diamanté ballgown, she waved gleefully and, in a moment of supreme irony, shouted her thanks to the crowd.

Moments later, Jade was reunited with her family and friends and there were tears of joy. But there was another surprise in store for her, and Davina McCall was almost hopping she was so excited. Here, to meet and greet Jade, was her favourite chat-show host, Graham Norton (who had since done a turnaround

127

following his pig jibes and had spent the last few weeks singing her praises and urging the public to vote for her to win). Lost for words, Jade hugged him tightly, and then, spotting her grandmother and grandfather waiting patiently in the wings, she ran into their arms, leaving Norton to stare after her. This was Jade Goody at her spontaneous best.

There were more surprises. On the huge TV screen outside the house appeared the face of Hollywood actor Johnny Depp, who, it turned out, was a great fan of her and the show and told her personally how he'd been hoping she would win. Tears rolled down Jade's face and she was momentarily, and uncharacteristically, speechless.

Then Davina went through the worst and the best of Jade's antics in the house. The pair of them sat for while, listening to all the minging and chipstick Jadeisms while Jade stuffed her fist in her mouth with embarrassment. When Davina took her back outside, the crowd's boos had subsided and there was now a genuine applause.

Could it be that Jade had gone from public enemy number one to celebrity hero overnight? It began to look that way. Even staunch critic the *Sun*, a newspaper that had printed such terrible things about her, had done an abrupt about-face, even going so far as to parade Jade around south London on a red double-decker bus, emblazoned with the newspaper's logo. Were they feeling guilty, or was this done simply for publicity purposes? Even the then editor of rival publication the *Daily Mirror*, Piers Morgan, was heard to say, 'Jade was refreshingly honest. A sweetie.' Talk about the fickle world of celebrity! One minute you're cursed and the next you're placed high on a pedestal.

So how was Jade going to fare from here on in? Was she going to cash in on what she assumed would be short-lived fame? Would she disappear into the night like previous contestants? Or would she hit the big time?

Put it this way: when the editors of celebrity-focused magazine *OK!* were choosing who to put on the front cover of their 'Special Collectors' Edition' to celebrate their tenth anniversary, the list of possible contenders was impressive and included class-A celebrity couples such as Victoria and David Beckham and Catherine Zeta Jones and Michael Douglas, as well as the hugely popular model-cum-media personality Jordan. Instead, they chose a picture of Jade, her partner, Jeff, and their baby son, Bobby, under the headline 'jade at home: world exclusive'. Inside were eleven pages of text and seventeen pictures devoted to the ex-*Big Brother* star and her family.

But just how did Jade go from being branded a pig by the media to being a cover girl of a market-leading celebrity mag? From a kebab-bellied laughing-stock to a slim mother with a cute TV-presenter boyfriend? Just what is it about Jade's personality that has brought her so much success? Many love her, and even those who claim to hate her or think she's an irritating attention-seeker have to admit that she's done extraordinarily well for herself.

THE CELEBRITY CURSE STRIKES

Despite Jade's elevation to stardom in the British public's eyes, the celebrity-curse factor was furiously at work. As her fame grew, hordes of parasites crawled out of the woodwork, scrambling over each other in their odious attempts to make money at the expense of their old mate, while previous lovers (allegedly) told lurid tales about the girl. And, of course, the journalists had their chequebooks at the ready.

Jade was able to cope with most of this madness but, when her father, Andy, talked to the press, it proved one blow too many. Playing the victim, he told stories of how embarrassed he'd been when his daughter had been overtly sexual on television, wailing that he'd been through a nightmare because of her.

It was enough. Jade felt that it was time for a confrontation and went to see him. Although she'd been to see him in prison as a child, it must have been very different to see him on the outside, and it couldn't have been easy to visit the father who she felt had let her down yet again. But, after some nervous chatting, Andy finally managed to tell her he was proud of her. It was better late than never, and, in yet another demonstration of her forgiving nature, Jade said that she would never forget the sentiment.

However, it turned out that her dad wasn't really able to change. One morning in the summer of 2003, Jade woke up to read newspapers splashed with more of Andy's lurid stories. This betrayal was too much for poor Jade. A healthy father/daughter relationship can be such a precious thing, but in her view, 'My mum has been my mum *and* my dad.'

Maybe the reason Andy was so weak was because his mother was a thief with a taste for crack cocaine. It's not much of a start in life – but then again, neither was Jade's, and she managed to turn her life around with a startling degree of success. While it's true that you can't choose what life deals you, Jade has demonstrated how it's possible to make the best of a bad deal and turn your life around if you give it your all. And that's exactly what Jade did next.

She got herself an agent and a personal trainer, who helped her to get fit and lose weight. After she'd got herself in trim, she found more television work and suddenly became a hugely sought-after celebrity, with magazines such as *Heat* falling over themselves to put her on their front covers. As *Heat* editor Mike Firth has acknowledged, what female celebrity fans see in Jade is a form of identification. While they might want to be Posh Spice or Madonna, Jade is someone with whom they can identify. As Jade admits, 'I'm not famous. I'm not a celebrity. I'm not a star. I'm just a face people will recognise.' It's this attitude that people admire and respect.

But there's more to the way in which people relate to Jade than her identifiable face on the magazine covers; people also want to read her down-to-earth interviews. She's not one of those celebrities who give controlled, bland, edited versions of their lives, saying what they want the media to believe of them. Indeed, when stars start to behave as if they're royalty and start to believe in their own hype, they alienate their fans. Jade is not like this, and that's why she's loved.

Not long after the opening of her beauty salon Ugly's, Jade took part in a call-in show on Radio REM FM in Marbella, a station where I regularly broadcast, and she had listeners in hysterics when she explained the difference between a Brazilian and a Californian wax. In her brash south-London accent, she told the local ex-pats, 'Well, in a Californian you have to take all the bum hairs, too, but in a Brazilian you leave a landing strip.' Wonderful.

LIFE AND LOVES

When she was still enjoying the first flushes of fame, Jade met and fell in love with Jeff Brazier, an ex-football player with Leyton Orient who was forging his own career as a TV personality. Young and attractive, when he met Jade he'd just appeared in the Channel 4 reality-TV show *Shipwrecked* and would later win a similar show entitled *The Farm*.

The two met through Jade's personal trainer, Kevin Adams, and soon became close. Neither had had a particularly idyllic childhood, which gave them something in common, something about which they could identify closely with each other. What began as a friendship soon blossomed into something more meaningful, and Jade confessed that Jeff was totally different to anyone she'd been out with before. Perhaps, she hoped, it would be the start of something beautiful, as she'd always dreamed of marrying and having babies.

But peace didn't reign for long. First, there was an accident that could have left Jade blind in one eye, just like her mother. It happened just after Jade moved into her new three-storey house in Essex. One can't imagine her being particularly adept at DIY, but she decided to have a go anyway. However, while she was trying to fix the house's telephone intercom system, she prised out two live wires, and then, when she tried to push them back in with a pair of scissors, she slipped and fell against the blades, which pierced her eye.

She fell to the floor, in agony and on the verge of fainting. There was blood everywhere. Petrified, she called Jeff, who was at her side in a flash. Having found her bleeding on the kitchen floor, he rushed her to the hospital.

Later, at Moorfields Eye Hospital, she was told that her eye had been saved and she wasn't going to lose her sight. Nevertheless, the accident had terrified her, and she was glad to have had Jeff around to call on. Reliable and supportive, he was displaying qualities that she would have loved her father to have had – qualities that perhaps indicated he would make a good father himself.

Coincidentally, even though her work schedule was particularly gruelling at this time – and despite the fact that she was on the pill – she fell pregnant. She was the same age her mother had been when she'd had Jade. Worried sick, she again called Jeff, who managed to talk her down into a state of calmness and set her mind to rest. Although he was only twenty-three years old, he showed a maturity that one would, indeed, hope an expectant father to have. 'My mum had me when she was sixteen, and she had a tough time,' he observed philosophically. 'Now I'm looking forward to bringing someone new into the world myself, and I want to be totally involved and experience everything. I'll be there all the time and will be very proud. I doubt Jade will be the best nappy-changer in the world, but I'll be happy to muck in.'

The joy that the couple felt on informing the press of Jade's pregnancy was short-lived. Was there was to be no peace and harmony in the Goody home? Apparently not. It seemed that, wherever Jade went, chaos followed.

Pregnancy was doing dreadful things to Jade's behaviour. She was suffering from particularly strong food cravings, and at one time she just *had* to have pickled-onion flavoured Monster Munch crisps dipped in hummus. Her hormones, too, were all over the place and causing havoc. She became stroppy and bad tempered. Jeff, it seemed, was in for a rotten time.

But, if Jade upset Jeff, she upset herself more. Unable to contain her violent mood swings, she is reported to have wailed, 'Me being who I am is a strain. I always said you need to be a lunatic to live with me, and pregnancy has made everything even worse.'

This must have been a miserable time for Jade. It's a horrible feeling, losing control and having to resort to 'acting out'. There seems to be no rational behaviour available. Instead, you sense that you are pushing away those you love, but are powerless to stop the chaotic thoughts that swirl around your erratic mind. It causes a terrible strain on otherwise strong relationships. (I will go deeper into this part of Jade's personality in the analysis that follows.) Fortunately for Jade, Jeff managed to stay grounded and remained committed. Indeed, Jade referred to him as her 'anger-management teacher'.

Their son, Bobby Jack, was born four weeks prematurely, weighing in at a tiny 5lb 7oz. As with all premature babies, Bobby's immediate health was a worry, but it wasn't too long before he was taken home, where they attempted to be a happy family. Jeff and Jade doted on little Bobby from day one, as did grandmother Jackiey. 'I hope he gets his dad's brain and not mine,' grinned Jade. Both she and Jeff were determined not to employ a nanny, intending to be hands-on parents to their son, which they've thus far managed to do.

Life for both parents at this time was very busy, but despite the steady stream of work they had also devised a top-secret plan: Jade was training to be a beauty therapist, and the pair were building a beauty salon. Fully aware of the fickleness of the crazy world of celebrity, Jade was determined not to blow everything and end up at square one, broke. Indeed, while some reports indicate that Jade is now a very wealthy woman, others have it that her money is dwindling. What is undeniable, however, is that she has amassed more riches than any other ex-reality-show celebrity. She might be a ditzy blonde in many ways, but she is also one smart cookie. There may well be some truth in the rumours that she has a cash-flow problem, but at least she has invested wisely.

Today, Jade's beauty salon is up and running, and she clearly loves the place, where she spends much of her time surrounded by good friends, including her best mate, Carly. Beauty therapy is her passion now, and she proves this by being a hands-on therapist.

While her career was taking an abrupt but successful turn, however, in the romance department things were looking less than rosy. For one thing, Jade was pregnant again and, with her hormones going crazy again, her relationship with Jeff was soon under threat when some deep-seated insecurities bubbled up to the surface.

It's a terrible thing to wonder whether your partner is having an affair. One minute you fear you're being paranoid (well, you usually are told you are, anyway!) and the next you've convinced yourself that you're right. Is he or she having an affair or not? Is my imagination running away with me, or is my intuitive instinct spot on? Am I going mad? It can drive you totally nuts.

Then Jade started to get late-night calls from a mystery person who informed her that Jeff was having an affair. Her mind flipped back and forth; one minute she was terrified that it might be true and the next she was telling herself that such allegations were merely cruel lies. She was still madly in love with Jeff, but her nerves were stretched to the limit and his mobile was ringing late at night. Could she trust him? It was awful.

And then stories began to appear in the press alleging that a girl had been having sex with Jeff while she'd been pregnant with Bobby. The revelation nearly destroyed her and, although Jeff declared the story to be outright lies, the strain on the couple intensified. The fights reached fever pitch, and after one particularly violent fight they were both arrested.

This particular row had blown up after Jeff had gone out to dinner, ostensibly with some work colleagues, but when Jade called him that evening a woman answered his phone. After spending a couple of hours in hysterics, Jade was ready to burst, and when Jeff returned she immediately launched an all-out assault.

Jackiey, who had been in the house at the time, had been so concerned that she'd called the emergency services. Jeff, meanwhile, fled the house, and after visiting the Accident and Emergency Department of the local hospital he handed himself in to the police. Jade was then arrested for assault.

While Jade and Jeff's relationship had reached new and dangerous levels of violence, life went on. Even though they split up (in as much as they were no longer living under the same roof), Jeff's commitment to Jade and Bobby remained strong and, when Jade's second baby was again born prematurely, he was as supportive as ever.

Once again, the arrival of a premature baby was a dramatic affair for Jade and Jeff, who at the time was working fifty miles away in Colchester, where he was taking part in the TV show *The Farm*. Unable to get away, he called Bobby's godfather, Lee Howells, and asked him to take care of things. Racing off at high speed for the hospital, a confused Lee drove in the wrong direction while Jade languished in the back of his car on all fours (no doubt giving audible vent to her frustration), but eventually he realised his mistake, turned the car around and delivered her safely into the arms of medical staff.

When she'd given birth to Bobby, Jade had been in labour for nine hours, but little Freddie's birth was much quicker. Jeff, who made it back to London in record time, just managed to make it, and he and Jackiey were at the hospital when Freddie entered the world and were able to give their support to the new mum.

In fact, it's fortunate that they were there, as the new mum certainly needed support, as both she and her new son had a tough time after the birth. Jade experienced complications and needed a blood transfusion while Freddie was in an incubator for nine days – a long time for a mother desperate to hold and bond with her baby.

It was an odd situation, with Jade and Jeff at Freddie's bedside, looking like any other loving couple doting over their newborn son yet, in reality, estranged. Although Jeff was a regular visitor to the house, where he played with the boys and was a generally supportive father, Jade was now the single mother she had always dreaded being.

Meanwhile, Jade's career remained strong and she was offered further lucrative deals. And then she met another guy. Enter one Ryan Amoo.

Although she confessed to being too busy for love, Jade did enjoy a few torrid months with Ryan. The newspapers, of course, seized another opportunity to have a go at Jade. One commented unkindly, 'Ryan Amoo is unique. He's the only man in the world who sees Amoo when he looks in the mirror and then sees another one when he rolls over in bed.'

Would the personal insults ever stop? It seemed not. But Jade knows this is all part of the media game. Staying glossy and groomed is expected of someone in her position, however tedious it might be. Dieting and breast enlargements are all part and parcel of her life now, as are choosing the right clothes to suit her figure, getting the best hairdresser, having the most expensive beauty products at her disposal and, of course, stuffing her wardrobe with Gucci and Prada.

It's all about taking the rough with the smooth, and Jade certainly seems to be more than able to be rational about the world she inhabits nowadays. Even when she was wrongly accused of shoplifting from Asda, she was able to turn it into a joke. When I asked her what it was like to have this particularly horrible accusation thrown at her, she responded, 'They called the newspaper before they called police. It was mad. Then, a few days later, me mate was down Asda and she heard this woman saying, "Hey, that's the jacket Jade was supposed to have nicked. I *must* get one!"'

Jade Goody seems to have few secrets, largely because she tends to wear her heart on her sleeve most of the time. With her, it's definitely a case of what you see is what you get, and this allows her a degree of freedom about which many other celebrities can only dream. If she wants to pop down to the shops in her slippers, for instance, then that's what she will do.

JADE ON THE COUCH

Just why is this Bermondsey girl, despite all the odds, doing so well in the world of celebrity? The nine other celebrities I have chosen to analyse in this book are, in many respects, very different to our Jade – and I think it's the word 'our' here that sets her apart from the others.

Could there be another chance for her and Jeff? And most importantly – what parts of her personality need to change if she is to avoid falling victim to the curse of celebrity?

At this point, you might well be asking, 'What are you on about? Jade Goody is already a victim. Look at the way the media has reviled her and hurled abuse at her. Doesn't that make her a victim?' Well, no. Being the victim of such abuse doesn't automatically mean you're a victim. Whatever was hurled at Jade, she threw straight back and refused to play the victim, taking all the jibes on the chin. She knew damned well that she'd grasped an incredible opportunity and that she would be the one having the last laugh.

Jade is, above all else, a spontaneous girl, and this often leads her to say things without thinking first. It's a tendency that often lands her in deep water, but it also endears her to others. She might not be the brain of Britain, but she's near the top of the scale when it comes to emotional intelligence.

Children suffering tough childhoods need to learn the art of survival very quickly. In Jade's case, survival meant keeping her family together, and so she took on the responsibility of caring for her mother. If she hadn't, she would have been taken into care. However, with looking after her mother day and night, she was too tired to concentrate at school, so for much of the time she chose not to go. Her education, of course, suffered. Consequently, when she was in the *Big Brother* house, the viewers heard her ask what 'a sparus' was and her state her belief that Rio de Janeiro was a man's name. Everything was 'minging' and everyone was a 'chipstick', and she claimed not to see the point in learning about history: 'Why would I wanna know about all those hysterical fings? Them days are gone.'

This lack of education placed her on the periphery in the house and set her up as the perfect scapegoat, and there were many there who ridiculed her. Add to this the mob hate that was gearing up across Britain and one might be forgiven for predicting that she would flee from public life entirely. However, Jade Goody was made of much stronger stuff. As she said on daytime chat show *Loose Women*, 'I'd already suffered much more than that. Of course it hurt, but most of it went over my head.' In this, she demonstrates an enviably resilient attitude, but where exactly does this resilience spring from?

It's all about attitude. Jade is the ultimate optimist. Even when things were tough and she was caring for a sick, frustrated mother who wasn't averse to thumping her one, she managed to see that there was a silver lining: her and Jackiey staying together.

On the other hand, a pessimistic attitude in such a situation can become a lifelong, self-fulfilling template for a child, causing them to focus only on setbacks and losses. Psychiatric hospitals are full of such cases, and it's the job of counsellors like me to help them learn about optimism.

Jade doesn't need to be taught this skill. She always sees the glass as being half-full and isn't one to moan about her woes. The power of her positive thinking keeps her spirits up in times of hardship, and she always has a dream on which to focus. For instance, on one occasion, when I asked her what her goals were at that time, she answered without hesitation: 'I would like to open an Ugly's in Los Angeles [she knows where it is now] and, yeah, perhaps in Marbella. Oh, and I'd like to get a part in [UK TV cop show] *The Bill* so I can dress up in a uniform.'

There is a fundamental difference between pessimistic and optimistic children that's worth mentioning here. Pessimistic children are most at risk of becoming depressed, having a belief that the causes of bad events are permanent, that they will never go away. In contrast, optimistic children bounce back from setbacks through the belief that the cause of bad events are temporary and will eventually be solved. At the lowest points in her childhood, Jade's thinking probably went something like this: 'Mum's in a really bad mood today, but she'll be OK tomorrow. I know she just punched me, but she doesn't really mean it. She's just tired and fed up. It'll all be all right tomorrow.' If she'd been a pessimist, the dialogue in her head would have gone something like this: 'Why me? Why do I have to have a sick mum? She hit me again. It's never going to end. It's not fair!' In the first example, Jade sees her predicament as something that will pass and visualises the future as rosy, whereas in the second it's all doom and gloom for the pessimistic child.

140

Another factor that differentiates pessimists from optimists is the way in which the former apply their emotional state globally, thinking, for instance, 'All teachers are horrible.' Optimists, on the other hand, tend to recognise that their emotional state derives from a particular situation; in the same circumstances, an optimist might think, 'Mr Smith is a rotten teacher.'

What causes one child to respond positively and another negatively? In fact, this is something of a mystery. You can have two children raised in the same environment and one will be a pessimist and the other an optimist. This happens even in the case of twins. While pinpointing the fundamental catalyst behind such attitudes is undoubtedly important, what's more important is being able to recognise the different ways of thinking and to help the pessimist think differently. Helping a depressive to change their naturally negative thoughts into positive ones is the key to helping them out of a dark place.

A wonderful therapeutic model for helping pessimists to change their mindset is a technique known as *cognitive behavioural therapy*, by which patients are taught simply to change all of the negative messages in their heads into positive ones. Obviously, it takes a while to change this deeply ingrained habit, but it can be done.

So the young Jade used to love to read the celebrity magazines, and now she's on the front covers – admittedly, not always looking her best, but with a lovely home and a lump sum in the bank. Her other dream was to own a beauty salon, and she's done that too. Then, after she 'made it' as a celebrity, she went back to school and is now a qualified beautician. She's bought herself and her boys some security.

Jade is the kind of role model that Samuel Smiles would have approved of back in 1859, because she gives out all the right messages to girls aspiring to be like her. They have seen the worst of her, and they've witnessed her survival. From being raised in one of the poorest parts of Britain and being a full-time carer to a sick mother while her dad was in prison, she got herself on to a popular reality show through her own efforts. Now, that's one hell of a positive message for underprivileged kids: 'If Jade can do it, so can I.'

A Message to Jade

There is one blot on your landscape, Jade. (Well, there has to be at least one; life's not perfect, remember.) Beware of your erratic hormones. They were all over the place when you were pregnant, and I'm guessing that you suffer from pre-menstrual tension. Three weeks of relative calm and then – bang! – you go off on one. Jeff, the father of your boys, gets it in the neck and life becomes chaotic. If you *do* suffer from PMT, you'll be feeling insecure and perhaps a little paranoid at this time, which could be the one week of the month when your sunny, optimistic nature suddenly darkens.

Well, Jade, I'm going to share something personal of my own with you. Many years ago, when I was your age, I suffered from PMT and my poor husband used to get spaghetti bolognaise over his head if he was ten minutes late home from work. It was just awful. I tried everything from oil of evening primrose to a carbohydrate-rich diet, eating little and often.

Nothing seemed to work, however, so I went to see a Harley Street specialist. He asked me, 'Would you describe yourself as generally quite neurotic?'

'No,' I replied, rather taken aback. 'Certainly not.'

'The reason I ask,' he went on, 'is because PMT usually affects a certain personality type and, if you *do* tend to be a little neurotic, that would be why you suffer so much at this time of the month. Try to modify the neurotic part of your nature, breathe deeply and calm down.'

'I'm not neurotic, though,' I told him, my voice rising. 'Haven't you got any magic pills?'

'Well, yes, I have,' he said, leaning in his chair, and as cool as you like he continued, 'but they have powerful side-effects. You'll probably get acne and grow a beard.'

'Sod that!' I yelled. Suddenly, a bit of PMT didn't seem so bad, and from that point on, every third week of every month, I would breathe deeply and thank God I had clear skin and no beard.

So, the next time you feel your hormone levels rising, Jade, go to Ugly's and get Carly to give you a calming massage. Oh, and keep breathing deeply. Of course, if you *were* to take the pills and you *did* end up growing a beard and getting spots, you wouldn't have too far to go for treatment...

Chapter 5

GEORGE BEST

Once upon a time, there was a young handsome lad who was born with a gift for playing football. He first found fame on the pitch during the mid-sixties, a time of swinging, dancing in the street and The Beatles. Indeed, this lad from Belfast was later to become known as the fifth Beatle. On the pitch at Old Trafford, he displayed footballing skills that were second to none. Some claimed that he was even as great as the iconic Brazilian player Pélé.

The lad was, of course, George Best, whose name became inextricably linked with Manchester United... and booze.

The pop group The Kinks wrote a number-one hit all about this new celebrity who was hitting the headlines as much for his flamboyant personal life as for his skills on the pitch. 'Dedicated Follower of Fashion' reached number one in the UK Hit Parade and contained the lyrics, 'They seek him here, they seek him there...' – and they did. Everyone did: the press, the girls and the hangers-on. He had it all: fame, money, birds and, of course, booze.

But then, one day, a waiter delivering vintage Champagne to his room asked him a simple question: 'Tell me, Mr Best. Where did it all go wrong?'

At that time, George didn't have a clue what the chap was on about. There he was, cavorting around his plush hotel suite with the current Miss Universe with £20,000 in cash – a small fortune in those days – scattered over the bed.

Yet it seems the waiter was spot on with his observations, as George was already on the slippery slope. By that time, he was twenty-one years old and his football career was already over. He had sacrificed his great talent for a seat on the celebrity merry-go-round. (How strange, then, that twenty-five years later he was to be crowned Greatest British Sportsman of All Time. It's a funny old game!)

When I began writing this book, George was knocking on the door of sixty and there was a continuous stream of disturbing pictures of this erstwhile sporting hero reported in the tabloids. The *News of the World* showed him sporting a fractured jaw. And then, just a week after he had appeared in a front-page story in a Surrey newspaper featuring a shot of him standing outside his local pub, three yobs in their twenties barged into the establishment and beat him up. Whether the attack was unprovoked or not was unclear.

On the very same day, one of the Sunday supplements carried a picture of his ex-wife, Alex, as she attended a film premiere. It seemed that the young woman who found fame by marrying a man old enough to be her father, who waltzed 'eyes wide closed' into a relationship with a notorious drunken womaniser, is now famous herself.

George earned his media medals, winning his celebrity status through talent and hard work. But then he threw it all away.

His great friend Michael Parkinson has concluded that we'll never know just how great the Manchester United footballer could have been, and indeed there are endless 'if only' stories about him – most tellingly, if only he could pass a bar the way he could pass a ball. We often forgive the shortcomings of our sporting heroes, especially when they're as charismatic as George, but even he pushed public generosity to its limit.

Doctors did everything in their power to help George combat his alcoholism; pills, potions, implants – you name it, he had it. Yet it seemed he couldn't help himself. Alcoholics Anonymous wasn't his cup of whisky, and neither was counselling. 'That,' he said, 'is for others. Not me.'

When he was given a life-saving liver transplant, his family and friends felt sure that this would signal the end of his drinking days, but no; on meeting a woman who'd also had a liver transplant after wrecking hers from drinking too much red wine, he leaped back off the wagon, much to the dismay of those around him.

It was at this point that the public seemed to stop caring. It seemed that he deserved no more sympathy. He'd proved himself to be an unworthy recipient of a major organ from which somebody else could have benefited – someone who wouldn't have abused it.

When Alex Best's autobiography *Always Alex* was published, in which George was portrayed as a wife-beater, it was the final straw. To the majority of the British public, violence against women is simply unacceptable behaviour. Indeed, in the criminal fraternity, wife-beaters are considered to be only a little better than child molesters.

Then the media published reports of George getting involved in drunken rows and fights with yet another woman, and even allegations of him abusing a minor sexually. Whether they were true or false, what could have started these terrible rumours?

Just what did the world of celebrity do to Best, the erstwhile street urchin from Belfast? Would he have been a drunk anyway, whatever career he followed? How on earth did a man who had so much going for him mess up so badly? And what about his now famous son, Calum? What was it like for him, growing up with a talented but tormented father? Does he share his father's alcoholic demons?

Followers of football like to think they know their heroes (and villains) well, but how well do they really know them? After all, they can really only see what's projected on to the screen.

In order to understand George Best, it's therefore important that we get to know him better. Only then might we understand why he self-destructed so horrendously. Why did he turn so violently against his second wife? What was going on in his alcohol-fuzzed brain?

Let's go back to the beginning, then, when at the age of fifteen Georgie Best was plucked from obscurity and raised to the highest footballing echelons during his time at Manchester United FC. This young boy with such a wonderful gift for the game threw it all away. But why? Did he have a choice in this, or were his demons always going to beat him? What we do know is that, if being one of the world's greatest footballers during the 1960s was fab, being a hell-raising dedicated follower of fashion was to prove highly dangerous.

I've worked with hundreds of people who have floundered in the depths of despair, in danger of drowning in their own personal addictions, yet I continue to counsel them because each has the ability to change his or her behaviour. And yet being in the company of these troubled people can be incredibly frustrating. Their monumental denial keeps them stuck fast and unable to progress. They are their own worst enemies. In essence, they are vulnerable and their behaviour is akin to that of a needy child. How often do you hear an alcoholic – or, indeed, any other addict – being described as 'pathetic'? To be pathetic is to be pitied – and, yes, George was to be pitied. As he lay ailing in his hospital bed for most of October 2005, one just knew the final whistle was about to blow.

For alcoholics to rid themselves of their addiction, they need to be understood, and this understanding needs to be spoon-fed back to them. The dilemma is that they waste an inordinate amount of energy on trying to keep a safe distance from others when what they crave most is to be close to them. This was the reality behind the sexual part of George's addiction. How can you feel alone when you're locked inside the warmth of another's body, exchanging endearing whispers of love? Simple. You can't.

So let's take a peek into the mind of the legendary George Best. What follows is, I believe, an accurate profile of the boy who never grew up.

BESTIE

'When I was little, I was always in bare feet. We children had shoes; it was just the sharing of them that was the problem. My sisters didn't like my sandals and I didn't like their high heels.' – *George Best*

Being barefoot as a child didn't mean that George was raised in poverty, and neither was he neglected. There's no *Angela's Ashes*-style tale of misery attached to George Best's early years. In fact, the opposite is true: he was loved and nurtured.

Home for George and his family was a house on the Cregagh

council estate in East Belfast. (George said that, if all the people who claimed to have lived in the same road as him had really lived there, it would be 'a hundred bloody miles long'.) A blue plaque has now been erected on the wall outside the house where he grew up, and where his father still lives. George's great friend Waggy reckoned it was put there to help George find his way home when he was drunk. Indeed, laughs have always been plentiful in George's life. No one could ever accuse the boy of not knowing how to enjoy himself. It's just that such enjoyment got out of control far too often.

In George's accounts of his childhood, he described how his family were very supportive of him. In the telling of one such tale, he spoke with soft pride of the time he was playing on some wasteland with his mates, with whom he'd built a bonfire. Along came a local bully and started to pick on George, the smallest of the boys. The bully was easily five inches taller than the young George, but soon enough he has been kicked to the floor. As they tussled on the ground, the bully cut his arm on some broken glass and cried out in pain. He ran off home, blood running out of his sleeve. That evening the boy's father knocked on the Best front door.

'"Your son has maimed my boy !" shouted the man to George's father.

George had told his dad what had happened, and though not a loud or violent one, his face reddened and he thrust it towards the man on the doorstep. "Your son is a bully and everyone knows it. Get away from my door. Now!" He guided George into the line of the man's vision so he could see how much smaller he was than the bully.

George always spoke fondly of his dad, Dicky, and in his book *Scoring at Half-Time* he narrated a number of endearing stories about him, most of them being tales of loyalty and love. In one such tale, George recalled how, on one occasion, he claimed that he felt a sliver of glass go into his foot but, when the blood was cleaned away, they couldn't see anything. Nevertheless, his dad took him to hospital, where a nurse poked around for some time but then concluded that there was no glass in George's foot.

'If my boy says he can feel glass in his foot then there's glass in the foot,' argued Mr Best. But it was no good; he and his son were sent packing.

Then, a couple of weeks or so later, as George was running home from school, he felt a pain in his foot. He examined the area and found a quarter-inch length of glass sticking out of the sole of his foot. When he showed his dad, Dicky promptly marched him back to see the disbelieving nurse.

In his tales of his home life in Belfast as a youngster, George gave the impression that in some way he wished he'd never been discovered and whisked off into the limelight. Indeed, when he and Eric McCordie (another Manchester United discovery from Belfast) first arrived at Old Trafford, the boys missed Ireland so much that, after just twenty-four hours, they fled back home. On George's return, however, his dad took control of the situation and called up Matt Busby. Before George knew it, he was back at the club.

It remained hard for George to settle, and when Christmas rolled around he was terribly homesick. Once again, he took himself back home to be with the family, even though his team needed him for a home match against Burnley the next Saturday. In what would prove to be a characteristic display of wilfulness, George demanded that he'd play only if Busby arranged to fly him to Manchester and then straight back to Belfast after the match. The manager agreed.

This was a defining moment in Bestie's life. Getting his own way was how it was going to be. Why did he keep doing whatever he wanted? Because he could. He realised when he was still a teenager that he'd made the big time, which in turn meant that he could indulge himself in whatever he wanted. If he made demands, they were met. This realisation of every whim sent a dangerous message to an impressionable boy who was already acting out his alcohol–dependency problems.

Meanwhile, George had upped his game. In fact, he was now playing more than one game. He was playing football at the highest level and was about to play the celebrity game, whose motto seems to be 'Play now and pay later'. He once confessed, 'Just as I wanted to outdo everyone when I played, I had to outdo everyone when we were out on the town.'

In his heyday, George had an incredible number of things going for him. He was held in great esteem and was supposedly an important factor in helping the Manchester United team to overcome their terrible memories of the plane crash in Munich in 1958 in which eight of their fellow team members perished. With his awesome dribbling skills, George toyed with defenders and was hailed as a direct heir of these late 'Busby babes'. But herein lay much of George's problem. He was hailed a genius who could do no wrong, but no one is all hero; everyone has at least a little villainy coursing through their veins.

In fact, there was a dangerous mix of ingredients in this cocktail of success. For a start, George was the first of many footballers who would become wealthy stars without a clue of how to deal with their celebrity status. Being the first of his kind was problematic in itself, but, back in George's day, famous footballers were high–profile heroes yet without all the wealth and hype of today's players. They played football, full stop. There were no lessons to be learned yet by witnessing the demise of the likes of Paul Gascoigne or Tony Adams, the latter of whom battled his way back from alcoholism. George was flying blind.

Combined with this, Britain was now in the grip of the swinging sixties. Liberation, free love, sex, drugs and rock 'n' roll were available in abundance, and George wasn't about to miss out on the fun. He'd already learned that he could pull other people's strings; soon he was adapting his technique to pull a string of attractive women.

And then there was the booze. In the early days of his career, it seemed to George to be the most natural thing in the world to get drunk and have a wild time with his fellow players. But in a very long section of his book *Scoring at Half-Time* titled 'The Drink', he related a bittersweet story about one of Scotland's folk heroes, Slim Jim Baxter, who like George was hailed a footballing genius. Unfortunately, by the time George came to tell this story, Baxter had already died after a lifelong battle with alcoholism. ('He was twice as bad as I was,' wrote George. 'He had two liver transplants, for a start.')

According to George, back when many footballers were drinking 'with gay abandon', and long before they were living with the consequences of this, Jim had been playing for Nottingham Forest FC. George remembered Jim waking one morning with terrible back pain. The Scot had been on one of his notorious benders. He was still suffering two days later, so he went to see his GP. (Naturally, he steered clear of the club doctor.) The doctor asked some probing questions about his drinking habits. 'How much would you say you drink a day, on average?' Not about to admit to his daily six or seven pints after training, and far more on a weekend, he lied, 'I suppose about two or three pints a day on average, Doctor.'

'Two or three pints a day!' exclaimed the doctor. "Carry on like that and you'll become an alcoholic.'

George admitted that alcohol was 'the petrol that drove his social life' and that he'd lived a life that many young men could only dream about, sharing his bed with beautiful women and jetsetting around the world, drowning in cash and Champagne. How could he *not* have got caught up in all the sheer headiness of it all? The temptation was simply too much for a man of his character. His competitive personality always compelled him to be leader of the Get Ratted Pack.

At one point in his autobiography, George wrote about society's changing attitudes to drink and drugs. He noted that in the swinging 60s, while drinking and driving was commonplace, figures in the public eye like Mick Jagger and Keith Richards were locked up for smoking cannabis. George observed how times had changed, with Mick receiving a knighthood whilst penalties for drunk driving get ever harsher.'

During this time, George had been simply one of the boys, out clubbing most nights and getting home way after his alarm clock had shrilled into life. Indeed, he never saw himself as being vastly different to his contemporaries, and since those wild days some of his erstwhile drinking partners such as Rodney Marsh have admitted to having had a serious problem at that time. But, lamented George, 'The belief among the public was that it was just me.'

Whereas most of his friends would realise their limit and go home to sleep it off, George would carry on. He would simply take himself off to one of the more obscure drinking dens that catered for what George referred to as 'gentlemen of the night'. These places catered for croupiers, musicians and others who were unable to wind down until the early hours of the morning.

According to George, his drinking crept up on him. This might well be true. All addictions start in this insidious way. One day it's great fun and the next you're lost in oblivion. One minute it's a laugh and the next it's misery. There seems to be no in-between time. If there *are* any warning signs, they're usually denied by the addict.

George also admitted to being shy, and this doesn't surprise me one bit, as drink is a great friend to the shy and reserved – at least, for a while. Add to this the embarrassment he used to feel about his 'unintelligible Irish brogue' and it becomes clear that George was destined to suffer from a dependent disease.

We now have a list of attributes as long as George's drinking arm to help us to understand why he became an alcoholic. And yet what a great time he had along the way! Back in his early carefree days with Man United, when he simply enjoyed himself out on the town, he had a great circle of friends, comprising not just other footballers; being the UK's first football celebrity, he rubbed shoulders with famous names in television, comedy and music. What they had in common was a love of having a good time, and George, being young and charismatic, was incredibly popular, and not just with women; men, too, liked his company. In his own words, he was one of 'the Manchester Rat (as in, arsed) Pack'. He didn't credit himself as being the leader, however, but he was the most famous of his circle, and the fact that his face could open doors (including bedroom doors) for his mates must have given him a powerful role in the gang.

George's stories in *Scoring at Half-Time* reveal so much about his fun-loving personality and give the whole picture of the man. I now understand why he was able to pull the birds – and not just any old birds. He didn't simply win the love of the prettiest girl in the village; he won the affections of many a Miss

World and even a Miss Universe. George was the kind of gorgeously shy guy that girls go for. On the surface, he was a famous, talented and wealthy footballer, but underneath he harboured a vulnerability that drew the girls to his side and a sexy edge that enticed them into his bed. There was a dangerous aspect to his personality that was a magnet to risk-taking girls, so in the risk-taking sixties he was destined to have a ball. With his Beatle haircut, his good looks and his bulging wallet, all George needed to finish off the image was a new wardrobe.

Enter George's best mate, Malcolm Mooney, a smart guy who George met at a party. The pair clicked instantly and it wasn't long before they were in the fashion business together. At this time, the chain stores were starting to encounter competition from smaller boutiques that were popping up all over the place. And it was at this time that the dress-obsessed Mods were born. Discos displaced dance halls and free love was available for the taking. The pill liberated women, and in turn the men found themselves in a sweetshop full of tasty goodies. At the centre of this were The Beatles, The Rolling Stones… and George Best, who at that time was just as prominent a figure as the two globe-dominating bands, his name splashed all over the tabloids and his face adorning the front covers of magazines. 'Bill Wyman, formerly of The Rolling Stones, said recently that in those days he and the boys would pick up the teen mags to see how well they had been featured only to get a bit vexed to keep seeing my teeth smiling at them from the front pages,' George reported in *Scoring at Half-Time*. Thirty years before David Beckham, George was the first player to attract a female fan base. Previously, the very thought of girls screaming at a footballer as if he were a member of the Beatles was ridiculous.

When Malcolm Mooney opened a boutique just off

Deansgate in Manchester, George and fellow footballer Mike Summerbee invested £1,000 each, while Malcolm got the exclusive rights to sell a chic line in footwear from Ravel. In his autobiography, George wrote colourfully of this time and painted a picture of flamboyant clothing, trendy haircuts and, of course, dazzling women. One gets the impression that he used to hang out rather a lot at Edwardia with Malcolm and the rest of the gang.

George didn't always pull the girls single-handedly, though. He had a group of friends who would help him in his conquests, and together they would turn each approach into a military-style operation. If a bus went by with a young girl on board, George would send a young boutique employee named Gary to fetch her back. Gary would sprint off, catch the bus up, leap on board, and the next minute George was wooing her.

On one occasion, a beautiful lady caught George's roaming eye while he was in Alvaro's restaurant in London with Malcolm. When their eyes locked, George wrote, his stomach somersaulted, and when she suddenly disappeared George sent one of the waiters to fetch her back. The girl turned out to be an American named Suzanne Valier, and as she lived in Switzerland she didn't have a clue who George Best was, so his celebrity status meant nothing. They exchanged telephone numbers and she went back to her very different world. George promptly charged Malcolm with the task of going over to Switzerland to find her and bring her back, with nothing but a name and a number to go on.

This is just one example of how those around him would do anything for George. No one ever said no to him. Instead, his every whim was indulged, and those around him did nothing to make him doubt his belief that he could do just as he liked, and have anything he wanted. When he got bored, he'd pester Malcolm until he shut up shop so they could head off to the pub, which was now his second home. He felt that he was above all others, and this belief was the primary factor that led to his downfall.

One of the downsides of being a celebrity was that people always wanted to fight George. According to him, he encountered this attitude more often in London than in Manchester, but he was usually able to escape unscathed, and more often than not he talked his way out of trouble. There were times, however, when he was belligerent with drink and would just go for it, and there were others when he didn't even see it coming. But then, there was a lot that he didn't see coming.

GROUPIES

Just like pop stars and famous actors, footballers from the sixties right up until the present day have attracted groupies. When pop and rock groups perform live, these girls wait in the wings, ready to satisfy the stars' every sexual desire, and George reported that it was the same for footballers at a match: 'What tended to happen was that a girl would target a player and then slowly but surely would work her way through the entire squad. Or, at least, those who were interested. It wasn't quite a one-night stand each time, but it didn't seem to take too many weeks for these girls to have been passed around.'

While this might sound like great fun, there was a downside. On one occasion, when Manchester United were playing in Southampton, the receptionist at the hotel at which the team were staying handed George a message, which he was shocked to realise was a death threat. He had to take the threat seriously, too, as the note referred to a girl he'd met the previous season.

The message had been written by the girl's enraged brother, who threatened to shoot George for ruining his sister's life.

George admitted that he had taken the girl out and later slept with her before heading back north. As far as he'd been concerned, that was that, but then she kept contacting him and became quite hysterical when she realised that he didn't feel the same way about her that she felt about him. And now George's casual sexual dalliance had come back to haunt him.

George wasn't killed, of course, but he'd been concerned enough to go to Matt Busby and ask his advice. Busby reportedly told him to go on to the pitch and just keep running and running. On seeing George's puzzled expression, the manager continued, 'Because, George, a moving target is much harder to hit.'

This wasn't the only death threat George received. His second was from an Irish political group. News of the threat was leaked to the papers, but George did his best to put the threats out of his mind as he ran on to the pitch at Old Trafford. At one match, as the players were warming up before kick-off, George wandered over the halfway line to have a chat with his old friend Mike Summerbee, but Summerbee acted terrified and backed off as George approached.

'Hello, Mike,' said George.

'Fuck off, Bestie. Keep away from me. He might have a machine gun.'

As celebrity curses go, this is a pretty extreme example, and yet it's one that recurs for footballers and, indeed, their partners today. David and Victoria Beckham have received both death *and* kidnap threats, and these have been taken very seriously indeed. Then there are the endless kiss-and-tell revelations about the dalliances of professional footballers off the pitch. Again, David Beckham has been at the mercy of such gossip, being accused in the press of infidelities, the Rebecca Loos story being the most damaging.

George was only too aware that the time footballers reach their peak coincides with when they are most interested in the opposite sex. It should surprise anyone that young athletic men in their prime with money, fast cars and fame so often prove an irresistible target for women. For the single men, the opportunities were (and still are) enormous; for the married ones, the temptation is worrying, but ever-present. He would frequently express surprise that over the years so few scandals were made public.

Some scandals, however, have come to public attention, and rape charges are rife now among footballers and groupies. Nowadays, however, the girls aren't necessarily referred to as 'groupies'; instead, they are often portrayed as innocent young girls who have been attacked and violated by athletic men who can't keep it in their pants. I have a strong hunch that some of the girls who end up in bed with these attractive and talented men are out for a good time before running to the press to wring as much money out of their conquests as they can.

The most recent high-profile footballer to be accused of rape is another Manchester United superstar, Cristiano Ronaldo, who with his cousin was alleged to have raped two French Afro-Caribbean women in a plush hotel in October 2005. Ronaldo was so incensed that he gave his side of the story in a world exclusive to the *News of the World*.

The story seemed to be almost identical to those of other sportsmen who have found themselves charged with sexual assault. Allegedly, the girls were dressed to the nines and already drinking before Ronaldo even arrived. According to him, they moved in on the boys and followed them to the bedroom, where they all had sex – consensual sex, according to Ronaldo – before going off clubbing until the early hours of the morning. Indeed, they were spotted drinking and laughing together in London's VIP Lounge and, when the boys eventually left, the girls followed in a separate car. When they were refused access to the boys' room at their hotel, however, the girls took a cab with a French paparazzo who had been hanging around, waiting to snap a celebrity. On the way back to Park Lane, the girls told him that they'd been raped and were going to go to the police – but they didn't. Instead, they waited thirty hours and then went to a hospital. Eventually, the police were informed and Ronaldo was arrested. The newspapers then posed the question, 'What will happen to Ronaldo's career?' As for the girls, they remained anonymous. The police made it clear that no charges would be brought against Ronaldo or his cousin.

By all accounts, the girls who had one-night stands with Georgie Best knew what they were doing and loved it. So did George. There was consent on both sides, and neither exploited the other. Everyone, it seemed, was a winner.

THE FAME GAME

George Best retired from football far too soon. The magical talent witnessed by millions was no longer – the boy who was described as having wings on his feet hung up his boots. From this point on, he was famous for his lifestyle only. His every move was reported in the papers and magazines, and it seemed as though he was going to live out the rest of his life in the centre of a media circus. And his company was in demand, from Prime Minister Harold Wilson to everyday blokes down the pub.

Many of George's friends, however, inhabited the world of

showbiz and music. Indeed, at that time London was overflowing with fabulous music from fantastic personalities. Heart-throbs like Cliff Richard, Adam Faith and Marty Wilde were in abundance, sending all the young girls wild.

George was great friends with pop star Kenny Lynch, who he described as being a hard worker who also liked to play hard, a man who loved life and laughing. George loved to hang out with Kenny, who appeared regularly on television, but of the two it was George's autograph that was sought after more often. 'People almost shoved [Kenny] out of the way to ask for my autograph or to share some words of wisdom with me,' George later recalled.

This was quite extraordinary, given Kenny's string of achievements. London was, after all, Kenny's manor. He had written 'Sha La La La Lee' for The Small Faces and had enjoyed chart success of his own with 'Mountain of Love'. He was friends with other big names such as Bruce Forsyth and Jimmy Tarbuck. On one occasion, when he accompanied George on a trip to Northern Ireland where his friend was playing in an International, the kids went crazy. One kid was heard to shout, 'Hey, come over here! It's George Best – and he's with Cassius Clay!' How tragic it was that some years later, instead of fans fighting for his company, he was hunted down by angry yobs who viewed him as nothing better than a wife-beater or child molester. Just when did George's fame turn slightly against him?

Those who knew George Best well remained loyal – loving him unconditionally. Even after his liver transplant, as he lay in his hospital bed recovering, a *Daily Mail* survey showed that George had been voted the fifteenth in a poll to discover 'Who are the Coolest Brits?' (David Beckham was number one.) This couldn't be a sympathy vote, said George, because the votes had been counted before his hospitalisation.

Why, then, were people still considering him cool? He hadn't played football for approximately thirty years. Only his love of women and booze had kept him in the papers. Could it be that people lapped up the endless stories of the ups and downs of a fallen legend, enjoying a kind of removed *Schadenfreude*? Was it his charisma? Did the public believe that they really knew him personally because he'd been around for so long? Whatever the reason, remaining in the glare of the media lights for over forty years was quite astonishing, especially for one who'd retired from professional football decades earlier.

Concerning the *Daily Mail*'s poll, George opined, 'I must have got the nostalgia vote. I'm a survivor of the '60s, and the 1960s remain the decade that provokes the most affection and nostalgia amongst the population. Deservedly or not, I have become a personification of that era. So I think that, combined with the British custom of fêting and honouring the recently dead, that's why I got the vote. I know I'm not recently dead, but I guess many of those people polled thought I might be by the time the votes were in.'

This quote revealed an awful lot about the man George Best had become. He knew that he'd messed up in many areas of his life, but he also knew that he'd been a bright light in the lives of millions of people over many decades.

Nevertheless, when he did mess up, he did so in a spectacular fashion. To have been a friend or a girlfriend of his during the good times was one thing, but to be his wife or son was quite something else. His first wife, Angie, mother of their son Calum, was relieved to George out of her life. 'I couldn't look after two babies,' she said, 'so the older one had to go.'

CALUM BEST

George's son Calum is a celebrity in his own right. A good-looking lad with some successful modelling under his belt (although he seems to have something else under his belt too that the ladies quite like), he appeared on prime-time television when he took part in the UK reality-TV show *Celebrity Love Island*.

In the interviews Calum has given, he reveals that, in spite of being raised by a loving mother, hundreds of miles away from the daily influence of his drunken father, he has suffered badly. Visits to stay with his father in London were fraught and, by Calum's account, George had been something of a selfish dad. This is not unusual for an alcoholic father, not to mention a celebrity, suffering from all the pressures that that entails.

Calum is not only a child of an ambitious mother (who is, in fact, Cher's personal fitness trainer) and an alcoholic footballing legend; he is also an only child of divorced parents. Add to this the fact that Calum is now living in the limelight himself and comparisons to his father will naturally and constantly arise (he loves women, like his father, and women love him), which in turn will put him under great stress. As he listens to constant comparisons between himself and his father, he must be asking himself, 'Have I inherited Dad's womanising and alcoholism genes?'

So, is Calum doomed? Is it going to be a case of like father, like son? Will the genes kick in? Or can he forge a male identity of his very own? Of course, it's here that the nature-versus-nurture debate becomes relevant: did Angie Best manage to keep enough distance between her son and her wayward ex-husband (both by getting the hell out of the marriage and also by remaining in Los Angeles) to ensure that Calum couldn't emulate George's bad behaviour? Calum doubtless suffered a great deal of emotional pain on witnessing his father's immature and selfish behaviour, but he must also have felt the agony of being torn between his parents, a situation that brings about feelings of guilt in a child and a loss of innocence.

As I mentioned earlier, Calum Best, like his mother, is now a celebrity. But what about his desire for autonomy? Can he ever shake off the label of 'Calum Best, son of George' and just be known as himself, a totally separate man with an identity of his own?

I don't know if Angie ever spoke to Calum about her life with his father. Many ex-partners of alcoholic husbands or wives believe that it's wrong to speak negatively of the absent party, but even so it's very, very difficult not to have some angry moments, times when all good intentions fly out of the window. On these occasions, the lid comes off and a tirade of emotion spews forth. For the hurt and pain to have no expression is almost impossible. Those who lose their emotional voice become depressed, whereas others who sporadically burst forth with withering accusations, thus releasing strong emotions, experience some momentary relief. However, if there's a child involved, this can be particularly damaging to him or her, especially if he or she then feels compelled to nurture the wounded parent.

In an interview with *Loaded* magazine, Calum said that he loved his father to death, but in the same year, in his column in *The Mail on Sunday*'s *Night and Day* magazine, his father chose to tell the public at large stories of Calum using George's credit card without his consent and running up a massive hotel bill in London, portraying himself as the wounded father. OK, this should have remained a private matter between father and son, but what could Calum have been thinking?

This is what Calum allegedly told *Loaded*: 'My dad gives me no money whatsoever. Not a cent. I pay for all my shit myself. I make my own money, whether people want to believe it or not. I don't give a shit.' He also noted that he spent his whole life acting like the father-figure in his relationship with George, only to be portrayed as a reckless, spoiled brat. However, there might be some bravado to this claim. If Calum *had* spent his father's money without permission, although there is no reason to doubt Calum's word that he didn't, he would have been in all likelihood acting in response to his anger about the way he felt he'd been treated by his immature dad.

While he was living in America, Calum played some football, and says he even won a few trophies, but today he's removed himself from any association with his father's sport and is working on a career of his own. He says that he'd like to get into acting, and that he'd like to earn enough money to enable him to look after his mum. This diligent, generous approach is – perhaps unsurprisingly – astonishingly different to George's rather self-centred behaviour.

So where can Calum Best find the positive male role model that he so desperately needs? Who is going to be his mentor? Sadly, although he sometimes wears a gold chain around his neck with a pendant bearing the word 'legend', he admits that he has no heroes.

ALEX BEST

George met his second wife, twenty-two-year-old Surrey girl Alex, at London's Tramp club in 1994. At the time, she was employed as an air hostess for Virgin Air. The couple married the following year at Chelsea Registry Office.

Judging from her autobiography, *Always Alex*, she walked into the marriage with her eyes wide shut and barely survived the ordeal. Indeed, by the time I finished reading it, I felt almost as battered as she allegedly was throughout her nine years with George. It's very difficult to reconcile the image of George that Alex portrays with the man who wrote about his life with such humour in *Scoring at Half-Time*, but this is a prime example of the dual nature of the alcoholic. It's like living with a man with two heads: one head you adore and the other you learn to fear.

When Alex met George, he was in his fifties and his star was fading fast. Nevertheless, meeting and, indeed, connecting with such an icon was too tempting for an ambitious girl like Alex to pass up. She chose to ignore the many warning signs that flashed in front of her pretty blue eyes, and she knew, long before she took her vows, that her relationship with George wasn't going to be all milk and honey. More like wine and gambling, in fact.

Take their first date, for instance. George took Alex out for a jacket potato and then proposed to her in his local pub, the Phene, which Alex reported as being smelly and 'all wrong'. Nevertheless, in Alex's account the establishment had suddenly taken on a magical glow, so the newly betrothed couple had a quick knee-trembler in the toilets.

Why didn't Alex walk? Did she perhaps hope that she might end up being a celebrity herself? Well, if so, she must be happy, having had her autobiography published and appearing on reality-TV show *I'm A Celebrity, Get Me Out Of Here!* Even so, she's paid the price; her tales of rows and drunken brawls and her descriptions of George's dreadful paranoia indicate a domestic environment that must have driven her to distraction.

While the couple's first experience of dining out was a jacket spud down a dingy pub, their engagement wasn't much better. He took her out for a pizza.

On the night before the big day, Alex hid George's house keys to stop him from wandering off and getting lashed in Tramp with the club's owner, Johnnie Gold. 'Now he couldn't escape!' she exclaimed triumphantly in her life story.

On the day of the wedding, the assembled congregation retired to the Phene for canapés and Champagne.

The couple's honeymoon, too, was a non-starter, with George telling Alex that he couldn't go because he had too many work commitments. Alex promptly went off to Portugal with a friend and George went on a bender.

It wasn't long after the wedding that Alex began to see the downside of being married to an alcoholic. Over the next nine years, her plea of 'Promise to calm down on your drinking' would become a mantra, while George's habit remained unchecked (he apparently once drank wine out of a fishbowl), although she protests that she didn't for one second think that George's drinking would define and ultimately destroy their marriage. Was her capacity for denial as strong as George's?

Of course, Alex isn't alone in turning a blind eye to the reality of life. It's that old chestnut, denial, again. 'Forgive me,' begs the abuser in floods of tears. 'I'll never do it again.' And, while the victim will never forget what the abuser has done, he or she will forgive. With alcoholic abusers, however, sometimes there can be no remorse when the drunk can't even remember the incident. During her marriage, Alex says she was on the receiving end of vicious beatings that George would later claim not to remember, a lapse of memory that of course enabled him to remain guilt-free.

It's this co-dependent behaviour that keeps a dysfunctional relationship afloat for so long. It can often take a very, very long time to wake up and smell the brandy, and this is especially true of Alex. During her marriage to George, she suffered a catalogue of injuries but continued to ignore the wake-up calls.

One morning, she woke and felt something crawling over her face. It was her lovely blonde hair, which George had apparently hacked off before scribbling all over her body with a marker pen. When she noticed George drunk and incoherent on the sofa and a pair of scissors on the bedside table, she couldn't help but think of an even more frightening scenario. What if he'd stabbed her in a drunken rage?

The dynamics between her and George were explosive, to say the least. On her twenty-fifth birthday, she wrote in *Always Alex*, he punched her in the face and blacked her eye. Her worried mother insisted that she inform the police and the press had a field day.

After another brawl with George, Alex fell awkwardly and broke her arm. It was reported that she said he hadn't meant to break her arm, but it was very upseting all the same. Nonetheless, Alex still loved George and secretly hoped for a baby with him. In the meantime, she bought herself a BMW.

By this time, George was very sick indeed, and one day he collapsed in the street. Alex was suddenly faced with the prospect of her husband dying unless he found help immediately. By this point he was sick every morning, even on the days he didn't drink. She found it tortuous, she wrote in *Always Alex*.

George got help, but it was yet another temporary measure, and soon he was drinking again. By the beginning of the new millennium, according to Alex, his brutality had escalated. There were more beatings and she suffered a suspected broken jaw. She nearly left him after this attack, but he was too ill.

Indeed, George was desperately ill. His liver was failing and the press were circling like vultures. He was hospitalised, subjected to eight weeks of treatment that saw him pumped full of drugs, and was then sent home. He was, said the doctors, dry.

Alex was ecstatic, and to celebrate she and George flew off to the Costa del Sol – a questionable choice of destination perhaps for a sick alcoholic.

Finally, after the couple first moved to Ireland and then returned to the UK, it became apparent that George was in need of a liver transplant. A liver was found and George duly went under the knife.

But, of course, it wasn't over, and incredibly George began to drink again. While the couple talked at this time about possibly having children, George just wouldn't quit the booze. At one time, his medical team advised him to sign himself into the Priory to get some extensive counselling, but George flatly refused, having decided long ago that such a course of treatment wouldn't work for him.

Meanwhile, life for Alex was like a tornado. One day she was being punched in the face, the next being whisked away to Venice on the Orient Express, a magical time she confessed in her autobiography.

It was the infidelities that finally convinced Alex that their marriage was doomed. George would fall into the arms, it seemed, of just about any woman who would give him a bed for the night, and Alex was finally exhausted by the dreadful series of events that she called her marriage. She lamented the lack of trust. There was, it seemed, no conquering George's demons. They were too deeply entrenched. It was time for Alex to move on.

Now, like Calum, Alex is a celebrity in her own right, while George sadly passed away in November 2005, a victim of his own addictive weakness.

GEORGE ON THE COUCH

It's a really depressing story. Who came second best to George Best? He did. And, ultimately, it was because of this streak of selfishness that the street urchin with a gift to die for effectively killed himself. Indeed, he was dead in a number of respects before finally shuffling off this mortal coil, having suffered multiple organ failure, in 2005. He was like an old man suffering from Alzheimer's, his relatives mourning him way before his body finally gave up the ghost.

Indeed, his family loved him unconditionally, and those whose lives he touched — people like Waggy, Malcolm Mooney, Mike Summerbee, Kenny Lynch and Michael Parkinson — would describe the George they knew well with a mixture of pride for having known him in his prime and frustration for his self-destructive behaviour. And the women he bedded must have a wealth of stories about the man who was either a sex god or a rotter, depending on how the night went.

George's first wife, Angie, has already voiced her distress about the man, as has his second, Alex, while Calum seems to be quietly getting on with his life. Whatever impact having a father like George Best has had on him, he's still young enough to work on being different.

Unlike two other celebrities studied in this book, namely Robbie Williams and George Michael, Bestie always refused to work with a therapist, which is unfortunate, as a course of therapy could have made all the difference in his life.

In fact, George's and my paths almost crossed on a number of occasions. The first of these occurred in the mid-nineties, when I was working as a therapist at the Charter Chelsea Hospital in London, just off the King's Road, where I would often see George walking with a newspaper under his arm. Of course, I knew about his ongoing problem with alcohol, but I managed to stop myself from approaching him to ask him if he'd consider therapy, as this would have been highly unprofessional and unethical. Nevertheless, I was sorely tempted to go up to him and say, 'For goodness' sake, George. Get a grip!' Hardly professional behaviour, true, but there are always exceptions to the rule.

Then, just a few months before his death, I was in Kingston at the same time that he was beaten up by a gang of men. I itched to visit him to implore him to get some counselling, but again I chose not to. You can lead a horse to water, after all, but you can't make it drink – or, indeed, stop it drinking.

So what about the bigger picture of George's life? Did his downfall begin at the age of fifteen, when he learned that he was rich and famous and could do whatever he wanted, or were the seeds sown further back in his childhood?

THE ADDICTIVE PERSONALITY

I've always found it fairly easy to work with people with addictive personalities. Generally speaking, they are warm, funny, creative people who are too sensitive for their own good – and George's personality was typical of an addict. I've always been able to look behind the way they behave and connect with the vulnerability that lurks behind.

Other therapists steer clear of addicts, finding them too frustrating to work with. They run out of patience and the intuitive clients pick up on this and walk. On one occasion, I had a heated debate with an experienced psychiatric nurse after suggesting that we should offer a certain patient hope and understanding. 'We can't offer these people hope,' she said to me. 'There is no hope for them.' No wonder her patients remained stuck. Even in the most dire circumstances, there is always hope.

Unfortunately, for George, the luxury of hope no longer existed. For him, reaching out for therapeutic help took reserves of courage he didn't possess, and so he turned it down in exchange for hollow-eyed nights of booze and meaningless sex. Confronting and solving our problems is a painful process, as people like George Michael will confirm, but, if we avoid this pain, we get mentally and spiritually stuck.

Even though his mother Ann died from alcoholism, Bestie's childhood was no tale of woe. He wasn't neglected, and he wasn't abused. His parents didn't abandon him, and there was enough money to buy groceries. He was free to run around barefoot with his mates until the time came when he was discovered and publicly declared a 'footballing genius'.

On his arrival at Old Trafford, however, George was dreadfully homesick. Perhaps the land across the water felt like a big, bad world in which he couldn't cope without the security provided by his loving, extended family. He was, after all, one of six children, and the Best household must have been a very lively environment. At his digs in Manchester, however caring his landlady might have been, he must have felt lonely.

George was a shy boy and found life away from home difficult, but it's how we deal with the problems thrown at us that makes the difference between happiness or misery. Building up our coping mechanisms is all-important. But George learned how to cope in a different and insidiously dangerous way: by drinking. Why did he need to go through all that heartache to feel good? The booze worked perfectly well. But, in seeking solace in alcohol, George was simply feeding his dependent personality, and soon he became so pickled and so entrenched in his addiction that escape proved ultimately impossible.

George Best, it seemed, never grew up. His growth became stunted in his youth, when he was offered the world on a gold plate and believed he was a cut above the rest. Unfortunately, some of those who loved him just let him get on with pursuing his dissolute lifestyle. It was, after all, normal behaviour for the time and, besides, they were *all* drinking and having a bloody good time. Unfortunately, the fact that his friends knew when to stop while George carried on partying into the night failed to ring any alarm bells.

Of course, maybe the bells did ring but George chose not to hear them. After all, why bother listening to a new tune when the one that's playing sounds wonderful? He had his friends to stop him feeling lonely, the bottle to find oblivion and confidence, and a bevy of adoring women who were only too willing to stroke his ego and make him feel alive with sexual stimulation. What possible payback could be worth giving all of that up?

This was the root of George's problem. In order to want to change, a person needs to be motivated. There must be something in it for them. But, as far as George was concerned, he already had it all.

By the time George's life started to fall apart at the seams – the divorces, the volatile relationships, the liver failure – his personality was too weak to extricate itself from the alcohol. He simply didn't have any resources left to draw on. It was at this time that his need for professional counselling grew most desperate. When someone reaches crisis point, they need the intervention of others. It's imperative that they surrender themselves into the hands of trained professionals whom they can trust, people who can contain their demons and help to discipline them, people who know all about issues such as boundaries.

George had no boundaries. He had no sense of ever having had enough, always wanting more and therefore cursed never to feel really satisfied. This was the main reason behind his perpetual search for more women, more booze, more love. His appetite was insatiable and legendary. Had he been taught the necessity for discipline, he might have been saved. It's one of the basic tools necessary for solving life's problems. Absence of discipline leads to chaos, which leads to even more chaos. When people feel chaotic, they tend to seek ways of escaping, and hey presto! They become addicted, usually to something harmful.

George linked his problems to the swinging sixties, when discipline was a rude word, and indeed this decade set a precedent. Now we live in a time where addictions have reached epidemic levels. In fact, today most people seem to be addicted to something or other. But, by seeking solace in these addictions, and by avoiding problems and resisting the pain and suffering that working through them brings, we're setting ourselves up to be mentally ill. This might come as a shock, but to some degree we are all mentally ill.

When my clients ask me, 'Do you think I'm mad?', I always throw their question back at them – do *they* think they're mad? – before telling them my belief that everyone's a bit mad, and that that's OK. This usually comes as a great relief, and it *is* very liberating to be able to say, 'Hey, I might not be perfect, and I might even be a little bonkers, but I'm an OK person – I'm not wicked.'

George's avoidance of difficult feelings and emotions led to him being buried alive under layer upon layer of neuroses. There are so many 'if only's attached to his life, but the most poignant must be if only he'd reached out for help back when he had a chance. But he didn't. Instead, he became chronically ill, both physically and mentally.

While it might be too late for George, here's a list of the tools that an alcoholic would find useful to have in his or her therapeutic toolbox:

1. **Take responsibility.** It's not everyone else's fault. You have a big part to play in what goes wrong in your life.
2. **Delay gratification.** Just hang on in there and trust that you can wait a little longer for what you believe you need right now.
3. **Find a little balance in your life.** This means finding both inner and outer peace. You might be the centre of you own universe, but you're only a part of the bigger picture of life.
4. **Be truthful and honest** with yourselves and others.

George Best neither loved nor respected himself, and it was this low self-esteem that eventually dragged him into the gutter.

Many people think of George Best as having a huge ego and loving only himself, but this is simply not the case. He actually sold his European Player of the Year medal for £150,000 – hardly the action of someone caught up in his own legend.

THE WHISTLE AND LONE PIPER BLOWS

Thursday, 27 October 2005 was the hottest October day on record. It was also a day on which news headlines and bulletins all over the world contained news of George Best.

It was reported that, after three weeks in the Intensive Care

Unit at London's Cromwell Hospital, George's health had taken a turn for the worse. He'd been admitted there three weeks earlier after complaining of flu-like symptoms, which turned into a chest infection. Then a kidney infection complicated matters. Then there was internal bleeding. Soon Calum was by his bedside, as was Alex, while his father and sisters flew over from Ireland to join the vigil.

In a statement to the public, Professor Roger Williams revealed that George was fighting for his life, while his agent, Phil Hughes, pointed out that the complications from which George was suffering were due to the medication he needed to take. Several Manchester United fans spoke fondly of him, although the comments were interspersed with regrets about his alcoholism.

George had always said that, when his time came, he wanted to be remembered for his football talent, predicting, 'They'll forget all the rubbish that's gone on and remember the football.' He was right.

'We won't forget our Belfast boy, your star will shine now in the sky, farewell, our friend, but not goodbye.'

The media went into a frenzy. A ghoulish grief gripped the nation. We had had the 'People's Princess', the 'People's Pope', and now we had the 'People's Legendary – Simply the best footballer'.

The *Sun* screamed, 'The biggest funeral since Di', and, for sure, his funeral was a *Who's Who* of football. Yes, indeed, the charming guy who was a footballing icon/genius/legend was the one to be remembered, while the weak man who lingered too long on his excesses, and caused much emotional pain to those who loved him dearly, was brushed under the carpet. Ah! Celebrity.

That said – the funeral was a deeply emotional affair. There was an outpouring of love and pride for both Bestie and Belfast. To the people of Northern Ireland, their boy had come home – to be laid to rest alongside his mum, Ann.

The rain was torrential as the cortege began its forty-minute journey along the long and winding road from old Dicky Best's home in Burren Way (where the coffin had rested overnight), along the narrow street where George had played barefoot, dribbling the ball so brilliantly. The crowds cheered and clapped. The red and white Manchester United scarves and the green of Northern Ireland were thrown at the funeral car – as were the flowers. Definitely reminiscent of Diana's funeral.

George Best was honoured with a state funeral – the first ever to be held at the great Parliamentary Hall of Stormont. It was unprecedented. The flags flew at half mast and, after a minute's silence, the piper played a lament. Then the coffin was inched painfully up the sixty steps by professional pallbearers. It was a wobbly affair, and how these strong men managed to keep their footing was nothing short of a miracle. It would have appealed to Bestie's naughty sense of humour.

For me, the most moving part of the day was witnessing Calum's grief. At one poignant moment, the twenty-four-year-old's blue eyes raised to the heavens in grief, before he placed a supportive arm around his mother, Angie. Angie, who had flown over from LA to support her son, was now being comforted by him.

Angie may have divorced George many years before, and understandably, couldn't be expected to have many positive words to say about him since, but she was, nevertheless, genuinely bereaved. After all, they had been young and in love, and just because she had brought their marriage to an end because of his bad behaviour didn't mean she didn't hold the memories of those first precious years close to her heart. They loved, they had a child together, and they parted because of one thing – her husband's boozing and partying too hard in the limelight.

Tragic… Celebrity Curse.

Chapter 6

JUDE LAW

What a cad! What a spoiled little boy! These and similar accusations have dogged the life of handsome charmer Jude Law. But is there any truth to them? Maybe it's Jude who is the victim, perpetually cursed to choose girls who are emotionally unavailable to him.

Jude Law is doubtless an accomplished actor. Still in his early thirties, he has an impressive string of theatre productions and movies to his credit. He has chosen his parts, and this has partly led to his great success in conquering America. Two roles that he played particularly well were the eponymous anti-hero in the remake of the classic sixties film *Alfie*, and 'Bosie' in *Wilde*, a film in which he acted alongside Stephen Fry. Both womaniser Alfie and spoiled Bosie displayed unsavoury character traits that bore some vague resemblance to Jude's.

Possibly insecure, it seems that Jude sometimes gives the impression of needing his women to adore him and put him first, and therefore trouble sets in when the beautiful but strongly opinionated women to whom he is attracted refuse to play it his way. Instead, they pull him into their web. Then he throws a tantrum and, in order to assert his masculinity, he will turn to a young girl who is only too delighted to sleep with an A-class celebrity – especially if it sometimes means that she gets a fat cheque from a tabloid newspaper for selling her story, too.

I've chosen to include Jude in this study of celebrities for two reasons: because of his apparent need of women's adoration (his connection to beautiful and successful women seems to define much of who he is as a man) and because there seems to be a certain kind of woman who find him adorable – for a while, at least; then it all goes horribly wrong.

In other chapters, I've spoken of boundaries and discipline. Jude, some may say, could do with focussing more on such perimeters. And for that matter, so could some of his women. In 2005, the tabloid press was alive with tales of Jude's wife-swapping and three-in-a-bed parties that allegedly took place in the well-heeled London district of Primrose Hill, a location that has since become a notorious area for drink- and drug-fuelled excess. Two of the women named in these tales and with whom Jude's life has now been publicly entwined are glamorous heiress and actress Davinia Taylor and musician Pearl Lowe, whose names have also been linked to Kate Moss.

Later, stories appeared in the press in which it was alleged that Jude had slept with nanny Daisy Wright. These stories were splashed all over the front pages of the Sunday papers and devastated his fiancée, actress Sienna Miller. When this revelation came to light, Jude's ex-wife, Sadie Frost, was quoted as saying, 'It's not my nightmare any more,' before then offering to play agony aunt to Sienna!

Did sexy Sadie ever really get over Jude, though? She was by all accounts devastated when they split up and never seemed to regain her balance afterwards. Instead, she threw herself into more wild parties and, as top disciple in the Moss Posse, those times were wild indeed (see Chapter 2, 'Kate Moss'). She dated toy-boys and wore see-through clothes (at the age of forty!) before announcing to the world that she wanted to leave London and move to the country to lead a quieter life.

Maybe Jude should go with her. It's for sure that life is not working out for him without her. He blamed Sienna's workload and partying for his straying, and indeed just days later the *Daily Mail* reported Sienna's misery, publishing photographs that showed cuts on her arm that looked alarmingly like they'd been self-inflicted, despite her publicist's assertion to the contrary. However, Sienna picked herself up and reportedly met up with Jude's friend Daniel Craig, the new big-screen James Bond, before fleeing the country to live with her father in New York.

So Jude's women have played an important part in his life since he became a celebrity. But, rather than focus exclusively on his love life, first let's take a look at his life and career.

HEY, JUDE

Jude Law grew up in Blackheath, southeast London, the youngest child of Peter and Maggie Law and younger brother of Natasha, a photographer, and his first name was, indeed, inspired by The Beatles song 'Hey, Jude'. Both Peter and Maggie are teachers, his father having been described as a 'school teacher with a pony tail' while his mother teaches English to refugee kids. When Jude was growing up, they were both heavily into amateur dramatics, which must have been a major factor in Jude's entrance into the world of drama. Nowadays, Peter and Maggie live in France, where they run their own theatre company.

Jude did not fare well in comprehensive school, where the bullying and violent behaviour of his fellow pupils were too much for him to bear, so his parents moved him to a private school in Dulwich, where he was apparently much happier. In this cloistered environment, he was no doubt able to sidestep conflict instead of challenging it head on, laying down a pattern of behaviour that he would take with him into manhood.

When he was twelve years old, Jude enrolled at the National Youth Music Theatre, where he met a kid named Johnny Miller, and the two struck up a friendship. In later life, the two men appeared together in the British movie *To Love, Honour and Obey*, but back then Jude appeared first in a production of Tim Rice and Andrew Lloyd Webber's hit musical *Joseph and his Amazing Technicolor Dreamcoat* before making his TV debut in Beatrice Potter's *The Tale of Gloucester*.

Jude was determined to take his acting career as far as he could, and so his decision as to whether he should stay on at school or take a part in the daytime soap opera *Families* was an easy one. There was no contest. And so, at the age of seventeen, he dropped his studies and entered the exciting but fickle world of acting, and he's never looked back — at least, as far as his acting career is concerned. Indeed, his career so far has been nothing short of phenomenal.

In his early twenties, Jude dedicated himself to the theatre, touring Italy in a production of *Pygmalion* before making his London debut in the hugely successful play *The Fastest Clock in the Universe*, which *Time Out* magazine voted Best New Play of 1992. However, his crossover into the movies didn't go all his way; his first film, *Shopping*, also starring Marianne Faithfull, flopped badly and he received poor reviews. However, it was during the shooting of this film that he met Sean Pertwee, who would become a good friend of his and his future wife, Sadie Frost. At the time, Sadie was married to ex-Spandau Ballet member Gary Kemp, with whom she had a son, Finlay.

After his rather shaky start in the movies, Jude returned to the theatre, where he starred in *Snow Orchid*, the Royal Court's *Live Like Pigs* and Arthur Miller's *Death of a Salesman*, among other productions. He finally landed the big break he craved when he appeared in Jean Cocteau's play *Les Parents Terribles*, a production that required him to be totally nude during the first scene of the second act. The play was a hit and so, apparently, was Jude, who promptly found himself up for a prestigious Olivier award for Best Newcomer. When the play was rechristened *Indiscretions* and transferred to Broadway, Jude went with it. However, at this time, Jude was working at the Barbican's Pit Theatre in London, so he had to commute to New York for rehearsals. No one could ever accuse Jude Law of not being dedicated to his profession; like other successful celebrities, he knows all about working hard.

In America, *Indiscretions* was a great success. In the Broadway production, he starred alongside Kathleen Turner and played his part so well that he earned himself a Tony nomination.

His confidence levels soaring, and having acquired an enviable reputation, Jude went on to play a part that suited his personality beautifully – the spoiled Bosie in *Wilde*, a biopic of the great Irish playwright Oscar, starring alongside Stephen Fry. The film turned out to be a box-office success and put Jude Law's name well and truly on the map.

Following this triumph, America was beckoning Jude, fast becoming one of Britain's finest young actors, and he grasped with both hands every opportunity that came his way – and there were many. His first role in the States was in a piece entitled *Music From Another Room*, in which his character was a hopeless romantic. After this he played opposite Clare Danes in *I Love You, I Love You Not*, which was shortly followed by the acclaimed sci-fi pic *Gattaca*, in which he starred alongside such bankable names as Uma Thurman and Ethan Hawke. After this, there followed a succession of Hollywood blockbusters including *Enemy at the Gate*, *Road to Perdition* and, of course, the much-publicised *Alfie*.

Jude's workload at this time was truly phenomenal. Soon after completing these films, he earned himself Oscar nominations for his roles in *The Talented Mr Ripley* and *Cold Mountain*, while other of his screen credits include *Sky Captain and The World of Tomorrow*, *Closer* and the Howard Hughes biopic *The Aviator*, in which he starred alongside Leonardo DiCaprio.

It seems that Jude was receiving good advice at this time from friends and colleagues in the business, because he managed to not be tempted to take just any offer that came his way. Instead, he chose his roles carefully, and his discrimination seemed to pay off. It seemed inevitable that major awards were on their way.

However, his offscreen life was a different story. Whereas he had control of his acting career, in both Britain and the States, it wasn't long before his personal life spun out of control.

LOVELY SADIE, FASHION LADY

Sadie Frost was born into a large Bohemian family in London in 1967. Her first acting role came at the tender age of three, when she featured in a TV advertisement for Bassett's Jelly Tots. Like her future husband, she was eager to be famous and so studied drama at the world-renowned Italia Conti School. When she hit her teens, however, she ran away to Liverpool to become a punk, and by the time she was nineteen she was married to Spandau Ballet's Gary Kemp, with whom she had a son, Finlay, before she and Gary went their separate ways.

Hollywood was an option for Sadie, but, instead of chasing a career in America, she chose to remain loyal to the smaller British film industry. Her most notable film role until this time was as a lusty society girl turned vampire in Francis Ford Coppola's *Bram Stoker's Dracula*. She later went on to star in a number of films made under the aegis of the production company Natural Nylon, which she co-owns along with Jude, Ewan McGregor (at one time Jude's roommate) and Sean Pertwee.

When Sadie first met Jude, she was already a fully paid-up member of London's über-trendy set. It wasn't long before they were an item, and shortly thereafter they tied the knot, marrying in 1997. Soon afterwards, Jude – five years Sadie's junior – suddenly found himself married not only to feisty Sadie but also to her wild lifestyle. There was no question that he adored her, however, as evidenced by a tattoo he had printed on his left forearm bearing the legend 'sexy sadie' (a reference to another Beatles song). It seemed that the two stars were destined to be together. They soon had three kids of their own, besides Finlay.

Despite such apparently settled domestic surroundings, however, Jude found that life in Primrose Hill was extreme. Sadie's entourage played fast and furious, and it soon became apparent to Jude that his wife was capable of loving more than one person at a time.

When the 'sexy Sadie' stories broke following the exposure of her best friend Kate Moss's cocaine habit, it became clear just how intimate the friends were. Drunken revelries, it seemed, were the order of the day at not-so-Prim-rose Hill. Indeed, one Sunday newspaper printed what seemed to be inside information about one of Kate Moss's birthday-parties at which

Sadie – by now a fashion designer and half of the Frost/French designer label – was a main player.

Following the publication of the extraordinary images captured by *Daily Mirror* photographers during an undercover investigation that showed Kate Moss to be a practised user of cocaine, Sadie and the rest of the Moss Posse were dragged into what was turning out to be a story rich with seediness and salaciousness. Had Kate *really* been part of a threesome with Sadie and Jude? From the way the tabloids portrayed the situation, all of the protagonists had been intimate with each other at some point, either in west London or in the not-so-sleepy countryside.

Sadie recently celebrated her fortieth birthday and has voiced her desire to move out of the tree-lined streets of one of London's more upmarket areas. Has she partied enough? Are her wild days of drunken binges over? Perhaps the nightmare in which Kate Moss has found herself has made her realise how dangerous this kind of lifestyle can be. Or are they all heading off together, taking their allegedly debauched lifestyle with them? Now that she's split from toy-boy Jackson Scott, Sadie has apparently been searching for a property to buy in the Oxfordshire area, close to Kate's £3-million cottage in Little Farringdon. A close friend of the group told *Grazia* magazine, 'Sadie wants to escape the fast pace of London but doesn't want to feel isolated, so she's keen to live as close as possible to Kate.' Sadie has also revealed that she wants stables and horses for Finlay and her three children with Jude: eight-year-old Rafferty, four-year-old Iris and two-year-old Rudy. This means selling the £5-million house she shared with Jude during their passionate but volatile marriage.

Of course, it couldn't have done much to bolster Sadie and

Jude's relationship when daughter Iris was rushed to hospital after swallowing ecstasy while Sadie had been at a family party in London's Soho and Jude was working away. It must have been a frantic time, and the newspaper reports accompanied images of a strained-looking Jude.

A spell of separation followed before Jude and Sadie finally divorced. The big question, of course, is, to what extent did Sadie's involvement with Kate Moss contribute to the breakdown of her five-year marriage to Jude? Did Kate tarnish the union, or was the whole incestuous Primrose Hill scene to blame? The one overriding impression of the affair is Sadie's misery when she and her husband split up, whereas Jude's emotions seemed to be channelled into anger. Maybe if he hadn't been angry he would have been as desperately sad as Sadie was.

ENTER SIENNA

At this point, it was Sienna Miller's turn to enter Jude Law's orbit. Like Jude, Sienna has a string of highly acclaimed movies to her credit, and few of their friends were surprised when she and Jude became one of the most popular couples on the celebrity circuit.

Soon, Sienna was sporting a £20,000 engagement ring following Jude's proposal on Christmas Day 2004, and shortly after pictures of the couple beaming happily appeared in all the celebrity magazines. On the surface, the union of Jude and Sienna – both A-list celebs and beautiful people – appeared to be a match made in heaven, but of course they were inhabitants of the volatile world of celebrity, so it really should have come as no surprise when it all went horribly wrong.

For a start, even before the stories of wife-swapping and orgies began to circulate, there had been allegations that Jude had conducted an affair with a lap-dancer named Erica Coburn. And, when he flew out to New Orleans in the summer of 2005 to film *All the King's Men*, he created his very own hurricane when he whipped up a storm with Daisy Wright, the nanny of his children.

Daisy – dubbed by some tabloids as 'delightful Daisy' – kept a diary of her fling with her boss and promptly sold her story to a Sunday newspaper. '[Jude] is a great lover and knows how to satisfy a woman,' she enthused. Allegedly, he was masterful and made her whole body tingle. She went on to gush that, on one occasion, 'he said it was very hard to find a woman who doesn't want a career and to party all the time.' Later that night, Jude allegedly whispered in her ear, 'If you're lonely, come and see me.' As the story goes, they ended up in bed together, which Daisy breathed was a 'mind-blowing' experience.

When the affair with Daisy Wright became public knowledge, Sadie told *New* magazine, 'I didn't see this one coming. It was a total shock to everyone. My heart goes out to Sienna. I feel very sorry for her. She is young and has a great career ahead of her. I have all sorts of advice for her. If she phones me, I'll have a long chat with her, but I can only give her advice if she asks for it.'

Jude proceeded to do what's known in the business as 'a Hugh Grant', publicly admitting to a month of sex with Daisy and then offering a humble apology. He confessed, 'I am deeply ashamed and upset that I've hurt Sienna and the people closest to us. There is no defence for my actions, which I deeply regret.'

Sienna's mother was not impressed. 'Some men just can't keep it in their trousers,' she was heard to say. 'He's done a terrible thing.' Yet she had nothing but pride for her daughter, exclaiming, 'She's an absolute trouper, my Sienna. She has always been really strong.'

Sienna moved out of the home she'd shared with Jude and stayed for a while in London's Dorchester Hotel. The pictures of Jude taken at around this time show him looking strained and morose.

But just what was Jude regretting? Getting caught? A friend of Jude's parents revealed that his mother, Maggie, thought her son should face up to his responsibilities and stop feeling sorry for himself, and others agreed. However, one source told *Closer* magazine that, rather than feeling contrite, Jude had turned the whole thing around and was blaming his fiancée's constant partying and hectic work schedule for his cheating. He apparently accused her of not being there to support him during his busy filming schedule, opting instead to concentrate on her own acting career. The same source revealed, 'He said, if she's not working or partying, she's sleeping, and he blames her for what he's done. He told her, "I said I was unhappy. I told you I needed you to be there for me. Why didn't you listen to me?"' Jude's publicist denies these allegations but, whatever the truth, Sienna is believed to have told him to go to hell. For a short spell.

The shock of Jude's indiscretions had a devastating effect on Sienna. 'She's been having heart palpitations, she feels so upset,' reported one of her friends at the time. 'She hasn't been able to eat and felt she might faint.' Indeed, *Closer* revealed that Sienna needed to consult her doctor because of her stress and loss of appetite.

Despite all the upset, however, Sienna took only one night off from performing her role in Shakespeare's *As You Like It*. It seems that Sienna's mum was right: the girl is a trouper. Nevertheless, Jude's betrayal was taking its toll, and Sienna's friends described at the time how she was 'an emotional wreck, struggling to cope'. No surprise there; her whole world had been shaken.

Then a headline appeared in the *Daily Mail*: 'troubled sienna and the five cuts on her forearm'. The recent pictures I'd been seeing of her had already been ringing alarm bells for me. Her publicist, Clara Marks, said that the marks on her arm were caused during a bizarre swimming accident. It seemed to me that she could have inflicted the wounds herself after her anger had been so all-consuming that she'd had to release it somehow. In my opinion, she'd needed to feel pain on the outside, and bloodletting was the way to achieve this, a bright-red scream without a rational voice.

Such actions are known in psychological terms as 'acting out'. When someone can't find the appropriate words to express a tremendous hurt, they act out the emotion instead. The angriest form of acting out is suicide. On one level, this is a kind of 'who's killing who?' in that the people left behind are also killed off.

In a recent TV interview, Sienna told her interviewer that, yes, she had been experiencing a tough time but that she was a strong girl with a great support system. However, I saw a girl struggling with conflicting emotions, and her body language told a tale of woe. She raised her scarred arm, indicating that on some level she needed everyone to know about her pain, and she continually rubbed her nose.

At the time, I had no doubt Sienna Miller would pull through, and the fact she missed only one night's performance at the theatre spoke volumes for her resilience. But if she really thought that Jude would stick to the 'commandments' she insisted he obeyed – such as wanting him to spend less time the Primrose Hill set – she was fooling herself. Although Sadie and Jude are now divorced, they still have three of their own children and one from Sadie's previous relationship. The kids are part of the package.

Of all the rules Sienna laid down, however, the one that required Jude to keep his temper under control was always going to be the one that he was least likely to be able to stick to, unless he got some counselling and took a course in anger-management training.

Soon after the split, however, more allegations hit the papers. Sienna, it was reported, had been unfaithful with Daniel Craig, with whom she starred in the UK gangster flick *Layer Cake* and who it turned out (rather unsurprisingly) was a mate of Jude's. When he found out about the affair, Jude allegedly flew into one of his famous rages and dumped Sienna (who had recently dumped him) and shortly afterwards was apparently seen having a cosy time with actress Salma Hayek.

Now, call me old-fashioned but I'm really not sure all this intermingling of flesh and bodily fluids is very healthy, either physically or emotionally. What about the saying 'Two's company but three's a crowd'? And how bizarre is it that, at the time, Sienna just happened to be promoting her new movie *Casanova*?

At the end of October 2005, her mother announced, 'Sienna is leaving England and going to spend some time in New York with her father, Ed Miller.' This is probably the break Sienna needs. She's had a rough time of late. However, she remains adamant that she didn't cheat on Jude with Daniel – but then, she also said that she didn't think either she or Jude was capable of fidelity. But, of course, if you want monogamy, you have to marry a swan.

THE EMOTIONALLY STUCK JUDE

One of the things that has struck me about Jude is that, besides at times appearing selfish and petulant, he doesn't seem to have grown up enough to hold down a mature relationship. The main culprits for this failure, he affirms, are everyone else. Sadie was to blame; Sienna was to blame; everyone else seems to be to blame for whatever goes wrong around him. It's all someone else's fault. Fundamentally, it seems that he perceives himself to be the victim, even when he's the one who has misbehaved and caused hurt to others.

Jude Law is a prime example of a human being who still believes he can have everything. Like the late George Best, he is a typical alpha male who takes outrageous risks and seeks out dramas, a man with the mind of a naughty little boy who, when he misbehaves, thinks he can charm his way out of trouble. I call this quality a 'vile charm'. He seems to think that, because he's handsome, he can mask this deeply unattractive quality. I would take a guess that, during his formative years, he managed to get away with all manner of misdemeanours.

When Jude was unfaithful to Sienna, some thought that she should give him another chance while others thought that it would be better for her to live with the situation for a while before making a decision. By all the newspaper accounts of her emotional state at the time, it appeared that she was ambivalent about sticking by Jude. How she must have hurt. How much she must have wished he'd never cheated and that they could be as they had been beforehand. But, like it or not, the damage had been done; Jude had destroyed all trust with lust.

So can Jude change? Maybe; maybe not. He does seem to need some way of controlling his anger. If he can do that, it will indicate that he's capable of further change. Although patterns of bad behaviour can be broken, however, the process is a long one. Old habits really do die hard, and a person needs to be highly motivated if he or she is going to break the habits of a lifetime.

Maybe Jude will find motivation with reconciliation with his ex-wife and family, should it happen, or possibly with a new and meaningful relationship.

If Jude and Sienna had been together for longer, it might have proved worthwhile to try to repair the damage and start over. But, of course, theirs was a whirlwind celebrity romance involving two very driven people: a talented, beautiful young actress with a great career ahead of her and man who needed to come first in his wife's life. A scenario like that was doomed to failure.

In my professional opinion, the only chance Jude might have of holding down a decent relationship in the future is to immerse himself totally in a life-changing course of therapy. He can't stick a plaster over his behaviour; he needs to change on a much deeper level, and that would take courage. For a start, he needs to find out where his anger stems from. I have a suspicion that he's really experiencing a whole glut of emotions that are being acted out as one massive explosion of anger.

Let's take a look at why Jude behaves in such a selfish manner. Here's an imaginary scenario:

Sienna finishes a hard day filming and goes out to party with her friends. Jude doesn't know how to react. If he's not invited, he will feel rejected. If he is invited, he'll still feel rejected when he's with her friends because he won't be the centre of her attention. So he gets moody and starts to sulk, and Sienna isn't certain what's happening. Why is there suddenly a bad atmosphere? She loves him. Surely he knows that? She doesn't think she's done anything wrong, but she's beginning to feel guilty and angry. They have a row, a stupid, fruitless argument in which nothing is learned and nothing is resolved.

Jude licks his wounds and feels that his fragile ego needs a boost, so he looks to another woman for comfort – ie sex. Enter the accommodating Daisy Wright. Of course, if it hadn't been Daisy, it would have been another equally willing woman. He is a celebrity after all.

This way of feeling, thinking and behaving can damage a relationship seriously. If Jude is ever going to change his philandering ways and learn to control his anger, he'll need to travel along a road he's never before travelled and face up to his inadequacies along the way. He will need to become stronger inside. Only then will he be able to face the darkness that threatens to destroy his long-term personal happiness and contentment. He needs to learn to take responsibility for his actions, especially when those actions cause others pain and misery.

One gets the impression that, all through his life, whatever Jude Law has wanted Jude law has got. Perhaps if he'd been made to tough it out in the school he found intolerable, he might have built up some emotional strength. While I'm not advocating keeping someone in an oppressive environment for their own emotional wellbeing, there are times when children need to weather the storm, to learn to stand up for themselves and fight their own battles. Standing up for yourself feeds your soul and waters your self-esteem. In turn, you begin to feel good about yourself and secure within your own skin.

TEMPER, TEMPER!

Jude Law, now in his thirties, seems to be spending a disturbing amount of time in a state of childish egotism. Anyone who has observed his angry outbursts or seen the photographs of him scowling at photographers will have seen this childish behaviour

He is evidently not secure within his own skin, and therefore emotionally needs to look to others to feed and water his fragile self-esteem.

I don't think Jude has every really lost his childish petulance: 'I want it! Why can't I have it?' But why does he behave like this? Well, the short answer is, because he can. Because he's always got away with it in the past. He's always been indulged. But indulging a child without disciplining him or her is a form of neglect. It is possible to love a child to emotional death.

When Jude lashes out at a photographer or kicks one up the backside for daring to snap a shot when he's in a bad mood, he behaves like a two-year-old. Maybe the only recourse, then, is to treat him like a two-year-old. He needs someone to say to him, 'No, Jude. Life doesn't work like this. You can't keep on hurting the people you say you love. It's cruel and will also keep you stuck in the emotional state of a two-year-old, someone who thinks he's the centre of the universe and that everyone owes him something.'

Jude comes across as a bit of a moaner. Doesn't he realise that life is difficult, or that, if he took more responsibility for his bad behaviour, he would be much happier? Life is a series of problems. If we moan about them instead of dealing with them, we become a pain to both ourselves and others. Solving these problems can be a very painful process, but by avoiding them we prevent ourselves from developing emotionally. Frustration, grief, sadness, guilt, regret and despair are all uncomfortable feelings, and sometimes, when we can't handle them, we become childlike and throw a tantrum. In therapeutic terms, this is known as having a *low frustration tolerance*. If we're unable to bear our frustrations, we literally flip.

Many celebrities are described as being hedonistic or

egotistical, and in all likelihood such people – like Jude – have from an early age been given messages that they are special. Yes, they might have special gifts and talents, and they might have worked hard to get to the top of the fame ladder, but somewhere along the line their emotional side seems to have got caught up in the belief that their celebrity status makes them better than everyone else. This kind of immature self-belief is a curse in itself. A celebrity curse.

Jude is a handsome specimen of a man, and with his looks, talent and wealth he could have his pick of beautiful women, but, unless he addresses the issues I've raised in this chapter, he will in all likelihood continue to destroy all of his relationships. One accusation commonly levelled at him is 'The only person Jude Law loves is himself', but this is simply not true. The fact is that he probably *doesn't* love himself at all, and this is the real problem. It's likely that deep down he knows he's behaving like a brat but doesn't know what to do about it, so he acts out, confirming the media and public's belief that he's a nasty piece of work. Such behaviour must make him feel miserable. The women who enter his world have the choice to walk away, but Jude doesn't have this luxury. He's stuck with himself. That is, unless he gets help.

ANGER MANAGEMENT

'Anger is the chief enemy of public happiness and private peace.'
– *Hyman Meltzer*

Anger is not always a destructive emotion. Constructive anger – ie that which is devoid of malice, hatred or hostile aggression – can be very useful. Most anger-based feelings are born out of fear. Frightened children don't have the maturity to help them express their fear appropriately. Some hit out at others, some suppress their emotions and become depressed, and some seem to be able to manage their emotions quite naturally.

When children grow into adults, they are required to express their anger in such a way that they don't cause harm either to themselves or to others. Unfortunately, not all make the transition, hence the need for anger-management courses and workshops. Indeed, today such schemes are extremely popular, helping many people whose anger is either making them sick or ruining their relationships. Such people are often suffering from what's known as *problem anger* — ie that which urges a person to hurt, punish, disparage or avenge, rather than build, protect or defend.

Jude and Sienna evidently experienced lots of anger throughout their troubled relationship, and they expressed it in a number of ways for two fundamental reasons. A lot of their anger was produced because they truly cared about each other. Because of this love investment, when one became fearful of losing the other, this fear would be transferred to anger, an emotion for which they have no mature vehicle for expression, and so they acted out instead.

Here's my take on their relationship:

Jude feels ignored and shouts at Sienna for ignoring him. Sienna doesn't like being shouted at and told what to do, so she parties even harder. Jude is angry at being ignored, so he finds an adoring substitute. When he is found out, he is too emotionally immature to own up to the fact he has betrayed Sienna, so he blames her. He genuinely feels that she is to blame, because in his mind she started it all by ignoring him. Because of her love investment, Sienna is devastated. Her anger is so intense that, in order to express it and get some release, she cuts herself. The pain of the bloodletting gives her a sense of relief from her internal anguish.

Jude then publicly apologises, and she accepts his apology but lays down commandments, in the process publicly humiliating him, just as he humiliated her by sleeping with the nanny.

Then Sienna allegedly sleeps with one of Jude's best friends. He storms into a rage and is then seen in public with another beautiful woman.

The way I see it, Jude is acting out this great big ball of anger. How different it could have been for their relationship if he and Sienna had been able to channel and communicate their fears and, ultimately, their anger.

Jude has demonstrated that anger can be a real problem if it's excessive, is out of control, lasts too long or is poorly timed. Negative expression of anger happens when someone needs to win an argument rather than solve a problem or needs to blame another person in order to preserve their fragile ego.

Jude is viewed negatively by others because of his out-of-control anger. There is an ugliness in his temper tantrums, and his poor behaviour distracts people from his great acting achievements. The problem is that anger begets more anger, propagating a self-perpetuating circle of misery. As I mentioned earlier, if he doesn't take responsibility for changing his behaviour and heal his weaknesses, if he doesn't indulge in a little self-scrutiny, he can never hope to grow or change, emotionally.

If Jude can find some way of containing his anger, he'll find

he has much more energy to use positively. He'll experience
less guilt and more self-respect. The goal is not to eliminate
anger altogether but to gain control over it by taking the
following steps:

1. Generally reducing levels of anger;
2. Stopping the anger from escalating too quickly;
3. Decreasing the intensity, duration and frequency of the angry outbursts;
4. Keeping the levels of anger at manageable levels.

Managing anger doesn't mean bottling it up, which will lead to either depression or an explosion of uncontained anger. Instead, it's important to learn how to defuse or express the anger appropriately.

Jude seems to get angry most when he feels unloved or ignored or when things don't go his way, generally, but his terrifying rages make people want to distance themselves from him, which is exactly the opposite of what I think he wants and needs. In my opinion, he has this need because he may have a low level of self-esteem and, when our self-esteem is low, what others think of us matters terribly. As George Santayana put it, 'What others think of us would be of little moment, did it not, when known, so deeply tinge what we think of ourselves.' When people say or do things to us that make us feel uncomfortable, this can threaten our self-esteem, triggering anger. In order to control this anger, the length of time between feeling threatened and behaving angrily needs to be extended. It's like asking a child who's behaving badly to take time out.

So, in order to learn how to minimise and, in turn, manage

anger, one must find out exactly why one's self-esteem is low, where the roots of this fragility lie. Only then can self-esteem be strengthened and raised.

People without healthy self-esteem are easily threatened by stressful events, as this tests their lack of worth. When confronted by a difficult situation – for instance, being criticised, judged harshly, ridiculed, rejected or ignored – they react by feeling unworthy, which threatens the ego. A threatened, immature ego can't withstand feeling vulnerable, so the vulnerability is converted to anger.

A valuable yet quite simple technique that can be very effective in combating such leaps into anger is to recite a dialogue when one feels under threat. It goes something like this:

'So you want to go to the party without me. For whatever reason, you do not wish for me to accompany you. *All the same*, that doesn't make me a bad person.'

Or this:

'You've just betrayed me and slept with someone else. *All the same*, that doesn't make me any less of a person. I'm still the same person with the same values.'

This can be a very empowering message in times of stress, and with repetition comes belief. With this kind of positive affirmation, we can acknowledge that, while we might not be perfect, we're certainly worthwhile.

Jude, you need to take an anger-management course. Sienna, so do you.

JUDE LAW

Since their divorce, Jude and Sadie have been photographed together. Apparently, they are comforting each other. Whether this is true or not remains to be seen, but it would be wonderful if they could stay together, if only for their children's sake. Of course, this isn't always possible, nor is it always right, but I've worked with many clients who wished they'd worked harder to hold their relationships together, having gone on to even more disastrous ones. But who knows? One day the magazines might include pictures of Jude and sexy Sadie in their countryside home with their children and horses, enjoying a stable, fruitful relationship. It's that thing called 'hope' again!

Chapter 7

KERRY KATONA

Sitting in the back of Austrian Count Philippe's plush limousine, Kerry Katona appeared to be apprehensive. Swallowing hard, she looked imploringly at the TV camera, as if asking for support. Then she muttered under her breath, 'I feel as if I'm in a social-services car on my way to meet a new foster family.' Then she gave a nervous laugh and added, 'Dead posh, sitting in it now.'

This was one of many poignant moments in what was an essentially fun reality-TV show entitled *My Fair Kerry*, broadcast in the UK in autumn 2005, in which the notoriously brash Kerry attempted to pass herself off as a member of the aristocracy. It was a considerable challenge for her: 'The jungle was a piece of cake compared to living with a count!' she blurted, referring to her other reality-TV appearance in the celebrity challenge show *I'm A Celebrity, Get Me Out Of Here!*, which she won after beating a host of other stars.

THE CURSE OF CELEBRITY

In *My Fair Kerry*, Katona had two weeks in which to turn herself from a humble, outspoken Warrington lass into an educated and sophisticated female fit to accompany a count to a ball. She had to learn all about deportment and etiquette.

The show's producers had their work cut out for them. As Kerry's mother, Sue, announced, 'It's being as common as muck that makes [Kerry] an A-list celebrity.' And, indeed, Kerry is known for her down-to-earth attitude. Her favourite meal, for instance, is reportedly, chips, peas and steak, served up with her mum's gravy. She speaks of having to 'go and wet me lettuce'. She is, by all accounts, as unpretentious as they come.

Nevertheless, Kerry has a special relationship with her audience. When she was in Vienna during the shooting of *My Fair Kerry* and needed a friend to talk to, she would turn to the camera and, endearingly, have a conversation with it, as if it was her best friend.

As it turned out, her mum had been right; Kerry gave it her best shot but didn't quite manage to pass herself off as one of the aristocracy. Nevertheless, she did succeed in winning the hearts of viewers with her down-to-earth manner and wicked sense of humour.

Celebrities such as Kerry, Abi Titmuss and Jade Goody are often branded as being pointless airheads with no discernible talent and as shameless attention-seekers who should disappear from the media and crawl back from whence they came. Others, of course, adore them and will buy any celebrity magazine in which they appear. But the fact is that these people *do* buy the magazines. Kerry, in fact, is particularly popular, a girl referred to by *OK!* magazine as 'our Kerry'. What music that must be to a girl who spent much of her childhood in the homes of four different sets of foster parents. Feeling that she belongs and that she matters to those in her life must be terribly important to her.

These days, Kerry is clearly buying into what the public want from a celebrity. Her fans really care about whether the guy she is with is being good to her and how her two little girls Molly and Lilly Sue are doing. She's the girl next door who managed to crawl her way up the celebrity ladder. Millions identify with her and many aspire to be like her.

When it came to light that Kerry was struggling with her personal life, pretty much every magazine and tabloid newspaper in Britain covered the story. After the much-publicised breakdown of her marriage to boy band Westlife's Brian McFadden, the nation saw her in pieces. She dropped three stone, bought herself some new boobs that promptly split open, and then suffered a nervous breakdown and flew off to undertake a £4,000 treatment plan in Arizona. The demons of her childhood, it seemed, had surfaced, and she needed to focus on getting well. Now divorced from her first big love, Kerry is a single working mum, but for a while childhood sweetheart Dave Cunningham stepped into the role left by McFadden.

Kerry's background reads like the screenplay of an afternoon weepie – with a punch – so make yourself a cuppa and prepare yourself for a fascinating story. I warn you: it's a real tear-jerker.

KERRY'S BACKGROUND

Kerry Katona was born on 6 September 1980 in Warrington, Lancashire, and suffered a remarkably tough childhood, being dragged from refuge to refuge by her mother – who was escaping a difficult relationship with Kerry's father – and then spending some time with her grandmother before being sent to four different sets of foster parents.

The disruption and sense of abandonment that Kerry must

have felt at this would have been extremely difficult to deal with. A very young child (and Kerry was very young when her mother left her father) has no coping mechanisms and little understanding of what's happening to him or her. It doesn't matter how wonderful the foster parents or how much love they lavish on their little visitor: that child wants his or her mummy. And a child who experiences this type of childhood most often spends their adult years searching for a lasting love.

When Kerry embarked on a relationship with Brian McFadden, she must have thought that all of her Christmases had come at once. And, when he announced that he was leaving, she was quite obviously crushed. For a while afterwards, it would have been difficult for her to tap into her mature ego state; instead, she would have experienced the break-up through the eyes and mind of a child.

It's little wonder that she hit the bottle after losing Brian, first spending time in rehab clinic the Priory and then taking off for a spell in the now infamous drying-out Meadows clinic in Arizona. She needed time and space in a contained environment where she could be cared for while she regained her strength.

Her childhood might have been difficult, but Kerry is a survivor, and that's what most people love about her. There is a vulnerability about her, but also a great strength, with many coping mechanisms in her therapeutic toolbox, and probably more than she realises. It was her underlying strength that enabled her to take on a series of projects that would eventually find her fortune and fame.

Kerry's life as a celebrity began with a spell of glamour modelling, after which she turned her attention to singing. Then, in 1999, she became a member of the Liverpool pop act Atomic Kitten, a girl group founded by ex-OMD songwriter

Andy McCluskey. Inspired by The Spice Girls, the Kittens seemed to be Kerry's ticket to major success, but she wanted out. She didn't like the travelling, it seemed, and suffered from homesickness. Besides that, of course, she had fallen in love with Brian McFadden.

In September 2000, Kerry announced she and Brian had been an item for a year and that she was expecting his baby. With hindsight, however, she may have regretted leaving Atomic Kitten, as they won critical acclaim with their debut album, *Right Now*, before going on to enjoy a string of hits. Nevertheless, even though she and McFadden are now divorced, I'm sure that she has no regrets. After all, she has two adorable little girls, Molly and Lilly Sue. And, whatever Brian says about his ex-wife, he is always quick to point out what a fantastic mother she is. In fact, she was voted Quality Street's Mother of the Year.

At times, the news coverage of Kerry and Brian's relationship has been a little one-sided, with her pain having been documented more than his. The truth is that, when any marriage breaks down – even one of just two-and-a-half years – everyone hurts, especially when there are children involved.

Not long after he split from Kerry, he began to date Australian singer Delta Goodrem, for which he was branded the most hated man in Ireland. However, this accusation also partly stemmed from rumours that he'd dumped Kerry over the phone, which he strenuously denies. 'I didn't just pack up and leave my family,' he protested in response to one such claim. Instead, he too hit the bottle hard for a while before picking himself back up and moving on with Delta, with whom he is about to move to New York. 'I can't base my life around whether Kerry is in a clinic or not, so I'm going to follow through with my plans,' he told *Closer* magazine when Kerry was at her lowest ebb, before expressing his hope that his ex-wife would be better soon.

But what of Kerry's deep-seated problems? I've no doubt that she will need to continue to work hard on herself – that will be an ongoing process – but at times she appears to be quite overwhelmed, and sometimes the need to escape these feelings will be intense. If she feels that she's losing control, she might become panic-stricken and maybe even suffer from panic attacks.

One thing she's doing right, however, is focusing on her career. Being in demand will be good for her self-esteem, and in the process she'll learn more and more about herself, which in turn will raise her confidence levels. These days, when pictures of Kerry appear in magazines, her face is imbued with an expression of pride.

As I mentioned earlier, for a while Kerry found love with Dave Cunningham. 'It's lovely to know I've got someone like [Dave] in my corner,' she told *OK!* magazine. The well-known publicist Max Clifford, a great friend of Kerry's (and, possibly, the first positive father-figure in her life), was also full of praise for Dave and said that Kerry couldn't have asked for more from him. Having Max in her life nowadays must help greatly in the healing of her wounds.

WORKING WITH DEMONS

During the summer of 2005, Kerry spent a month in a faraway place, putting herself in an unfamiliar and tough environment. Really tough. As anyone who's spent time in one will confirm, a psychiatric hospital is no holiday camp.

Initially, Kerry's fans were shocked at revelations in the press that she was suffering depression. It was difficult to believe bubbly, smiley Kerry could be suffering so much that she needed to remove herself from society. But, of course, she had been masking her inner pain – amazingly well, it's true – but then cracks started to appear and she hit a crisis point.

While she was in the clinic, Kerry's two daughters, Molly and Lilly Sue, were looked after by her mother and also by Brian and his family. At the time, Kerry voiced her relief that she and Brian were back on friendly terms: 'The fact that Brian and I are mates again is brilliant. We were young and made mistakes and now we realise that we can hopefully become good friends again.'

But why did Kerry choose to travel so far away from home for treatment? Why not a clinic in her home country, England? Her reason for crossing the Atlantic, she says, was that she needed a complete break away from life in the UK. Yes, the Priory had demonstrated that they could help her, but the events in her personal life had been the real reason behind her opting to seek treatment in America. And partly, of course, she was seeking some peace and quiet. 'She is isolated,' reported Max Clifford while Kerry was undergoing treatment, 'but she is happy with the isolation. She can totally open herself up without thinking everyone is watching her. She is anonymous there and she knows everyone else is going through the same thing. In many ways, that isolation is an important part of why she is feeling better.' This makes a lot of sense, as a psychiatric hospital is exactly the right environment for a person to explore themselves and find out who they really are, what it is about their past that has contributed to their depression and exactly what they want out of life.

So what about Kerry's past? Just how much does the trauma of her childhood affect her life today? There is much talk about her wrestling with her inner demons. Can she really rid herself of them and move forward without being weighed down by so much emotional baggage?

My analysis of Kerry that follows contains an assessment and a recommended treatment plan for her to follow if she wants to keep on top of her emotions and control any potential chaos. As I mentioned earlier, there are so many different therapeutic interventions available that people become confused as to what therapy really is – and, of course, when one is at a crisis point, it's almost impossible to make decisions. The feeling of being out of control can be overwhelming, and sometimes the advice given by others isn't necessarily correct.

The thought of going into therapy, too, can be confusing and terrifying. Some people, like the late George Best, resist counselling and reject the idea completely, while others are reluctant to go but find life so unbearable that they take a deep breath and take the plunge, and if they're lucky (which most are) they find the right person to help them, someone qualified with whom they can connect. Elton John was able to recommend an appropriate therapist to Robbie Williams, and Robbie trusted Elton's judgement enough to give it a shot.

The socialite Tara Palmer-Tomkinson, too, is familiar with the types of clinics that Kerry has tried. Six years ago, the notorious socialite checked herself into the Meadows clinic in an attempt to tackle her cocaine addiction. From her column in *Closer* at this time, it was clear that her heart went out to Kerry, remembering her own difficult experience as an inpatient. Champney's, it wasn't. There was no pool to lounge around in while swapping stories with rock stars, and she couldn't call a taxi and escape because the clinic is in the middle of the Arizona Desert. Instead, like all the other inmates, Tara had to adhere to the clinic's strict rules, eat their bland meals and abstain from wearing revealing clothes. That said, Tara admitted, without the nurses and counsellors at Meadows, she would have never got her life back. (Strangely, it wasn't long after this that Kerry was sending Kate Moss similar messages of hope.)

Kerry's recovery wasn't speedy. Indeed, recovery is, by necessity, a long, hard road. There is no quick fix. Some of today's treatment programmes are designed to be cost-effective and act simply as a sticking plaster over an open cut, whereas longer therapeutic intervention heals the wound. Kerry is bright and brave and has huge potential, but in order to conquer the demons that threaten her health and happiness she needs to keep walking down the road of self-awareness.

But just what form do Kerry's demons take? In fact, they seem to be similar to many of the demons I find residing in the troubled minds of some of my clients. Indeed, most people who seek counselling have experienced a childhood trauma of some kind, some having suffered mental, physical or emotional abuse while others felt rejected, abandoned or unloved. While it's clear that Kerry's mother loved her, when she sent her daughter to foster parents, Kerry didn't necessarily *feel* loved, and this sense of abandonment will have left the child in her feeling unlovable.

Hopefully the treatment she received at the Meadows has shored up her self-esteem, which must have sustained serious damage during this episode of her life. Indeed, it is in the shadows of low self-esteem that internal demons lurk, speaking in tongues of evil. They are the voices that constantly put you down and rear up unexpectedly just when you think you've conquered them. You know you're winning the battle of the demons when your strong positive voice wins the battle of the inner dialogue. When your subconscious has grown to accept, and feel comfortable with, this new, more logical voice, you're well on the way to being comfortable with yourself. Only then will you be rid of your demons.

Many people I've counselled have actually been able to put an image to their demons. One girl I treated spoke of a 'little man' in her head who kept telling her what she must and mustn't do. Her road to recovery was long and difficult, but eventually she got the better of him and, although she came to realise that he would always be lurking somewhere in the shadows of her mind, *she* won control of *him* instead of *him* rigidly controlling *her*.

Kerry's demons moved into her head early on in life, and it's therefore not surprising that her safe and secure family life with Brian came undone when the demons of her abandoned childhood surfaced and she, too, became undone.

KERRY ON THE COUCH

Assessment
name: Kerry Katona
date of birth: 6 September 1980
marital status: Divorced
children: Two daughters, Molly and Lilly Sue
profession: TV presenter
presenting problems: Ongoing reactive depression
childhood issues: Inconsistency; lack of positive father-figure; feelings of abandonment
recommended therapeutic intervention: Psychodynamic counselling and transactional analysis

themes: Abandonment; insecurities; chaotic behaviour
strengths: 'Good enough' ego strength; motivated and hardworking; strong support system (mother, lover, friends, fans)
prognosis: Excellent

Loss and Grief in the Life of a Child

To be able to live happily in the present is a gift, but in order to be able to feel happiness and satisfaction one needs to explore one's past. Only then can one look to the future with confidence.

If one can share one's past experiences with a skilled counsellor and learn to understand them, first through the eyes of a child and then with a more mature, adult mind, one can move out of the emotional quicksand and on to firm, dry land.

As soon as I read about Kerry's childhood, I was reminded of noted psychologist John Bowlby's attachment theory, which describes the tendency of people to establish bonds with others and how the grief response is triggered when these bonds are threatened or severed. Bowlby's view is that attachment comes from a continual human need for security and safety. Attachment needs, he says, go beyond the physical – food, warmth, comfort, etc – and the quality of the attachment during childhood determines how well the child will be able to establish deep and meaningful affectional bonds later in life.

More recent research suggests that, following any emotional trauma, it is necessary for the patient to undertake what are known as 'tasks of mourning'. These include the following:
- Accepting the reality of loss;
- Experiencing the pain of grief;
- Adjusting to a new environment;
- Investing in new relationships.

From the ages of about two to five years, children grow in independence. When separated from a primary carer they are unable to grasp the permanence of separation. They will then demonstrate behaviour aimed at the restoration of the absent person.

A child who experiences loss or a death during this phase of development will need help in order to understand the irreversible nature of the situation, but often the need for this reparation lies dormant beneath the surface of defences – that is, until they attempt to forge a meaningful relationship as adults. Then their dependency issues will become apparent.

Booking oneself into a rehab clinic or seeking out a 'good enough' therapeutic experience can help to heal the early wounds that such separation inflicts, and only then will one be able to move away from a place of weak dependence to reach one of strong independence.

'Good Enough' Therapy

There's a worrying trend today in the world of therapy in which short, sharp treatment plans seem to be taking the place of longer, more in-depth counselling. Going into rehab has, it seems, become fashionable. However, while it's true that rehab can be tremendously effective for many people, it's not without its pitfalls. Sometimes, for instance, patients in such clinics collude with other patients, while others might compete unhealthily with each other. What's most important is the follow-up counselling that will enable clients to integrate fully all that they've learned about themselves. One needs time in order to change deeply ingrained negative habits into a more positive way of living. And you can't buy time.

Kerry has worked hard to get where she is today, in both her internal world and the way she lives her life under the media spotlight. My guess is that, given time, motivation and a hardworking ethos, she is perfectly capable of reaching her personal potential. As I mentioned in my assessment, the outlook is excellent. Buy why would I recommend ongoing psychodynamic counselling? And what exactly is it?

To work psychodynamically with a client is to build a close, trusting relationship, known in counselling circles as 'the working alliance'. This is a unique kind of relationship that differs from any other that the client will have experienced. In order to be able to work on this kind of level with another human being, the counsellor will need to be a highly trained (to at least diploma level) individual. After this initial training, they will then require regular supervision and undertake ongoing therapy themselves. And then they will need to continue to research their subject – reading and attending workshops and seminars – in order to update their knowledge.

Transactional analysis is another highly effective therapeutic intervention, and one that I feel would be excellent for Kerry. With this kind of analysis, the counsellor works with the three ego states – child, adult and parent – in which the human emotional core resides.

When we are children, we have only one ego state – unsurprisingly, that of a child. In this state, the mind is immature and has yet to acquire the coping skills that are gained by the time we become adults. Then, the third ego state – that of a parent – begins as a learned way of thinking; in other words, people who have had critical parents will instinctively parent their inner child with a critical voice. In transactional analysis, the client is helped, firstly, to acknowledge and understand this inner child and, secondly, to nurture the child with a loving parental voice. At this stage, if the patient's adult ego state is underdeveloped, it will need to mature into that of a responsible, disciplined grown-up.

The ultimate goal in transactional analysis is for the client to be able to balance the time they spend in each ego state. To behave like a child all the time is disastrous – just look at the late George Best to see the dangers of this situation – while spending most of one's time in the parent ego state means that one is constantly hammering away at one's self-confidence. To be an adult with no inner fun-loving child to balance the rigidity of life is really to have no life at all.

Transactional analysis is a highly effective therapeutic method that helps clients to grow and change – which is, after all, the required outcome.

Kerry the Client

Kerry isn't mentally ill and she isn't entrenched in a serious addictive disease, but she *does* have some deep-seated insecurities, and it's these insecurities – her demons – that threaten her mental wellbeing. She seems to have conquered her drinking problem, but the real issue is the depression from which she seems to suffer every now and again.

It's a truism that a problem aired and shared loses its power, and by extension depression is often an emotional state brought about by the suppression of angry feelings. Anger arises when we are afraid, and fear is an emotional state to which Kerry was no stranger when she was a small, vulnerable child. These unresolved fears remain buried, but they're still there and they will eventually surface. When this happens, a person will at first become anxious, but as the anxieties escalate they will experience a panic attack and a feeling of being out of control will threaten their mental stability.

(Incidentally, many clients have told me of their terror of dying in the middle of a panic attack. In truth, the worst that can happen to someone experiencing a panic attack is that they will faint. Then, when the blood and oxygen supply returns to the brain, they'll come around. This is a quick process and causes no physical harm. Once this phenomenon is understood, the panic attacks will subside.)

There was an endearing scene in *My Fair Kerry* that gave an insight to Kerry's neediness. On one occasion, the count wanted her to learn to shoot, but she refused. She just couldn't and wouldn't pick up a gun. When I watched this scene, I instantly thought of the Disney classic *Bambi*, when the young fawn's mother was shot, leaving him alone. Here was a woman who would lay down her life for her children, a strong young lady who would always fight for what she felt right. This might be another reason why the public loves her.

Kerry won't have fully 'found herself' after spending just a month in a psychological hospital, but the door to her eventual self-discovery has nevertheless swung open. She will have an understanding of her demons, over which she now needs to win control. The isolating environment at the Meadows might have given her a break from being at the centre of media attention, but constantly focusing on her feelings for such a short space of time could have been damaging. There's always the danger that such rapid therapy will open an emotional Pandora's box and that, when the patient returns to their normal, everyday life, their pent-up emotions will come spilling out. Having no counsellor on hand to help contain these often overwhelming feelings can prove to be highly dangerous.

THE CURSE OF CELEBRITY

(I've seen it happen time and time again. A person comes into a psychiatric hospital and is encouraged to 'open up'. They share their feelings in groups, paint dark pictures in art therapy and then work more in depth with their one-to-one counsellor, before meeting up with their allocated psychiatrist, who will check to see how they're doing – and then their insurance runs out, or their personal funds dry up. With half-explored secrets out in the open, and the bleeding wounds exposed, they are sent home, often to the same environment that was causing the suffering in the first place and in a more dangerous state of mind than before they opened up. Those who already know all about rejection will experience the end of such short-term treatment as rejection, while the 'I'm not worthys' will feel even more unworthy.)

When Kerry was heading into unfamiliar territory in Count Philippe's plush limousine, she transferred all of her childhood feelings on to her current experience. She immediately felt childlike and was reminded of what it's like to be in the back of a social-services car, heading for the unfamiliar home of an unknown family. She lapsed into her child ego state.

This one short scene in *My Fair Kerry* is rich with information for a counsellor. Indeed, an exploration of this phenomenon could lead Kerry to a complete understanding of her inner child. She could grieve for that little girl who was lost, lonely and afraid, and then move on with a nurturing parental voice inside.

Kerry's childhood experiences, and the feelings that accompanied them, were so powerful that, when she found herself in an uncomfortable situation, the painful memories flooded back. Quick as a flash, she felt small and vulnerable, as if she'd travelled back in time to become the little girl she thought she'd outgrown. But, if she ever comes to understand this phenomenon of the present transferring to the past, she'll have the choice of not going there. Instead, she can say to herself, 'I am no longer a helpless child with no choices. I am Kerry Katona. I am a mother of two children. I am an adult and a parent. My feet are firmly on the ground, and I choose *not* to go back in time. I've been there and done that a hundred times – too many times – and it stops *here*. This is not the home of more foster parents; this is a home I choose to be in.'

This kind of thinking demonstrates the value of both transactional analysis and psychodynamic counselling. By speaking to herself in a calm and controlled way, Kerry will be able to make the transition from a frightened child ego state to a nurturing parent ego state (ie transactional analysis), while psychodynamic counselling will enable her to naturally transfer the feelings of her childhood experiences on to a situation in her present-day life. By understanding that she doesn't have to panic about these old feelings, that they're in past and no longer threatening her, she can live in the present, in the knowledge that she's a grown woman and that what she fears is going to happen has already happened. It's over.

(Incidentally, this therapeutic method is really effective when working with the victims of child sexual abuse, enabling the patient to realise that the panicky feeling of being out of control resides in their past, and that that's where it needs to stay.)

Kerry has admitted to getting homesick, and for this problem a mixture of psychodynamic counselling and transactional analysis often proves effective. When I work with a client who is homesick, I take them back to their childhood to find the roots of this disempowering feeling, and this approach, I believe, would benefit Kerry. Why does she get so homesick? Does she remember feeling homesick as a child? And what is the one overriding memory that she has of being away from home when she was little? Once she'd grieved over these memories, she would be in a position, emotionally, to move away from home in her adult ego state. And, if her child ego state surfaced, she could mother her using her nurturing parent ego state.

Of course, this gentle probing wouldn't happen all at once. By necessity, therapy is a slow process of feeling, grieving, acknowledging and, finally, understanding. The process involves the jettisoning of a lot of negative emotional baggage, too, thus empowering the patient.

Despite the apparent chaos of her life, Kerry comes across as someone who is great fun and very entertaining, with a deliciously wicked sense of humour. She's also demonstrated her stamina and determination, particular in participating in *I'm A Celebrity, Get Me Out Of Here!* However, it seems that being the focus of entertainment for millions exhausted her and burned her out, and because of this fatigue, combined with her personal problems, she just had to get away. It's the stuff of which nervous breakdowns are made.

But what about her depression? Today, barely a week goes by without news of a celebrity succumbing to depression. However, I'm certain that Kerry isn't clinically depressed; it's more likely that her depression is a reaction to difficult life events. But then, life *is* difficult, and misery isn't caused so much by what life throws at us as by how we deal with it.

In order to combat her depression, Kerry needs to ask herself some searching questions. What is her depression telling her? What can she learn from it? How can she use her past experiences to keep her in a better place, both internally and externally?

When speaking to *OK!* magazine about Kerry's recovery

and her fears that she might never conquer her depression, Max Clifford made an important observation when he said, 'She knows from all the therapy and from all the conversations she's having with the staff there that she's on the mend. She's also met people there who have gone through the same thing and had similar childhood experiences. She's realised that, in some cases, what other people have gone through is worse than what she has been through – and they have come out of it, so she can too.'

This understanding of others' pain and being able to empathise with them is a huge developmental step. Being able to experience herself and her life as a part of a bigger picture is an all-important skill for Kerry to learn, as it quietens the voice inside that constantly asks, 'Why me?'

I've facilitated numerous group-therapy session at London's Charter Nightingale Hospital, and those that people found the most difficult to bear were the 'loss and change' groups. This is perhaps unsurprising. After all, when we lose someone or something precious, it's a natural reaction to fall apart, emotionally, with the knowledge that life will never be the same again. It might be good again, but what has been lost can never be returned. The cold reality of this fact is hard to swallow, and for some the feeling of loss will tip them over the edge and they'll need help to be brought back to mental health. This is the job of the counsellor.

It's this uniqueness of the relationship between counsellor and client that can bring about the healing process, the necessary one-sidedness of therapy sessions in which the client talks and shares their misery while the counsellor listens, absorbs and feeds back the pain in a way that the patient can digest it.

In those highly charged group-therapy sessions I mentioned

earlier, in which people from all walks of life shared their individual and unique losses, I heard tales of death, divorce, physical trauma, redundancy and the loss of once healthy minds. Slowly, the losses were shared and grieved over, and together these courageous individuals drew on all of their fragile inner resources to address tentatively the necessary changes they needed to make. Some, of course, got there quicker than others, and all of my clients move at a pace that's right for them. When I'm asked, 'How long is this going to take?', in all honesty all I can do is shrug my shoulders and answer, 'As long as it takes.' It might not be a satisfactory answer for someone who is struggling and desperate to get out of their dark hole, but it's the only honest one I can give. Some clients have surprised me and galloped towards the finishing line while others whom I initially thought would make fairly swift progress have depended on both me and the whole process of therapy for some considerable time.

If Kerry was to ask me, 'How long?', I'd give her the same answer. Then I'd ask her how long she thought it might take. What were her expectations of both me and the therapy? Then I'd ask her what her goals were, both in the short and long term, and then I'd work on being her facilitator and helping her to reach those goals, someone prepared to travel alongside her as she walks the road of emotional wellbeing. With Kerry, I'd work through her dependency issues, enabling her to arrive at an independent place before moving into the healthy state of interdependence, where relationships aren't about desperation and neediness but about friendship, sharing and, of course, passion. In my experience, I've come to realise that fighting demons with assistance isn't such a bad idea, as they're usually less powerful than we might think.

Chapter 8

ABI TITMUSS

Blonde, voluptuous and magnificent, with smooth, translucent skin, and a heart-shaped face, graceful and confident and yet at the same time both provocative and innocent, Abi Titmuss has nevertheless been voted Miss Pointless Celebrity. She is the latest blonde goddess to thrill media and public alike, and her ardent worshippers will buy any magazine or newspaper that features her face and body. She is adored by millions. And yet she is also ridiculed.

It's a universal truth that sex sells, and being a sex symbol can bring wealth and fame. Abi seems to possess the wondrous mix of a childlike innocence and jezebel temptress that intoxicates both men and women alike. She teases men into believing that she's bisexual, thus heightening the sexual tension she exudes. In this, she follows in the footsteps of other sex icons who have gone before her. She is a modern-day Samantha Fox.

There is, however, another side to her personality that few realise exists. Her autobiography, entitled simply *Abi Titmuss*, is reminiscent of the erotic sexual writings of authors like Molly Parkin, Nancy Friday and Erica Jong. Her imagination where sex is concerned is highly charged, and the fantasies she shares with her readers are both subtle and mind-blowing. She writes of a wide variety of sexual possibilities.

Abi Titmuss has made no secret of the fact that she loves sex, but the press has no doubt hyped revelations of her highly charged sex drive. There is much more to this girl than meets the eye.

FABBY ABI

Abi Titmuss was an only child who always wanted to be a vet, and even changed her subjects at GCSE level in order to give her the flexibility to go on to be a vet if she so wished. She also dreamed of being an actress. In fact, she became neither; instead, she took up nursing. 'Nothing will ever fill the void or give you the same feeling as caring for someone,' she told readers of *Now!* magazine. 'But, equally, it's no fun having no time for yourself and no money. I miss nursing very much. But you need to keep practising your registration, so it's not as simple as just walking back on the ward.'

Abi has a natural beauty, but much of her powerful sexual allure comes from her confidence. She appears to love herself and enjoy her body and, when a woman is comfortable within her skin, she is open to sharing it with others. She is fascinating, enticing and gives the impression she wants to be devoured. A slight smile showing gleaming white teeth. A toss of golden locks and poses betraying a supreme confidence. Pure seduction.

Abi first came to the attention of the tabloids while hanging on to the arm of TV presenter John Leslie and was portrayed as a loyal nurse who loved her man. At the time, Leslie was involved in a sex scandal, and what the press wanted to know was, 'Just who *is* this girl?' At first, all they knew was that she was a nurse, but after being thrust into the limelight – and while her boyfriend was in the middle of a sex scandal – Abi seemed to find the media attention as intoxicating as the tabloids found her. Soon stories appeared about her being partial to group sex, and these shocking revelations caused her to lose her nursing job.

She didn't waste much time in finding alternative employment. Having ditched Leslie, she landed a place in the reality-TV show *Hell's Kitchen*, in which she competed with other contestants to survive in the kitchen of notoriously difficult ex-footballer restaurateur Gordon Ramsay. Overnight, she became a household name, largely thanks to her wild sexual antics.

Today, Abi is a highly sought-after name, especially where any kind of nude modelling is involved. She is Britain's current object of lust, displaying the kind of natural curves for which Marilyn Monroe is remembered rather than the androgynous lines of a supermodel like Kate Moss. She is perfectly at ease in front of the camera and alludes to enjoying a woman's body as much as a man's, although she has confessed to being more bi-curious than bisexual.

While appearing on *Celebrity Love Island*, another reality-TV show, she fell for one of her fellow contestants, ex-soccer star Lee Sharpe. On screen, they sizzled, and later, off screen, they became an item. She succeeded in holding on to Lee, despite fierce competition from the female winner of the series, Jayne Middlemiss, who referred to her on screen as 'flabby Abi' and observed caustically, 'Abi is a big fat slag. I wanna punch her face in.' Was this vitriol born of envy? After all, with her pretty face and curvy figure, Abi must be no stranger to the emotion, particularly when exhibited by others.

Jayne's outburst shocked and upset Abi and totally ruined the end of the show for her. 'I came out of the show thinking I was going to be happy and excited, but I felt horrible when I saw that. I was crying when I left in the speedboat. It was awful. She wasn't like that to me in there.' The criticism directed at Abi after Jayne's 'flabby Abi' taunts were cruel and hurtful, yet she rose above the jibes, deciding not to bitch back.

Abi knows that she's not a natural catwalk model. 'I was in a bikini, being shot from all angles, and wasn't doing anything for five weeks,' she told *Hot Stars* magazine. 'I've always been curvy, and I think men like that – and I think it's a good image for a girl in the public eye. People said, "That's how she looks without an airbrush," but all the photos for the lads' mags are airbrushed. My problem is that I don't stand in the right way. It's all about posing and lighting.'

Jayne Middlemiss isn't the only female celebrity to have it in for Abi Titmuss, either; Jordan, too, has had a little dig, calling Abi an 'ugly rat' during the filming of *Celebrity Love Island*. Abi admits that her unkind comments made her cry all day.

Abi is clearly a sensitive creature, but this is perhaps not surprising. When her friend Calum Best became very friendly with another friend of hers, Rebecca Loos, people assumed that she would be jealous of their liaison, either because she had a thing for Calum or a thing for Rebecca, yet Abi says that she simply felt lost, lonely and very, very single. However, there's also a possibility that she was slightly embarrassed that the viewers expected her to be the first to get it on with Calum – or, indeed, anyone. She had a reputation, after all. She'd been hailed as a sex symbol, after all, and the public expects such people to live up to the implied lifestyle.

Abi has since sworn off participating in any more reality-TV shows. So what does she want out of life now? She says that she loves writing and would also like to be a TV presenter, implying that acting might still be on her agenda. Although many believe that she might find it difficult to break into serious acting, as she already seems to be pretty firmly typecast (some sizzling home movies appeared in the public domain, along with a purported sex tape involving her and John Leslie that was leaked on to the internet), she did appear in the football flick *Goal! 2*, shot in sunny Spain. Maybe her breakthrough on to the big screen shouldn't come as that much of a shock; after all, Madonna turned herself into a sometime movie actress. It's all about priorities and how much you really want something.

In the introduction to her autobiography, Abi reveals that she's always been a bit naughty, talking candidly of how, at sixteen, she discovered a high sex drive that strengthened as she grew older. When she was younger, the kind of men she lusted after were working guys, like rugged builders. 'I remember one guy in particular who was working on a house near where I lived,' she remembers. 'I was seventeen.' He was older.

But what, besides an acting career, does Abi Titmuss really want? What about her personal life? When asked, 'Where would you like to be in five years' time?' she replied instantly, 'I just want to be happy. Probably married with children. But I can't imagine it at the moment. I'm an only child, so I've always wanted a big house with lots of children.'

Unfortunately, of all the curses heaped on sex sirens like Abi, attracting shallow men who can't keep it in their trousers is the worst. For a start, there was John Leslie. He wasn't a fling; Abi had a five-year relationship with him. 'I was very much in love with him,' she recalls. 'We're still in touch. We wish each other all the best.' Although John was cleared of any offences levelled at him, his career nose-dived in the wake of the highly publicised scandal.

Then there was Lee Sharpe, with whom Abi embarked on a relationship after he admitted on national TV that he'd fallen for her. There were pub lunches here and a night in a hotel there and Abi told *Hot Stars* magazine, 'I want to shout about Lee from the rooftops.' Then an article in *Closer* painted a picture of the happy couple and revealed, 'The loved-up glamour girl and the ex-footballer prefer to snuggle up in front of the box rather than hit the clubs.'

But in the same interview with *Closer*, Lee confessed to having a problem, admitting that he'd split from his last girlfriend on the brink of marriage because he had 'commitment issues'. He also admitted to 'falling hard' on first meeting a woman but that it took him a long time to take the next step.

Then a story appeared in the *People* newspaper that must have shattered the sensitive Abi. It seemed that Lee's long-standing secret lover, Kathryn Shaw, had revealed all to the paper, which ran the headline: 'lee met up with me for sex under the motorway bridge… and then fled to bed with abi'. Although she confessed that she and Lee had never been an official item, she divulged that they had known each other for twelve years and liked to meet up for drinks, chat and sex. According to Kathryn, these trysts often took place at 'a little halfway point in between where he lives and where I live. Maybe we'd stop off for a drink in a pub and do… whatever. It's really nice. It's not really mucky or horrible. It depends on where he is and what he's doing. We keep in touch all the time. We do a lot of texting. I've got about forty texts from him on my phone at the moment.'

The story went on and seedily on. Apparently, after meeting Kathryn for a steamy romp near the M62, Lee then headed south to attend the V Festival in Chelmsford, Essex, and, later that day, while he was with Abi at the event, he sent another message to Kathryn that read, 'It was very horny, babe, must do it more often, and soon. X.' According to onlookers at the festival, Lee and Abi had a string of rows that day and there was a definite tension between them, with Abi flirting with her male friends, in front of a fuming Lee – even though he'd only just had sex with another woman.

The interview then reported that Kathryn laughed off the idea of Lee and Abi getting married and having babies. 'I think Abi is just a publicity stunt. If she can help him with the publicity, maybe that's what he's doing.'

Coincidentally, Lee Sharpe's autobiography, *My Idea of Fun*, was published in the same week as these revelations appeared in the *People*.

For many celebrities, being used in this way is standard procedure. Many find it difficult to know if any potential love interest is genuinely interested in them or just seeking some self-exploitation, and so they need to keep their guard up all the time. This can create a whole host of problems involving trust.

Abi's response to the *People* article was to go to the gym and take it out on the treadmill, trimming two stone off her curves. The tabloid pictures of her at this time showed her to be a picture of health, curvy but firm, with none of her assets compromised by the vigorous workouts.

Abi's problem was that, like many sexy glamorous women whose identity is entrenched in being curvy and blonde, she wasn't taken seriously. The public didn't look beneath the surface; instead, they just saw what Abi projected: silky nakedness, a mane of gold-blonde hair and, in all, a woman who uses her assets to achieve fame. Abi traded on her erotic allure, just like Marilyn Monroe before her and many, many more before her. The Ancient Romans, after all, had Venus, while the Ancient Greeks had Aphrodite of Knidos, the first universal blonde and the world's original model of sexual fantasy and power, a divine goddess whose form was to fill the erotic imaginings of men and women for centuries to come.

Abi is the UK's lust of the moment, her body a well-fed celebration of femininity. If Aphrodite represented love in all its forms, then so does Abi. If Aphrodite was the most beautiful of all the great mythical gods of the Mediterranean and the crucible of all erotic energy, Abi can be seen as her modern-day equivalent. In fact, it would come as no surprise to me if the men reading this book skipped straight to this chapter first, not so much to read about what makes Abi tick as to look at the images of her voluptuous body. Men are bewitched by her sexual imagery, and to many it doesn't matter what's fact and what's fable; it's the fantasy that's important.

So, if Lee Sharpe was, as Kathryn Shaw indicates, using publicity to raise his profile and help to sell his autobiography, what about Abi's taste for self-publicity? And what about this Aphrodite-type image? Is her allure dangerous? And, if so, to whom? Just where is Abi's lusty thirst for fame going to take her? Will this overnight sensation soon be replaced by a younger model, or is there more substance to her? Can she build on the foundations she has set down, or is she too flimsy? Volatile or emotionally fragile? These and many other unanswered questions serve only to add to the mystery surrounding the sexy blonde.

Victorian men used to fear the kind of powerful blonde imagery that Abi portrays, whereas today's men find it irresistible and addictive. Indeed, like alcohol or cocaine, dazzling blondes are all at one time stimulating and exciting yet also terrifying, and it's this cocktail that makes girls like Abi so intoxicating – for a while, at least.

ABI ON THE COUCH

'Is this lovey-dovey stuff, or do you want a bit of rough?' – *Robbie Williams*

In this section, I'll be discussing the difference between lust and love and explaining why love rats have a phobia of commitment. First, though, let's look at the link between sex and food. It's fascinating stuff!

Sex and Food

After counselling hundreds of people with eating disorders, I'm convinced that there's a close link between sex and food. When I worked on the Eating Disorder Unit at the Charter Nightingale Hospital, what I saw convinced me of the importance of helping people to understand just how much their sexual identity is entwined with their eating habits. So, if you want to know what someone's like in bed, just watch the way they eat their food.

From the way Abi Titmuss ate her way through *Celebrity Love Island*, it's clear that she enjoys her food in the same way that she enjoys her body. I'm certain that she takes her relaxed body image into the bedroom and she turns herself on as much as her partner. It's a very close, very intimate means of communication with herself and her lovers.

Too many women feel pressure from the media to change their body shape, to diet and control their food intake, ultimately losing their sexual spontaneity. At some point, these insidious messages can creep under the skin and an obsession can set in.

However, the likelihood of this happening to Abi is, I believe, slight. She doesn't pick at her food or play with it; when she eats, it's clear that she's enjoying it. Yes, she ate a lot in *Celebrity Love Island*, but the truth is, she was bored and was eating more than she would normally, while an injury that left her inactive for a while meant that she put on a few pounds, but she wasn't particularly worried. She knew that, once she was off the island, she could get back into her regular fitness routine and shed the excess weight.

Along with her body, though, Abi is able to feed her feelings, too. To understand this phenomenon, one first needs to bear in mind that Abi's way of experiencing eating is in complete opposition to that of an anorexic, a hugely complex illness whose sufferers have trouble not only ingesting food but digesting *any* goodness, including positive feelings and messages. For example, a mother can say to her anorexic daughter, 'You're a good person and your father and I love you, and you can beat this illness. You are *not* fat.' However, because the daughter can't digest anything good, her mind will turn the messages into something she can *digest*, something negative along the lines of, 'You're lying. I am a bad person and I don't deserve to eat. I can't do this. I'm a fat bitch.'

Abi, although upset by Jayne Middlemiss's harsh criticisms, didn't swallow her feelings and digest them in a way that would cause her lasting pain. Instead, she chewed them around for a while and then spat them out. While this demonstrates a certain fragility in Abi's emotional makeup, it also demonstrates a great strength, and this way of experiencing herself as a good-enough person indicates that she can withstand any heartache that comes her way. If this is true, it means that this particular aspect of the celebrity curse won't destroy her.

So, if Abi's self-esteem is healthy, what is the risky area of her life in the public arena? In my view, this area is men. The type of men she attracts, and the kind of man who can commit to her, seem to be poles apart. Abi seems to be searching for a man she can trust and who is not afraid of making a commitment.

Daddy's Girl?

Abi was an only daughter, and like all girls her relationship with her father was crucial. It has been shown that the bond between father and daughter affects the sort of person women eventually choose as a mate and, incredibly, has a direct influence on the age at which they reach puberty.

Research has shown that women — like men — who have suffered emotional neglect have a tendency towards promiscuity, experiencing the same confusion between sex and love discussed in the chapter on George Michael and lurching from partner to partner in search of intimacy through intercourse. Alternatively, they can withdraw and become frigid, keeping themselves shut away from both their sexuality and men.

As an only child, Abi would have been prey to the complex hypothesised by Freud that relates to the myth of Oedipus, a man who supposedly killed his father and had sex with his mother. In his book *They F*** You Up*, Oliver James explains Freud's belief as follows: 'As small children, all of us long to posses our opposite-sexed parent and kill off the same-sexed one. As time goes by, we realise that our same-sexed parent is much stronger than us, and to avoid posing a threat to them we repress our sexual attraction and identify with their conscience — adopt their moral precepts as our own. In short, that conscience is the result of fear and based on that of our same-sexed parent.'

Freud got a lot right, but he also got some things wrong, and it seemed that he exaggerated the importance of the Oedipus complex in forming conscience. It would appear that being loved by one's parents is far more important than fearing them.

It's a widely acknowledged fact, however, that girls often unconsciously seek out men who are similar to their fathers. If a girl grew up with a controlling father, she is likely to fall for a controlling partner. Similarly, if a girl's experience with her father has been close and affectionate, where appropriate normal flirting has been experienced safely, she is likely to end up in a contented relationship.

Unfortunately, in today's world of child sexual abuse, many men are scared of being touchy-feely with their daughters, and this has robbed many little girls of experiencing normal affection from their fathers. It is an important developmental stage for a girl to go through – to be able to flirt, but for her father to maintain the boundary, thus building a sense of trust that she can take with her into womanhood.

Abi's overtly sexy image scares a certain type of man (and it would have absolutely terrified the Victorians!), usually the type who will choose a 'Madonna'-type woman who will settle down, marry and have babies, whereas men who feel safer with lusty, short-term affairs find her exciting and stimulating. While I must make it clear here that Abi is in no way a whore, the kind of blatant sexuality that she projects can be viewed as possessing the same sense of rampant sensuality and danger often associated with the oldest profession. And the category into which a woman's image fits – Madonna or whore – will determine whether she is experienced as a lover or a wife. When men have affairs, they tend to keep their 'Madonna wife' at home and take on a 'whore lover' elsewhere, often after the wife has become a mother.

How, then, can Abi find the right man who is capable of

loving her, instead of falling for the love rats that find her irresistible but can't commit to long-term love? But, then, just what *is* love? It's an age-old question, but how can love be defined? It's too big and too diverse a concept to be fully comprehended. Lee Sharpe was heard to mutter to her, 'I've really fallen for you, Abi,' but what exactly does this mean?

The start of any new romance is fraught with difficulties, but embarking on a new relationship in the glare of publicity adds even more pressure. This is a particularly odious aspect of the curse of celebrity: the media wants to rush the new lovers into making decisions concerning their personal lives and for them to share their intimacies, with often disastrous results. But how is it that some celebrities' love lives go from strength to strength under such pressure while others' crumble?

When celebrities fall in love, it's a heady time, as it is for everyone who experiences the emotion. Their feelings are intense and they can't imagine they'll ever row, let alone break up. The sex is fantastic. They can't keep their hands off each other. Gazing adoringly into each other's eyes, each expression is captured by the paparazzi and splashed all over the latest gossip magazine. They wonder how they ever managed without this new, all-consuming passion. They're certain that they are completely in love and it will last forever.

Of course, such rash assertions so often turn out to be nothing but optimism. Too often, celebrity relationships founder under the glare of the media spotlight. 'J-Lo and Ben Affleck are in love,' say the papers. Oops, no they're not. Now they've fallen out of love.

'Brad Pitt and Jennifer Aniston are head over heels in love, and they're getting married. It's a celebrity love affair made in heaven!' Hang on – now he's in love with Angelina Jolie!

THE CURSE OF CELEBRITY

'Renee Zellweger has married after a whirlwind romance.' Hold on a minute – now she's asking for an annulment on the grounds of fraud after finding out that her new husband doesn't want the kids she was hoping for.

'Tom Cruise is marrying his new love.' *Another* new love?.

Why is it that celebrity love is rarely everlasting? Is it because celebrities occupy a strata of society in which temptation is particularly rife? Certainly. Is it because they spend too much time away from their partners? Quite likely. Could it be that they're really together only because high-profile celebrity couples get more publicity? Possibly. The reasons are plentiful. But this isn't the whole picture, and it certainly doesn't explain why some celebrity couples remain strong while others break up.

In his groundbreaking bestseller *The Road Less Travelled*, Dr M Scott Peck attempts to define love, describing the differences between 'the myth of being in love' and the 'real true love' that, in order to survive, needs to be disciplined. 'When a person falls in love,' he writes, 'what he or she certainly feels is "I love him" or "I love her". But two problems are immediately apparent. The first is that the experience of falling in love is specifically a sex-linked, erotic experience. We do not fall in love with our children even though we may love them very deeply.'

According to Dr Peck, the way in which people love their children, families and same-sex friends (unless they're gay) is very different to the way in which they fall in love with a sexual partner. In a nutshell, one must be sexually motivated in order to fall in love, and the very nature of falling in love is fraught with difficulties. For a start, explains Dr Peck, it's only a temporary state of being: 'No matter whom we fall in love with, we sooner or later fall out of love if the relationship continues for long enough. This is not to say that we invariably cease loving the person with whom we fell in love, but it means that the feeling of "ecstatic lovingness" that characterises the experience of falling in love *always* passes. The honeymoon *always* ends. The bloom of romance *always* fades.'

Look at it this way: a baby doesn't have any boundaries. He can't tell the difference between who he is and who his mother is. He is at one with both his mother and the universe. He *is* the universe. When he waves his hands in front of him, he doesn't know where he ends and the world outside begins.

Later, a sense of self begins to develop, and this is when he begins to realise that he is separate and different. When he cries with hunger, if there is no mother there instantly to feed him, this is the point at which his sense of identity is born. (Interestingly, it's in these early months of life that the digesting of good and bad food and feelings develops and most chronic eating disorders are triggered.) Now the baby recognises his voice as being separate from his mother's. He begins to know his limits – that is, where he ends and she begins. These limits are his boundaries.

Now, here's the link to falling in love. When people fall in love, they go back to being babies with no boundaries. They are at one with their lovers. When they gaze lovingly into their eyes, they experience a kind of self-love, just like Narcissus did in Greek myth when he gazed at his reflection in a pool and fell in love with himself.

Then, after around six months into a relationship, the boundaries snap back into place and people see their lover as once again a separate entity. These differences now need to be tolerated.

This is where discipline comes into the equation. The ultimate goal of a successful love-based relationship is a true and mature, give-and-take kind of love where a person can tolerate the differences that exist between him or her and their partner and still care deeply for them.

The point at which the boundaries snap back into place is the point at which many celebrities, who have so many choices and so much temptation, abandon what could have been a meaningful and lasting love. Many celebrities don't seem to possess the motivation required to discipline themselves to work through difficult times when it's so easy to move on and find another exciting and instantly gratifying romance. Those that do have the discipline and motivation to work through their problems and tolerate emerging differences in each other often enjoy a long-lasting love. This happens when both parties extend their limits (boundaries) and reach out to each other with a genuine wish to nurture. In this sense then, falling in love is very close to real love.

But if falling in love is all about sex, how on earth can it last? And, if Abi wants to find lasting love, what needs to change? How can the falling-in-love phase move on to marriage and children with a man who can commit? Well, the change must come from within, and it will occur only if this is what she really, really wants. She might be quite happy to stay as she is, playing out her fantasies, but the time may come when she wants more than this. And success in this area will come when, firstly, she gives out messages that suggest she is more than just a sex object – the type that narcissistic males go for but aren't strong enough to commit to – and, secondly, when she can extend her limits, enabling her first to be attracted to a man and then to move through a process of investing herself into his world, and thus become committed to him. She will thus incorporate this external love object – him – into herself. As she loves him, he will become a part of her, and if this kind of love is reciprocated then Abi and her partner will have a great future together.

An Emotional Void

There's just one more point to discuss in this chapter on Abi. She was an only child who chose to go into a caring profession: nursing. Nurses have an innate need to care for others, but a big part of this often stems from the fact that they really want to be loved and cared for themselves. Nurses have a reputation for being people who particularly enjoy sex. They are also mainly warm, loving people who often give too much of themselves, leaving a void inside.

It's also often the case that, rather than being spoiled or indulged, only children are needy of love. In later life, many of them describe feeling lost, lonely and really single – which is just how Abi said she felt when she appeared on *Celebrity Love Island*. We all carry a small child around inside us, and, while the child within Abi is full of feminine spirit, it's her masculine side that needs to be built up, the side of our personalities that helps us to be more in control of our emotions. There needs to be a healthy balance between both masculine and feminine sides.

Abi is a smart girl, and still young. I have a hunch that, as she grows and matures, her critics will have to eat their words about her being a pointless celebrity.

Chapter 9

PARIS HILTON

Unlike Britain, America has no real history and no royal family. Where Britain has Princes William and Harry, the nearest equivalent in the US is New York-born Paris Hilton, heiress of the world-famous family of hotel magnates. And, while William is destined to marry one day in St Paul's Cathedral, London, Paris has revealed that she harbours a similar desire to marry there, or at some other exclusive venue.

But Paris? A *royal*? This is, after all, a girl whom − thanks to the internet − millions have seen fellating her boyfriend. Sarah Ferguson was almost sent to the Tower for a toe-sucking incident that made front-page news!

So how was it that Paris Hilton thought that she stood a chance of marrying in one of the UK's historic cathedrals? It could be that, enmeshed into her self-belief system, she harbours thoughts of omnipotence and grandiose ideas. In other words, she might well think rather a lot of herself!

The reason I've opened this chapter with a comparison

between Paris and the royal princes is because they share a similar type of celebrity status, in that Paris is the only celebrity covered in this book who is famous for having been born into a world of wealth and fame, the latest in a long line of wealthy and famous people.

Of course, William is much further up the celebrity ladder, as he was born to be king. He has royal blood, and his celebrity status stems from his line of biological descent. But then, Paris, too, was born into a privileged position and today can afford anything her heart desires – and, had she married Paris Latsis, she would have accumulated even more wealth. (When she broke off their engagement and had to give back the huge betrothal gift he had given her, she reportedly complained that it had been too heavy to wear anyway.) Like William and Harry, she will never have to worry about having to work for a living.

Nevertheless, Paris *does* work incredibly hard at everything she does, from participating in US reality show *The Simple Life* to advertising burgers on billboards. (More erotica: all meat but no veg and big red lips. Very hot.) So, although she was born a celebrity, what has kept her in the limelight, just like the other celebrities included here, is hard work and being highly motivated.

But just what is it that motivates a girl who is already incredibly rich to become a model, an actress and a musician, not to mention a supposedly unwitting porn star? If she doesn't need the money, just what is it that she *does* need? It can't be just a matter of feeding her ego, as she already received a vast amount of media attention before embarking on her other projects.

Paris is a stunning and highly entertaining woman, with a huge personality to match her bank balance. I must admit that, before researching this book, I knew very little about her besides the fact that she was an American heiress. It strikes me, however, that the Hiltons are a close-knit family and Paris speaks affectionately about her younger sister, Nicky, whom she refers to as 'my other half'.

In fact, there is much about Paris that is kind. For instance, one person who attended the Lycée in LA with Paris has attested to how incredibly loving and kind Paris was to animals. But another side of Paris seems to be caught up in petty rivalries. She seems to possess a need to prove herself to be the best at all things, and one gets the impression that sometimes those in her sphere can bear the brunt of her ambitions. This is one side of her character that threatens to bring the celebrity curse down upon her. She has to be the leader of the pack. Everyone scrambles to be her best friend, and Paris seems to relish this power.

Getting to know Paris has been fun, but I fear for her. Just look at how she's sold herself to the media.

HOT PARIS HAS HER BURGER AND EATS IT

Paris Hilton is dressed in a skimpy black bathing suit. In one hand she holds a sudsy sponge and in the other a hose. As she washes a luxury Bentley sedan, she occasionally bites into a big, juicy hamburger. As she devours the apparently delicious morsel, the famous socialite leans forward and coquettishly confides, 'It's hot.'

These adverts for Carl's Jnr burgers could be shown only after the 9pm watershed in the US, and the overtly sexual imagery outraged Stateside parents' groups. When Mike Boddie saw the advert, he was worried. Boddie, the boss of North Carolina company Boddie–Noell Enterprises, who possess more franchises of fast-food manufacturer Hardee's than anyone else in the US, declared, 'I don't want to risk offending some customers [with the ad], even if it might sell more burgers.'

Indeed, some critics labelled the ad 'soft porn', and this allegation, combined with Paris's past reputation in the porn arena, merely added to the public interest. News of the ad spread like wildfire and sales of Hardee's burgers skyrocketed.

This, essentially, is Paris in a nutshell: someone who isn't afraid to capitalise on her sexuality in order to increase her already considerable wealth and fame. But, while being born into a wealthy family might seems to be no bad thing, it has its downside too, and after we've had a look at her life story I'll tell you what that might be.

But, first of all, while the whole world knows the girl in the gossip magazines, just who *is* Paris the heiress?

PARIS WHITNEY HILTON

She could have remained a quiet little rich girl, known only by the people moving in her immediate circle, but so relentless are her personality and energy that she was always destined to be a big noise in the world of celebrity.

But why on earth is a fabulously wealthy heiress, a socialite running her own club (Club Paris) and a successful TV personality with her own show, *The Simple Life*, included in these pages? What could possibly go wrong in her privileged world to bring the curse of celebrity down on that pretty blonde head? This is a fair question, and maybe everything in her life will remain rosy, but if tragedy does befall her, or she hits a spell of depression, my guess is that she'll have very little in her therapeutic toolbox to help her navigate these troubled waters. (See the section entitled 'The Toolbox' later in this chapter for more on this subject.)

Twenty-two years before footage of her performing oral sex found its way on to the internet, baby Paris was born, the first daughter of fabulously wealthy Kathy and Rick Hilton, great-granddaughter of hotel magnate Conrad Hilton, granddaughter of Barron Hilton and grand-niece of Nicholas Conrad 'Nicky' Hilton, one-time husband of Elizabeth Taylor. She has one younger sister, Nicky, and two brothers, Conrad and Barron.

Whereas today Paris is known as a socialite, TV personality, occasional model, actress, musician, writer and unwitting porn star, her career began with the occasional modelling job and a few small film roles, most notable of which was an appearance as herself in the 2001 high-fashion satire *Zoolander*, starring Ben Stiller. Then, in 2003, Paris starred in a fish-out-of-water reality show entitled *The Simple Life*, in which a camera crew followed her and Nicole Ritchie (daughter of singer Lionel) as they spent a month on a working farm in Altus, Arkansas, getting involved in the day-to-day running of the business. Providing an hilarious juxtaposition of genteel city-girl aristocracy and hardworking scut labour, the show – a take-off of the 1960s sitcom *Green Acres* – was a hit and went on to spawn sequels over the next couple of years.

Then, in 2004, Paris released a very pink and sparkly hardback book entitled *Confessions of an Heiress*, whose frothy pages are filled with dozens of vibrant photographs depicting Paris doing what Paris does best: posing. She poses with friends and family. She poses with her beloved Chihuahua, Tinkerbell. Then she has a rest and poses all over again. While there is some text in the book, in which she reveals a few hitherto secret facts about her (her hair is naturally curly, apparently, and she has big feet), most of the book is devoted to presenting the blonde heiress in all her sparkly glory.

In 2005, Paris appeared in a remake of the 1960s classic horror flick *House of Wax*, but the role in which she is perhaps best remembered, and for which she is perhaps most well known, is the one she played in *that* home movie, released online in November 2003 by her former boyfriend, Rick Solomon, ex-boyfriend of Shannen Doherty. Paris was nineteen years old at the time.

Entrepreneur Solomon is but one name in the long cast list of figures who have played Paris's love interests. She has also reportedly dated Leonardo DiCaprio and a host of other actors, including Edward Furlong, Jared Leto, Jamie Kennedy and Simon Rex. Then there have been musicians, including Deryck Whitby, Rob Mills and Nick Carter, and then Greek tennis player Mark Philippoussis, who was followed by Greek tycoon Paris Latsis. At the time of publication, Paris is with twenty-two-year-old Greek heir Stavros Niarchos.

Following her break-up with the confusingly named Paris Latsis, Paris reportedly said, 'I've seen the break-ups between people who rush into getting married. I don't want to make that mistake.' At first, there was confusion about whether or not the two Parises were still, in fact, an item (after all, this comment from Ms Hilton came on the back of the Greek tycoon gushing about giving his family grandchildren), and then the couple were seen at LA's Spider Club in LA embracing so passionately that onlookers were left blushing.

But then it seemed like only five minutes later that she was caught sneaking into LA's Element Club with twenty-year-old Stavros Niarchos, ex-boyfriend of Mary-Kate Olsen. According to the *New York Post*, Paz was so desperate to devour Stav that she asked the nightclub's bosses to dim the lights so no one would see her. (It seems that, while Paris might end up walking down the aisle in Westminster in white, it probably won't be virginal.) But, when she heard that Mary-Kate Olsen was seen 'all up close and personal' with Latsis, Paris and her Greek lover allegedly had an almighty row.

Elsewhere in her life, it seems that Paris is somewhat fickle in the way she makes and breaks friendships. For example, in early 2005, it was reported that she had announced that she was cutting Nicole Ritchie from future editions of *The Simple Life* and replacing her with another friend, Kimberley Stewart, daughter of Rod.

Then, when a gossip magazine article charted the top-twenty celebrity skinnies, including among their number Nicole and Kimberley, photographs of Paris taken less than a month later showed her looking very skinny, apparently down to six-and-a-half stone. In one magazine, pictures of Paris and Nicole appeared on the same page and their bodies were compared.

There is much trivia written about Paris. She is apparently Swarovski's most die-hard fan. (It's the world's largest crystal company. Apparently, Paris even has a crystal-encrusted hairbrush.) One UK Sunday supplement has calculated that, judging by her lifestyle, she will die in 2056, at the age of seventy-nine (no doubt swathed in pink like romantic novelist Dame Barbara Cartland). She has admitted to living on junk food. After dropping out of school, she drank and smoked considerably. And, although she has never held her hands up to smoking marijuana, she has been spotted apparently smoking what looked like a joint.

But there's more to Paris than trivia. Despite being born into phenomenal wealth, she has also made a fortune. And, for all her youth (she is still in her early twenties), she has an impressive list of past loves. Many of these romances are said to have ended in heartache, but just how does Paris deal with this? On the face of things, it looks as though, in order to get over one failed relationship, she runs headlong into the next. Never a good idea.

But what about her dramatic weight loss, noted above? Is this solely evidence of her rivalry with her girlfriends, or is she pining for Paris Latsis? Is she heading for crisis? Will she burn out from all the partying?

PARIS ON THE COUCH

The Toolbox

When we fall down emotionally during childhood and adolescence, we have to pick ourselves up, dust ourselves down and get on with life. If we're lucky, we learn from mistakes, and what doesn't kill us makes us stronger.

Those who have enjoyed privileged childhoods often don't learn these life lessons, generally being shielded from real life to a much greater extent than children in families suffering hardship. This is why Paris Hilton and Jade Goody possess such different personalities. Jade lived through many traumas and needed to find a strong set of coping mechanisms in order to survive. Her therapeutic toolbox, although not complete, is pretty full, containing such useful tools as optimism and a strong sense of survival.

Other celebrities analysed in this book have suffered troubled or difficult childhoods in which they've been forced to deal with issues such as abandonment, bullying, rejection or simply not being accepted for who they were or what their needs might have been. During these painful times and the years that followed, they constructed coping mechanisms to help them deal with their problems, tools that can be used as needed. Such tools might include a positive voice to counteract a negative dialogue or a positive-visualisation technique to aid relaxation, a wise old owl to ask how best to deal with a difficult situation or an angel to ask for guidance. Coping tools are collected over a number of years, and the more life throws at someone, the fuller their toolbox becomes.

But, still, how could someone as privileged as Paris Hilton possibly be in danger of falling foul of the curse of celebrity. Doesn't she have everything a young girl could wish for? Well, maybe, but I've had experience of numerous women from privileged backgrounds (usually older than Paris, true) coming to me for help, claiming that they can't understand why they're feeling depressed and don't know how to cope with feeling so bad. These women often feel guilty about being unable to cope because they simply can't understand what's gone wrong. They are confused and don't like to bother others with their troubles because, when they do, they are met with the response, 'What on earth could you have to worry about? You're so rich, your life has to be so much better than mine.' While it's true that, when problems hit, having money always helps (if your health fails, for instance, you can buy the most advanced treatment and be treated by practitioners and surgeons at the top of their profession), nevertheless the old saying 'You never know what's around the corner' is as true for these clients and for Paris as it is for the rest of us ordinary mortals.

Back in the sixties, The Beatles declared, 'Money can't buy me love,' and they were right. Where romance is concerned, Paris has already had her fair share of heartache, having been betrayed and humiliated by her past loves. But how much sympathy does the general public have for Paris? She doesn't seem to be the kind of person to engender such an emotion in others. Men might desire her and women might want to be like her, but the envy she evoked in others must leave her in a very lonely place. Perceived by many to be frothy and frivolous, few take her seriously, and she is often the butt of jokes while many of the snippets of trivia that appear in gossip magazines seem to be tongue-in-cheek.

For Paris to be able to find a long and lasting relationship, with both boys and girls, she will have to change – no easy task, as Paris the heiress has already forged a powerful image for herself, and labels have a tendency to stick. The fact that the world at large views her on the whole as being a shallow pink butterfly who trades on her sexuality to boost the public's awareness of her must make her desperately unhappy, and it's entirely possible that she defends herself against such misery by sometimes being beastly to those close to her. In analytical terms, this kind of behaviour is known as *projection*, and Paris might well unconsciously project her misery on to others in order to feel good about herself. She has to be top dog, and for that to be the case someone close to her often has to suffer. Nicole Ritchie might have suffered a lot for having been Paris's on/off friend.

A Dangerous way of Bonding

Back in the 1990s, I wrote a paper about the dangerous way in which women bond today. The paper dealt principally with eating disorders and was well received by some experts in the field of anorexia and bulimia. Since that paper appeared, the epidemic of girls striving to be thin has risen by an alarming rate. Many of these cases can be put down to the enormous peer pressure that many (if not all) girls endure during their teenage years.

The overt bullying that occurs in schools has often been cited as a primary cause for depression and, consequently, the development of eating disorders in young girls, but what's less well documented is the covert way in which girls compete with each other on numerous levels, and one of the most dangerous ways in which they compete is directed at their bodies. With this phenomenon, if one friend is a size eight, the next friend will eat less, take an inordinate amount of laxatives and/or binge/vomit themselves into a size six, a pattern of behaviour that can then develop into a vicious circle. They smoke because they think it will help to keep their weight down – and, of course, if lunch is replaced with a diet coke and a couple of cigarettes, they *will* lose weight. If one girl admits to taking ten laxatives a day, the next will take twenty. If one exercises for two hours a day, the next will run for three. These days, they can even visit websites where they can chat with other girls engaged in the same pursuit and, alarmingly, even buy 'anorexic bracelets'.

Of course, much of this behaviour stems from the representation of women in the media. Not a week goes by without some glossy magazine gasping with horror at the mounting numbers of skeletal celebrities. 'Eat more cake!' the text cries, and yet elsewhere in the pages there are conflicting messages and endless dietary advice. Why? Because, along with sex, food and dieting sells. But where will it all end? Might there be a possibility of change in the way women bond in the future? Yes. Eventually. But I think it will take quite some time. The popularly held conception that one can never be too thin or too rich is one that is now deeply ingrained in the female psyche. For some female celebrities, their central, real self becomes split into three: the real self, the public self and the female image they feel they ought to resemble. If it's Paris's goal to be both the richest and the thinnest, she is going to become well and truly undone.

During one TV interview with Britt Ekland, the Swedish actress spoke about the crippling osteoporosis from which she now suffers and for which she blames her yo-yo dieting. Speaking frankly, she gave warnings to younger women behaving in the same manner, telling them that it wasn't worth having a decade of being thin and hungry for the sake of vanity if, like her, they then had to spend many decades in agony. Shirley MacLaine has also given similar advice. If only more celebrities would speak out against such damaging behaviour.

One of the most promising articles I read recently was on the subject of teenage pregnancy. It seems that underage girls in America are now saying no to sex, thus cutting the incidence of both unwanted pregnancies and sexually transmitted diseases. Yet, only a few decades ago, the pressure was in the other direction: young girls were pressurised into having sex, by both boys and their female peers. 'Have you done it yet?' was a constant question and, if you hadn't, you were 'square'. Because of this attitude, many girls had sex as a direct result of peer pressure. Now it would seem that the opposite is happening.

Can this be the result of girls being taught how to be assertive? If so, it could indicate the beginning of a turnaround of damaging attitudes. Maybe this shift in attitudes will extend to the concept of physical appearance and bring about a new way of thinking in which thinness is no longer perceived as desirable, thus reducing drastically cases of osteoporosis, kidney and liver failure, heart attacks and, of course, chronic mental illness in women.

Hopefully, more and more celebrities will jump on the MacLaine and Ekland bandwagon and follow these two brave women's example, not only to the general public but also to younger celebrities who, if they don't stop competing to be the thinnest, will suffer greatly in middle age – if, indeed, they make it that far. Maybe the next one of the countless pencil-thin celebrities out there, none of whom are anorexic or consciously trying to send the message that it is good to be thin, feel like skipping a meal or ten, they might instead visit some of the many emaciated girls in psychiatric units across the world who see these celebrities as women who have it all and hope to emulate them. Perhaps if they look into their gaunt faces and dead eyes, they might be shocked into reconsidering some of their diet choices. Then, maybe girls all over the world will be able to bond together healthily and reclaim their bodies. Then, perhaps pleasure will replace lonely misery and great, active sex will replace the boring treadmill.

As for Paris Hilton, she is still an utterly professional young girl who is currently having the time of her life. Being rich and famous might be wonderful, but, as another heiress found out, it wasn't all plain sailing. Christina Onassis was also perceived as being a rich little girl who was blessed with having it all, but she found her heritage to be an awful curse.

CONCLUSION

Many of today's celebrities are driven to be risk-takers and high achievers. This drive originates in the early days of their development, and the way in which they manage their success depends on a unique combination of their inner and outer worlds. The ten celebrities included in this book have known at some time or another what it's like to feel cursed as a direct result of their fame, although all would no doubt rather deal with this curse than disappear from their fans' screens and magazines. The same incredible energy levels it took for them to make it keep them fighting for survival.

The public self of a modern celebrity becomes an external persona who will go to extreme lengths to make his or her child fantasies of fame come true. Success reaps great rewards, in the form of the adoration and power the celebrity craved during childhood. Many celebrities are narcissistic characters desperate for their next fix of public adoration to counteract their often chronically low self-esteem. Being recognised by the mass media is the polar opposite to feeling invisible.

Robbie Williams, George Michael and Victoria Beckham have endured much personal trauma, and all in the glare of the bright lights of the media, but ask them if they would rather have stayed in obscurity and they would no doubt be horrified by the suggestion. Jade Goody was publicly humiliated and, in effect, bullied by an entire nation, but she turned the experience around and now lives a life she could only have dreamed of during her difficult childhood. A less ambitious girl would have run back into the shadows of her former life.

Each chapter of this book has focused on the life and psychology of someone who has succeeded in becoming a celebrity. But what about the curse of celebrity in general? It's fairly safe to say that the celebrities who manage to live fairly normal lives, without too much media intrusion, are those who have found a comfortable place within themselves and know how to behave appropriately in the outside world. They have grown into mature adults and are able to process their thoughts before giving voice to them. They behave in ways that are of no interest to the paparazzi or tabloids, and for this reason they are perceived as not being particularly newsworthy.

Human nature being what it is, we often want to know what's going wrong in other people's lives so that we can feel better about ourselves: 'Oh my goodness, thank the Lord that's not happening to me!' Or 'Just look at that dreadful behaviour. You wouldn't catch me doing something like that.' When Kate Moss's hedonistic life fell apart, and she was nicknamed 'Cocaine Kate', the general public reacted with scorn. Yes, she had been pushing her boundaries to a place where she was destined to hit a crisis point, but by getting herself into hot water she enabled many to

CONCLUSION

feel holier than thou and many others to think, 'There but for the grace of God go I.' And so a scapegoat was born. But closer inspection of Kate's personality type reveals a similar character to that of the tragic Paula Yates.

The truth is that scandals light up the lives of millions of ordinary people, which is why any celebrity who behaves badly, is hit by illness or creates a drama in some other way will make front-page news. When this occurs, there's no point in moaning about it or attacking the media for, when a star climbs aboard the *Celebrity Express* and joins the ranks of the rich and privileged, they give up all hope of anonymity in the process and become public property – which is, after all, the point. Attention once craved may become insufferable and intrusive, and press gossip – whether true or not – can be most degrading, but such is the price of celebrity. So be careful what you wish for…

We humans have always loved a gossip, but since the 1970s gossip and scandal have moved into the public arena, becoming front-page news for an increasingly star-struck readership. Today, while the tabloids are full of stories about the royals, Hollywood icons and sporting heroes, they also run inconsequential stories about the lives of a new breed of celebrities, the people Piers Morgan scathingly refers to as 'Z-listers', encompassing stars of reality-TV shows and people who are invested with celebrity status by marrying into celebrity or by being the children of stars. While Piers hinted that such people were worthless celebrities and looked down scornfully at the likes of Jade Goody and Kerry Katona, these girls are nevertheless great role models, and way back in 1859 *Self-Help* author Samuel Smiles would have given them much credit for their positive influence on other young women and their aspirations of upward mobility. In doing so, they have opened doors to others aspiring to fight their way out of the lower social classes and to find a better standard of living for their families.

Samuel Smiles attacked idleness and selfishness and promoted self-discipline, integrity and honesty – the very three personality traits that elevated Jade Goody from being seen as a pig by the public to being hailed as a class-A celebrity. He also argued that national progress would be stagnant without individual enterprise and was adamant that celebrity role models had responsibilities and national duties. He loathed the worshipping of mere wealth and power and would surely have wagged a finger at the goings-on at Primrose Hill. However, he was all for self-awareness and self-improvement and saw celebrities as being able to add to the value of a nation's economy.

As it turned out, *Self-Help* did very well for Smiles, making him a celebrity in his own right. It was a kind of bible of the times, giving the message that the energetically upwardly mobile individual provided a positive role model for the general public to emulate.

THE DANGERS OF CELEBRITY

When John Lennon took himself and his family off to America, believing that they would be safer there than in the UK, he was gunned down by obsessed fan Mark Chapman in 1980. UK TV presenter Jill Dando was murdered by a stalker named Barry George. Victoria Beckham has received death threats and been the target of kidnap plots.

Meanwhile, George Best's celebrity status destroyed the genius in George Best – and, eventually, George himself. A big part of his curse was due to his immaturity and lack of discipline, but the media also played an important role in his demise, and the constantly high expectations of him to produce world-class football only added to the pressures that sent him running to the pub, the bookies' and women. The media condemned him for squandering his talents, and he beat himself up for not being able to handle the pressures of life at the top.

But what of other celebrities? What about, for instance, Karen Carpenter? Karen was a magical singer but was riddled with insecurities. She attempted to ease the intense pressure of life in the fast lane by focusing her perfectionist obsessions on her body with tragic results, and later died from complications caused by her anorexia. Later, the erstwhile child star Lena Zavaroni did the same.

Possibly the most famous celebrity to admit to an eating disorder, however, was Princess Diana, who both craved and recoiled from the media attention that her royal status attracted. Diana could whip up a media frenzy like no other, reeling in people in the same way that she guzzled food, only to reject both soon afterwards. Her ambivalent nature played havoc in both her life and the lives of those with whom she came in contact – all under the perpetually clicking shutters of the paparazzi. When Diana signed up for a life of a celebrity, she was in effect surrendering most of her rights to privacy, but her views on her own celebrity status vacillated; she once confessed, 'I read everything that's written about me' (rather like Victoria Beckham), but in her devastating interview with UK current-affairs show *Panorama* she revealed, 'I don't actually like being at the centre of attention.' According to journalists, however, she was a skilful manipulator of the media and most stories about her that had supposedly been 'leaked', according to them, had been either inspired or planted by her.

When Diana was killed in a car crash on a Paris underpass, Britain mourned its princess and, it seemed, the entire world shared in its grief. Many felt that she'd experienced the very worst aspect of the celebrity curse, and today conspiracy theories surrounding her death abound – What really happened in that tunnel? Was she, in fact, murdered? – all the while giving the newspapers a reason to splash her image on their front covers once again. Princess Di was always one of the few women in the world who could guarantee front-cover exposure on a regular basis, and even now her face sells papers.

Of course, the overriding irony of the intrusion of press and public alike in the lives of celebrities is that their celebrity status actually depends on public recognition!

WANNABES

For every one person who gets elevated to celebrityhood, there are millions who fail to achieve such ambitions. These are the kids who remain in the wings of the theatre and the shadows of those who have made it. Depressed and pining at their perceived failure, they merely exist, half-alive. Such would-be stars turn up in droves to participate in auditions for talent-seeking programmes like *The X Factor* and *Pop Idol* and fall apart in desperation when told that they're not good enough.

Not good enough for what, exactly? Have we lost sight of the fact that we can be happy, contented and satisfied with normal everyday living – holding a family together, working in a job where we feel fulfilled and simply being independent people who are relatively happy? Do we really need to live our lives in the bright lights, adored by all, in order to feel good about ourselves?

Living with a sense of failure through not achieving childish fantasies of fame can be dangerous and oppressive, and it can cause some people to fall into deeply depressive states where, angry and feeling let down by life, they direct their anger inwards upon themselves. The most vulnerable of such people might even decide to take their own meaningless existence away, but in other extreme cases the anger might be directed out on to society, and when this happens the anti-hero is born – the serial killer, the stalker or the random, one-off murderer who becomes obsessed with one individual celebrity. Such individuals, of course, find their own notoriety.

The celebrity culture walks hand in hand with such practices as breaking boundaries, taking risks, flaunting the rules that govern society and pretty much doing as you damn well please. The behavioural traits that it engenders are redolent of omnipotence and narcissism. Celebrities, after all, have more money, more sex and more social opportunities. They are removed from the rest of society and looked on as different. Better, even. Placed upon pedestals and adored by hordes of fans.

On the face of it, one wouldn't perceive such privileged people to be cursed, but they are. They have a whole set of unique difficulties to cope with and obstacles to overcome – and, quite often, they fall. They complain about being trapped or suffocated by press intrusion. They wail when a relationship goes wrong because of infidelity. They demonstrate the best and worst aspects of humanity.

Having choices in life is terribly important, but having too many is another kettle of fish entirely, and temptation often proves impossible to resist. Jude Law knows this human frailty only too well, as did George Best.

One of the worst celebrity curses of all, however, is that which threatens to destroy the central, real self. When this aspect of their personality is compromised in favour of their public face, the celebrity disappears into a dark hole. (This is probably what happened to Robbie Williams when he left Take That.) What's even worse, though, is when this way of being leads to the fragmentation of the personality, a fate that befell George Michael.

George Michael started life out as Georgios Panayiotou. He didn't like him much, though, and decided to get rid of him. Soon, what George saw reflected back at him from the mirror was a new, lovable boy who could realise his ambitions – ambitions that he was terrified would remain just out of his grasp. George Michael worked well for a while, but all the time Georgios knew, deep down, that he could be of only temporary use, that he was a fake. He suffered confusion regarding his identity, and for a while he floundered, but he worked hard on himself and pulled through.

As Robbie Williams said, 'Nowadays we don't have to die.' He was talking about Kate Moss and Pete Doherty at the time, but the same is true of all celebrities. While the curse of celebrity certainly exists, it *can* be beaten.